ECHOCARDIOGRAM

The beginner's textbook for cardiac ultrasound

Mia Santos, RCS, RVS, CCT

PREFACE

Unveiling the hidden mysteries of the heart through sound waves welcome to the captivating realm of cardiac ultrasound. In the world of modern medicine, the power of technology merges seamlessly with the delicate intricacies of the human heart. Join me on a journey to explore the wonders of cardiac ultrasound, a groundbreaking Imaging technique that allows us to peek into the very core of the most vital organ. In this textbook, we will dive into the principles, applications and cutting-edge advancements of cardiac ultrasound that continue to revolutionize the field of cardiology. So, fasten your seatbelts as we embark on a voyage to unravel the secrets of the heart, one sound wave at a time.

Because of you...

The existence of this book is indebted to a group of extraordinary individuals who have had a profound impact on my life.

Dr Angel Castaner deserves special recognition for his unwavering support and mentorship, guiding me through every step of the way. His remarkable ability to balance toughness and empathy has been instrumental in my growth.

Steve and Nikki opened their doors to me when I needed it the most. Their generosity and belief in my abilities allowed me the freedom to hone my skills and flourish. It is undeniable that without the presence and influence of these exceptional individuals, this book would not have come to fruition.

Forever grateful

Table of Contents

Unit 1 - The Basics

Page 1	Chapter 1
	1. Anatomy And Physiology.
	2. Blood Flow
	3. The Conduction System
Page 10	Chapter 2
	1. Embryology And Fetal Circulation

Unit 2 - The TTE

Page 16	Chapter 3
	1. Basic Physics
	2. Image Quality
	3. Modes
Page 29	Chapter 4 - Windows & Views
	1. PLAX
	2. SAX
	3. A4
	4. A2
	5. A3
	6. Subcostal
	7. SSN
Page 45	Chapter 5
	1. Basic Protocol
	2. Measurements

Unit 3 - Pathology

Page 56	Chapter 6 - Valvular Heart Disease
Page 80	Chapter 7 - Cardiac Pathology
Page 110	Chapter 8 - Congenital Heart Disease

Unit 4 - Other Modalities

Page 126	Chapter 9 - Stress Echo
Page 128	Chapter 10 - Tee

Unit 5 - Physics

Page 136	Chapter 11 – Introduction to Ultrasound Physics
Page 143	Chapter 12 – The Doppler
Page 147	Chapter 13 - Artifacts
Page 151	Chapter 14 - Optimization

Page 156	INDEX A
Page 157	GLOSSARY
Page 167	REFERENCES

UNIT 1

The Basics

Chapter 1

Anatomy of the heart

The heart is a very unique and complex structure. No other organ in our body can compare. It has its very own muscle type, fibers and cells unique only to the heart & its own electrical system. We will break down the basics of the heart's structure and electrical system.

Structure

- Top of heart - Base
- Bottom of heart - Apex
- Four chambers
    - Right atrium - RA
    - Left atrium - LA
    - Right ventricle - RV
    - Left ventricle - LV
- Four valves
    - Tricuspid valve - TV
    - Mitral valve - MV
    - Pulmonic valve - PV
    - Aortic valve - AV
- Great vessels
    - Aorta
    - Pulmonary arteries (2)
    - Pulmonary veins (4)
    - Superior & Inferior vena cava

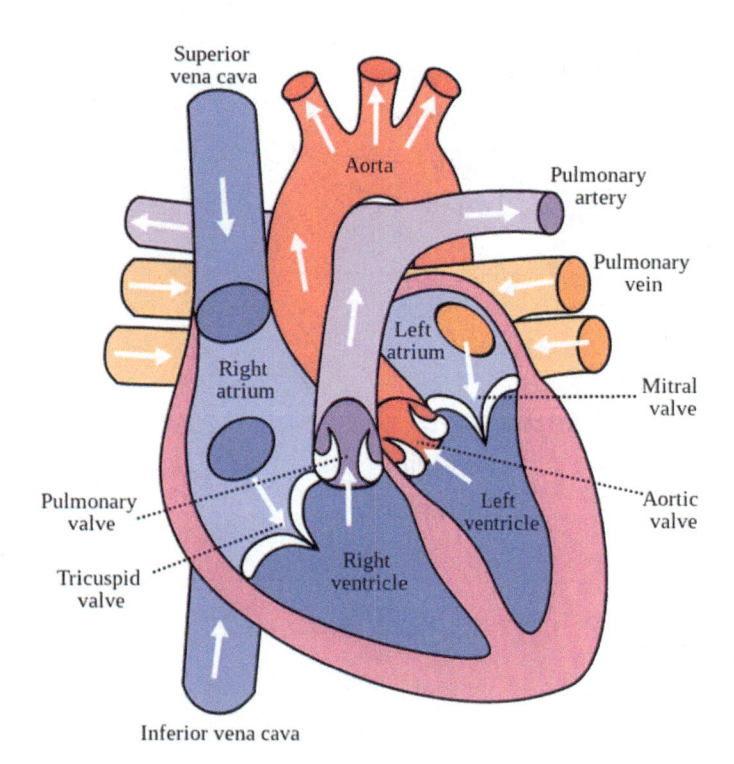

The chambers

The heart has a top, a bottom, a right side and a left side. The top of the heart is the base, and the bottom is the apex. The top right and left chambers are the atria (atrium). The bottom right and left chambers are the ventricles (ventricle).

The atria are the receiving chambers of the heart. Both venous and arterial blood enter the heart into the atria. The ventricles are the pumping chambers of the heart. They also pump both venous and arterial blood.

The valves

Remember, it is all in a name

Semilunar valves are the pulmonary and aortic valves. The **PULMONARY** valve separates the RV from the **PULMONARY** artery. The **AORTIC** valve separates the LV from the **AORTA**. The atrioventricular (AV) valves are the tricuspid and mitral valves. They separate the atria from the ventricles, thus, atrioventricular. The tricuspid is on the right and the mitral is on the left.

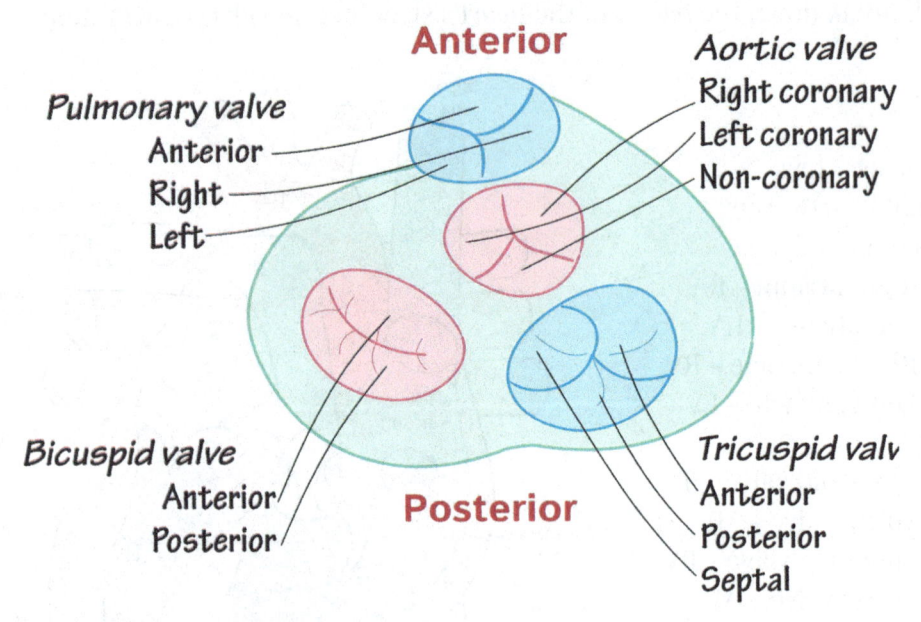

Pulmonary valve
- Anterior
- Right
- Left

Aortic valve
- Right coronary
- Left coronary
- Non-coronary

Bicuspid valve
- Anterior
- Posterior

Tricuspid valve
- Anterior
- Posterior
- Septal

The **chordae tendineae** Are strong, fibrous connections between the valve leaflets and the papillary muscles.

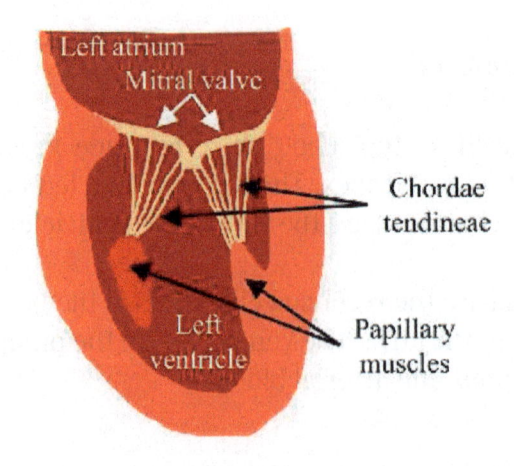

2

The great vessels

The great vessels are the large main vessels that are attached to the heart itself. IVC, SVC & pulmonary arteries supply and carry blood to and from the right heart, the aorta and pulmonary veins supply and carry blood to and from the left heart.
The aortic Arch has three arteries that bifurcate (branch off) off of it.

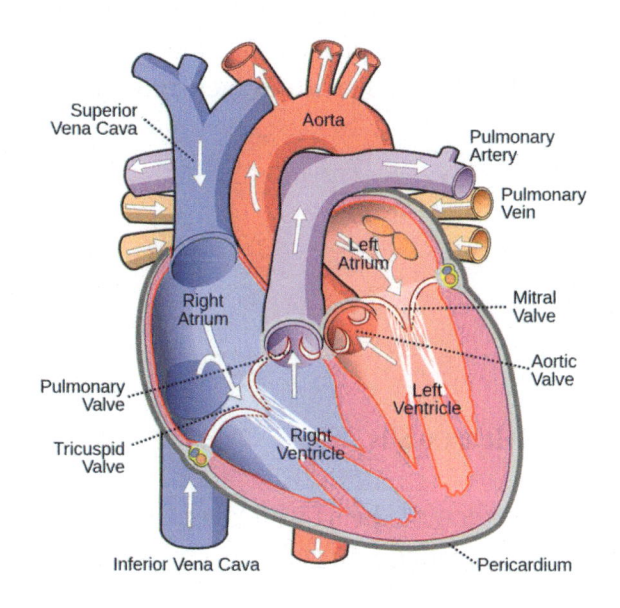

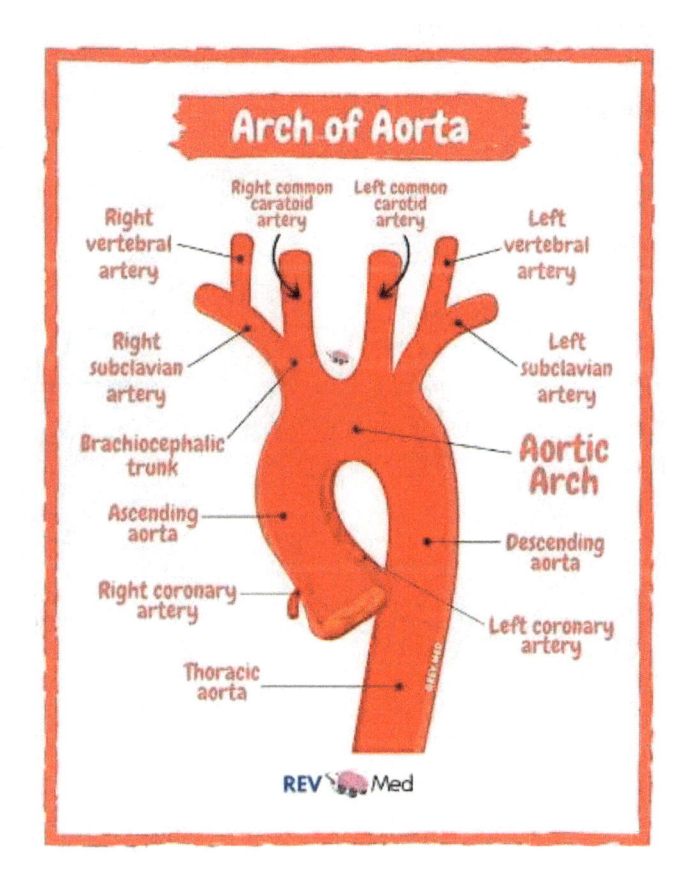

Coronary arteries of the heart

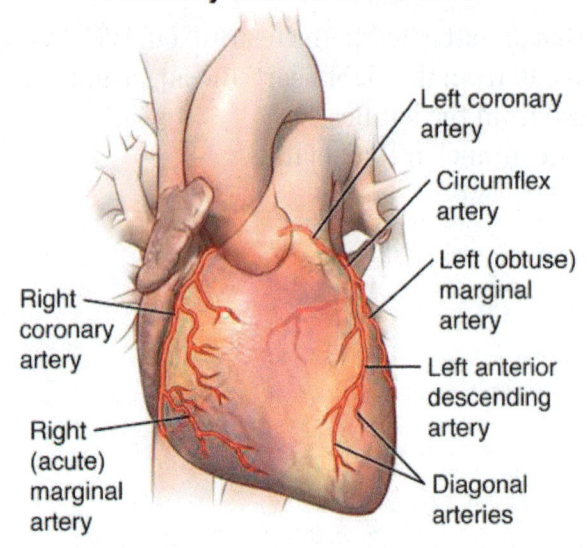

In addition to the great vessels, it is also important to know the main coronary arteries. The coronary arteries are on the outside of the heart and supply the heart muscle with oxygen and nutrients.

Heart walls

In echo, not only do we have to know the difference between the heart wall layers, but we also must know the wall segments as well. Wall segments are divided into sections and positional sides of the heart. There are three segments,
 1. Basal = towards the base of the heart
 2. Mid = middle section
 3. Apical = towards the apex

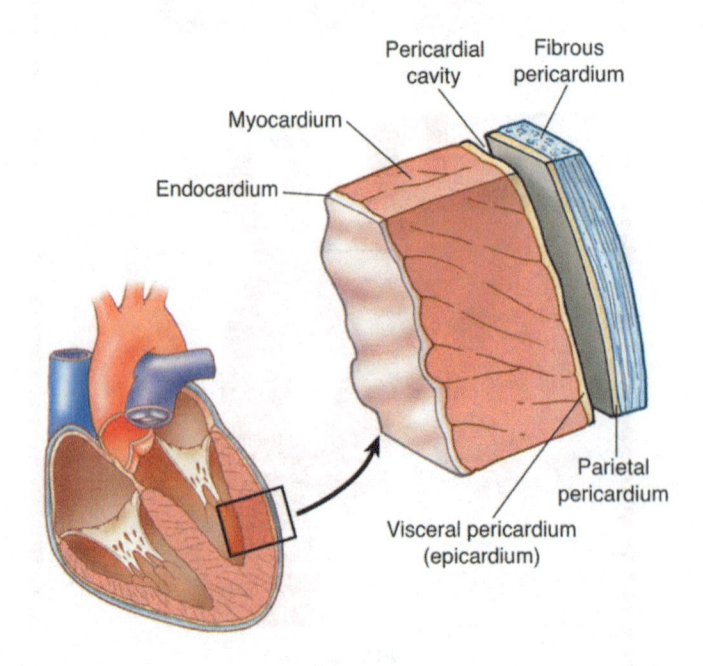

Segmentation of the left ventricle

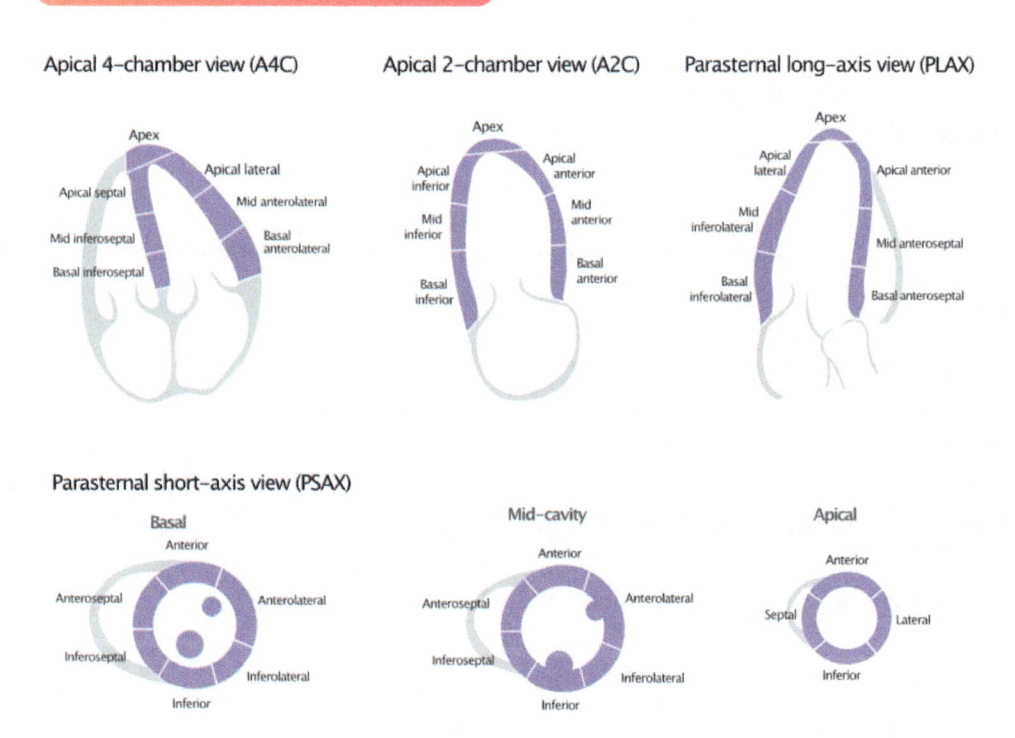

Apical 4-chamber view (A4C)

Apical 2-chamber view (A2C)

Parasternal long-axis view (PLAX)

Parasternal short-axis view (PSAX) — Basal, Mid-cavity, Apical

Blood Flow

First, do you know what the difference between a vein and an artery is?
1. Is it that veins have blue blood while arteries have red?   NO!!!! All blood is red!
2. Is it that veins have deoxygenated blood while arteries have oxygenated blood?   NO!!!

The #1 difference is that veins carry blood TOWARDS the heart and arteries carry blood AWAY from the heart.

Hint: **A**rteries = **A**way

Pulmonary veins and arteries are the only reason that makes #2 false. The pulmonary veins carry oxygenated blood from the lungs to the heart. The pulmonary arteries carry deoxygenated blood from the heart to the lungs.

Our circulatory system is divided into two parts, the pulmonary and systemic. The pulmonary system delivers blood to and from the lungs, while the systemic system delivers blood to organs, tissues and the rest of the body.

The pulmonary system returns blood that has been depleted back to the heart, which then gets pumped out to the lungs. When the blood is in the lung it gets replenished with O2 and other nutrients.

The pulmonary system:
1. All veins except the pulmonary vein
2. Pulmonary artery
3. Right heart

The systemic system returns oxygenated blood back to the heart to get pumped out to the rest of the body.

The systemic system:
1. All arteries except the pulmonary artery
2. Pulmonary vein
3. left heart.

Blood is transferred from the systemic system to the pulmonary system via capillaries.

So now let's piece together anatomy and blood flow. Let's start with the RA.

RA»TV»RV»PV»Pulm A»Lungs»Pulm V»LA»MV»LV»AV»Aorta»Arteries»Capillaries»Veins»IVCs»RA

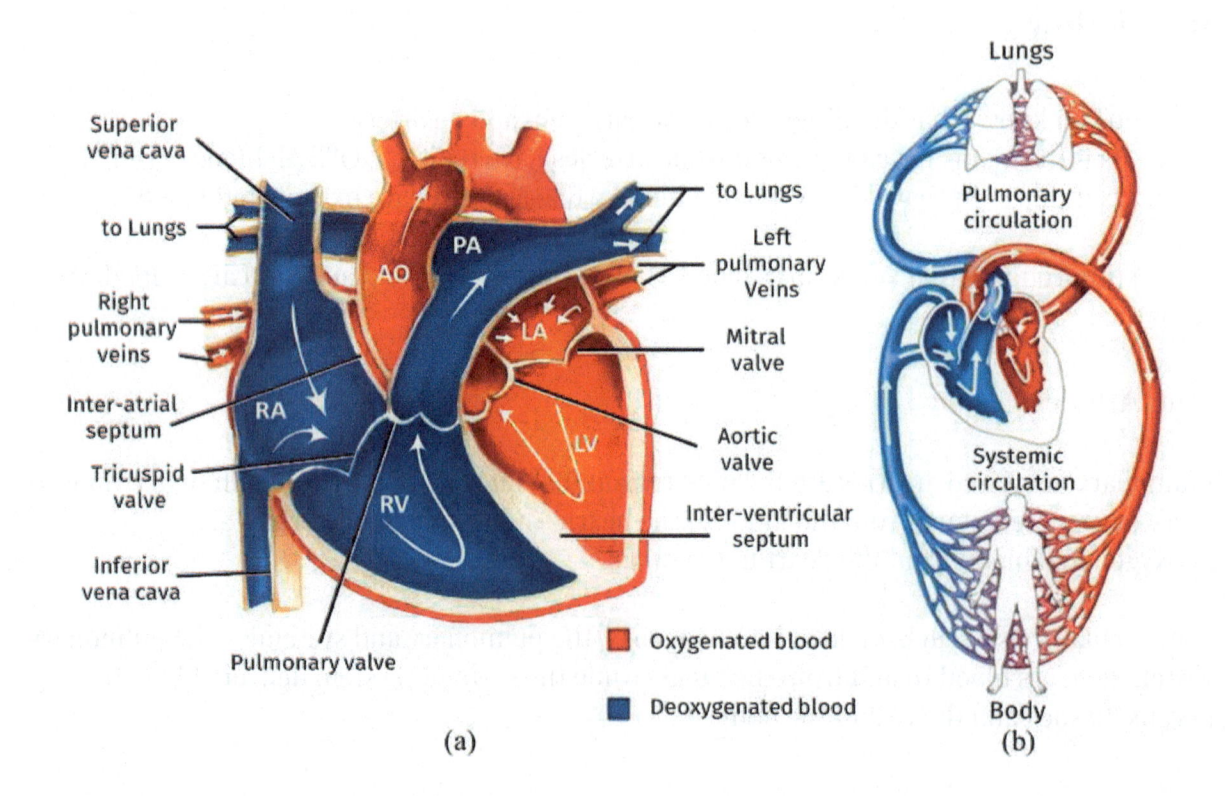

The conduction system

The conduction system is the electrical part of the heart. Its purpose is to stimulate charged ions in the heart that cause the myocardium to contract. Before we dive right in, let's go over some basic terms.
Contraction - when the heart squeezes and pumps blood out
Relaxation - when the heart relaxes and opens back up to receive blood.
Systole - when the heart contracts
Diastole - when the heart relaxes.
Depolarization - Igniting of cardiac cells, causing systole.
Repolarization - Regeneration of cardiac cells, causing diastole.

Depolarization = Systole = Contraction
Repolarization = Diastole = Relaxation

The conduction system consists of very specialized cardiac cells that have a property called automaticity, the ability to spontaneously ignite impulses. There is a very specific pathway of nodes, branches and fibers that cause the heart to function in a specific order.

They are, in order of conduction:

1. Sinoatrial node - SA node
2. Atrioventricular node - AV node
3. Bundle of his - BH
4. Left bundle branch - LBB.
5. Right bundle branch - RBB
6. Purkinje fibers - PF

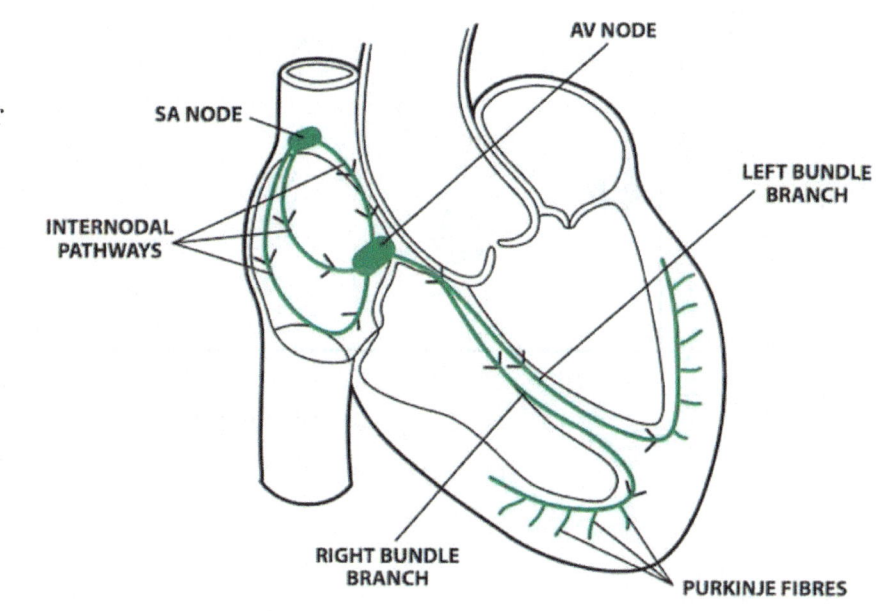

The SA node is the "pacemaker" of the heart. It is the first to ignite and start the cardiac cycle. The impulse then travels to the AV node & BH. It then simultaneously travels through the bundle branches and Purkinje fibers. This entire process is responsible for one complete cardiac cycle, or one single heartbeat.

Action Potential

Action potential is a measurement of the membrane potential waveform of the cardiac myocytes signifying the electrical activity of the cell during the contraction and relaxation of the heart. specific ionic currents contribute to each phase of the cardiac action potential. An action potential has three phases: depolarization, overshot, and repolarization. there are two more states of the membrane potential related to the action potential. The first one is hyperpolarization which precedes depolarization, while the second one is hyperpolarization which follows repolarization. There are four main cardiac ions, sodium, calcium, potassium and magnesium.

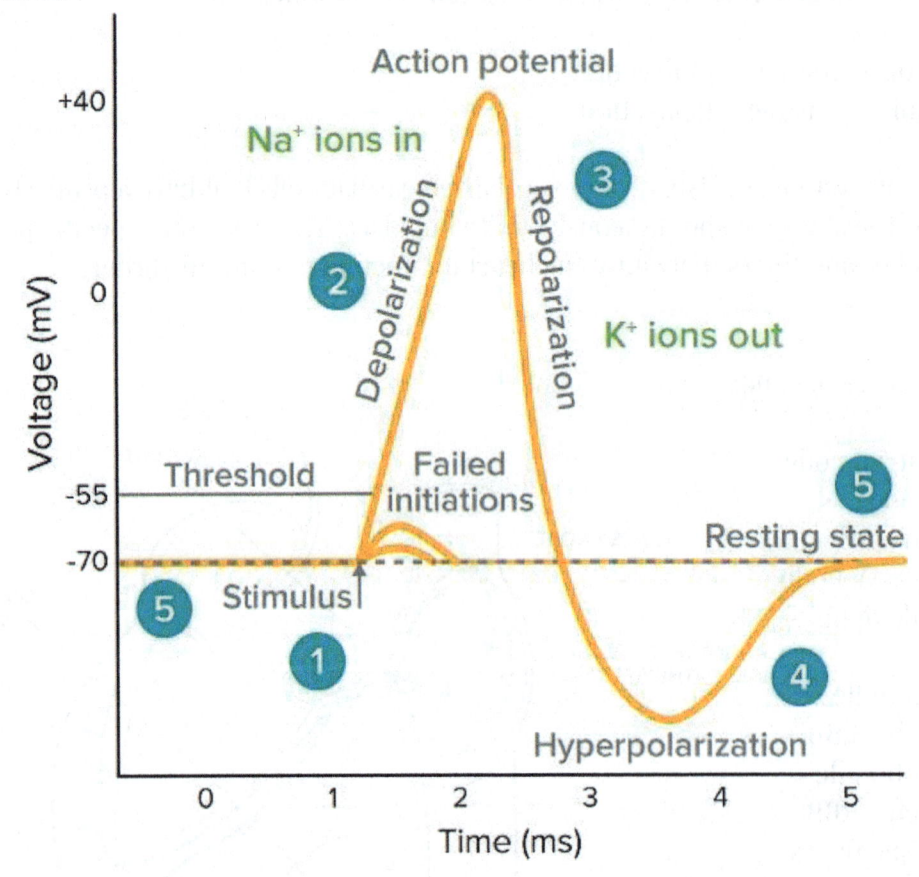

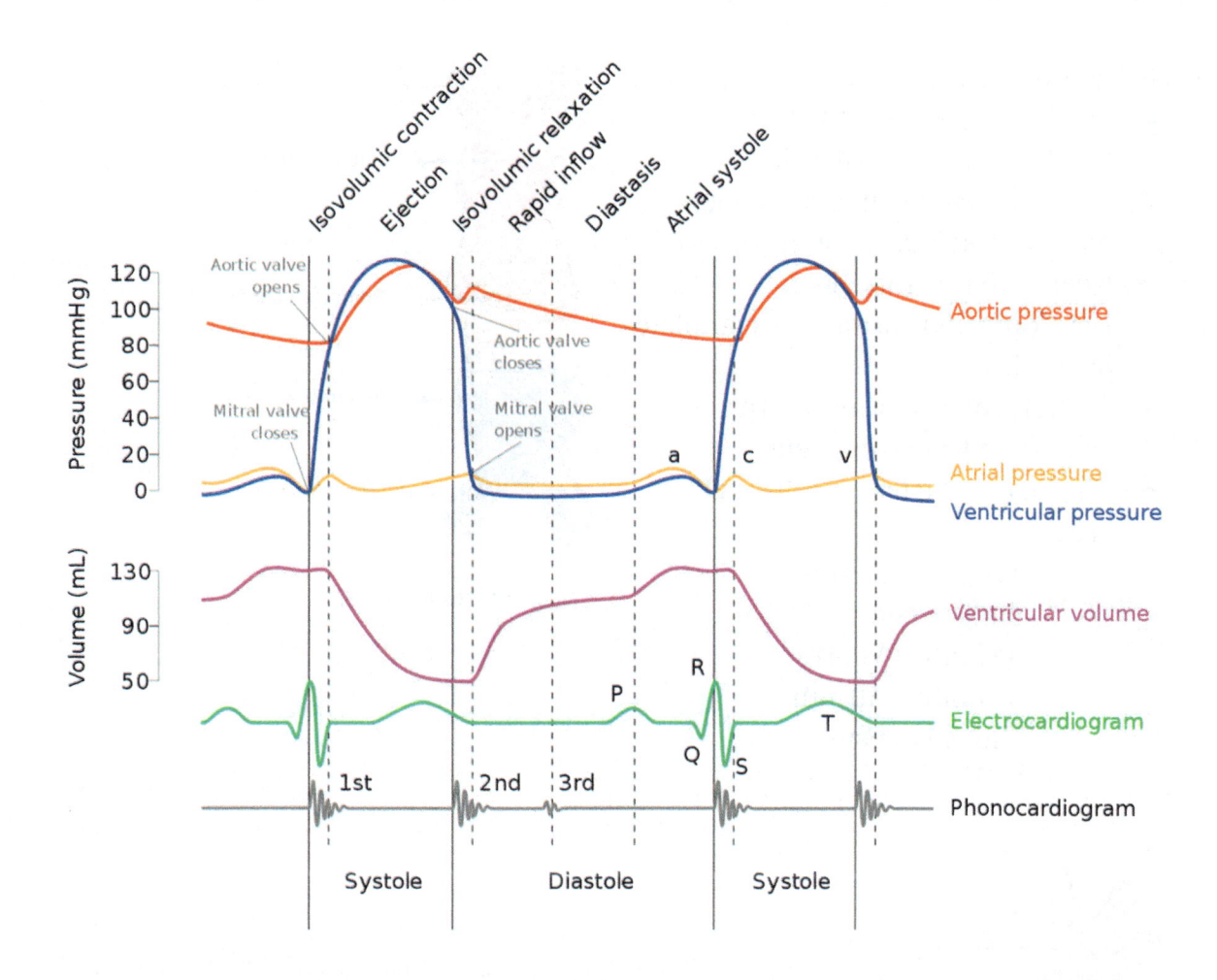

Chapter 2

Embryology & Fetal Circulation

Embryology: the study of the formation and development of an embryo and fetus

Early Development
- The human heart is the first functional organ to develop.
- It begins beating and pumping blood around day 21 or 22, three weeks after fertilization. Development is ordinarily complete by week 9.
- A single tube is formed with a venous and an arterial end.
- The heart tube has five distinct areas.
    - Truncus arteriosus
    - Bulbus cordis,
    - Primitive Ventricle
    - Primitive Atrium
    - Sinus Venosus

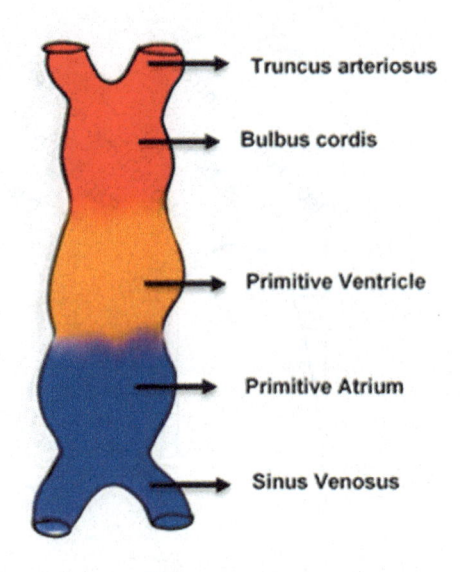

Figure 1A. The heart tube

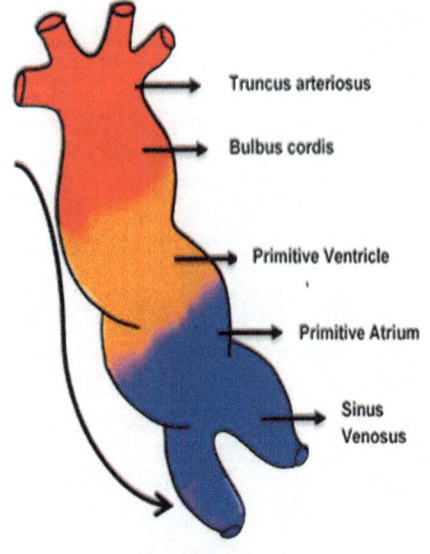

Figure 1B. Cardiac looping

- Cardiac looping begins around the 22nd day of intrauterine life. It results from elongation of the cardiac tube while both ends of the tube are fixed.

- Left-right polarity is established when the primitive ventricle is bent into a loop that moves anteriorly and to the right. At the same time, the caudal portion of the tube bends dorsally, cephalically, and to the left.

- By day 28, the heart consists of the common atrium, common ventricle, and common outflow tract.
- During this time, blood is pumped from the distal end through the sinus venosus upwards to the truncus arteriosus.
- Development of the four-chambered heart with two outflow tracts involves the simultaneous formation of three septa that separate atria, truncus arteriosus, and ventricles.

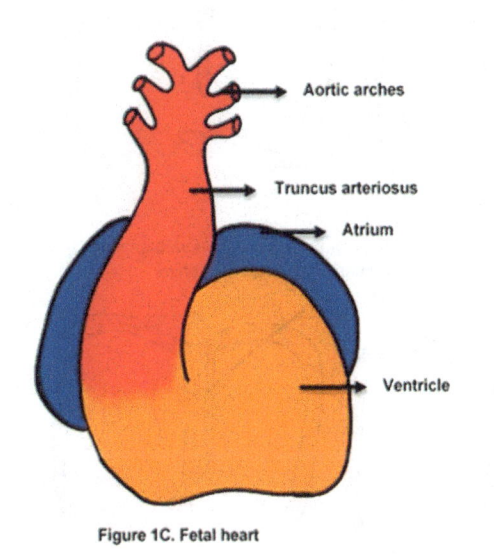

Figure 1C. Fetal heart

Embryonic » Final Structures
Truncus arteriosus » Ascending aorta and pulmonary trunk

Bulbus cordis » Smooth portions of right and left ventricle

Primitive ventricle » Trabeculated right and left ventricle

Primitive atrium » Anterior (trabeculated) portions of right and left atria

Sinus venosus » Posterior portion of the right atrium and coronary sinus

Endocardial cushions » Aortic, pulmonary, tricuspid, mitral valve

Separations

Atrial
- Primitive atrium is a single cavity. The primary atrial septum (septum primum) appears as a thin-walled sagittal fold in the roof of the common atrium and grows down towards the endocardial cushions.
- The opening between the septum and the endocardial cushions is called foramen primum. (Figure 2A). Tissue resorption at the superior end of the septum primum results in the formation of the foramen secundum (Figure 2B), before the foramen primum is completely closed by the septum. This occurs between the 5th and 6th week of embryonic life.
- Simultaneously, another enfolding appears in the roof of the common atrium to the right of the septum primum and septum secundum (Figure 2C). The inferior end of the septum secundum fuses with the lowermost part of the septum primum and the endocardial cushion, causing complete separation of the two atria inferiorly (Figure 2D). Incomplete closure of the foramen secundum by the superior end of the septum secundum results in the formation of the foramen ovale.

- Oxygenated blood coming from the inferior vena cava enters the left atrium and is preferentially directed to the right atrium through the foramen ovale by some primitive right atrial structures. This fetal interatrial communication (patent foramen ovale) normally closes after birth due to high left atrial pressure.

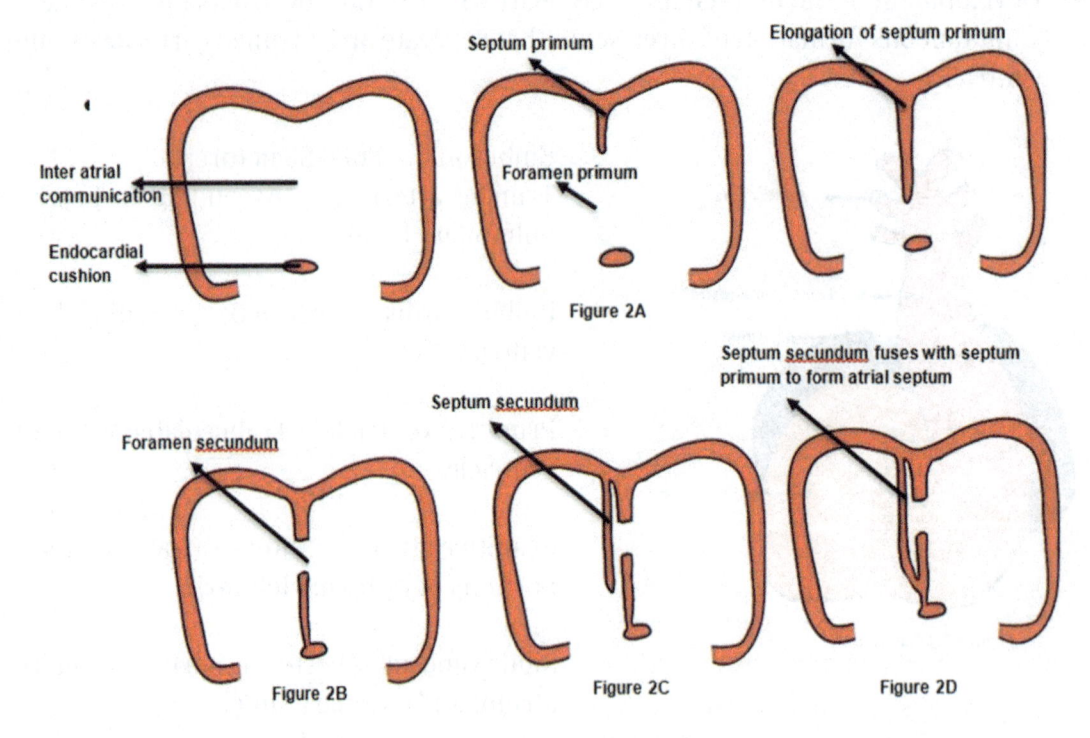

Figure 2. Formation of Atrial Septum

Ventricular
- The interventricular septum has three components- the muscular, inlet, and infundibular (outlet) septum.
- Muscular interventricular septum forms by proliferation of tissue upward towards the endocardial cushions from the apex of the heart.
- Membranous interventricular septum is formed by the downward growth of the aorticopulmonary septum towards the muscular interventricular septum and posterior-inferior proliferation of tissue from the endocardial cushions.
- Fusion of the membranous and muscular parts of the interventricular septum forms the complete interventricular septum.
- The infundibular septum is in continuation with the atrioventricular canal.
- Subsequent defects in the formation of these different components can lead to muscular, membranous and infundibular ventricular septal defects.

Partitioning of the heart into four chambers

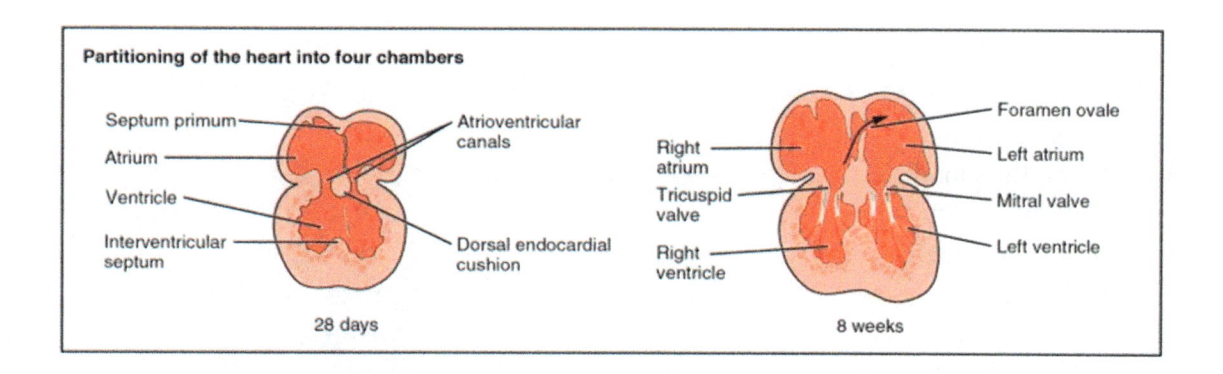

(Figure: diagrams at 28 days and 8 weeks showing septum primum, atrium, ventricle, interventricular septum, atrioventricular canals, dorsal endocardial cushion; and at 8 weeks: right atrium, tricuspid valve, right ventricle, foramen ovale, left atrium, mitral valve, left ventricle.)

Truncus Arteriosus
- The bulbus cordis elongates and forms three parts- the proximal part forms the trabeculated portion of the right ventricle, the middle part forms conus cordis which is the outflow tract and the truncus arteriosus which forms the ascending aorta and pulmonary trunk.
- Truncus arteriosus undergoes two separate processes: septation and spiraling. There are two swellings along the truncus arteriosus- truncal swellings more distally and conal swellings proximally. The truncal swellings, similar in appearance to endocardial cushions, divide the lumen into the proximal ascending aorta and the pulmonary trunk. Fusion of the truncal and conal swellings establishes the right ventricular origin of the pulmonary trunk and the left ventricular origin of the aorta. The aortopulmonary valves develop at the lines of fusion of truncal and conal swellings. (Figure 4)
- Spiraling of the septum allows the pulmonary trunk to cross the anterior and to the left of the aorta.

Fetal Circulation

The fetus gets all the needed nutrition, oxygen and life support through the blood vessels in the umbilical cord. This comes from the mother through the placenta. Waste products and carbon dioxide from the fetus are sent back through the umbilical cord and placenta to the mother's circulation to be removed.

The fetal circulatory system uses 3 shunts.
1. The shunt that bypasses the lungs is called the foramen ovale.
    a. This shunt moves blood from the right atrium of the heart to the left atrium.
2. The ductus arteriosus moves blood from the pulmonary artery to the aorta
3. The blood then reaches the inferior vena cava. Most of this blood is sent through the ductus venosus.
    a. This is also a shunt that lets highly oxygenated blood bypass the liver to the inferior vena cava and then to the right atrium of the heart.

Inside the fetal heart

Blood enters the right atrium. When the blood enters the right atrium, most of it flows through the foramen ovale into the left atrium.

Blood then passes into the left ventricle.

This is the large artery coming from the heart.

From the aorta, blood is sent to the heart muscle itself and to the brain and arms. After circulating there, the blood returns to the right atrium of the heart through the superior vena cava. Very little of this less oxygenated blood mixes with the oxygenated blood. Instead of going back through the foramen ovale, it goes into the right ventricle.

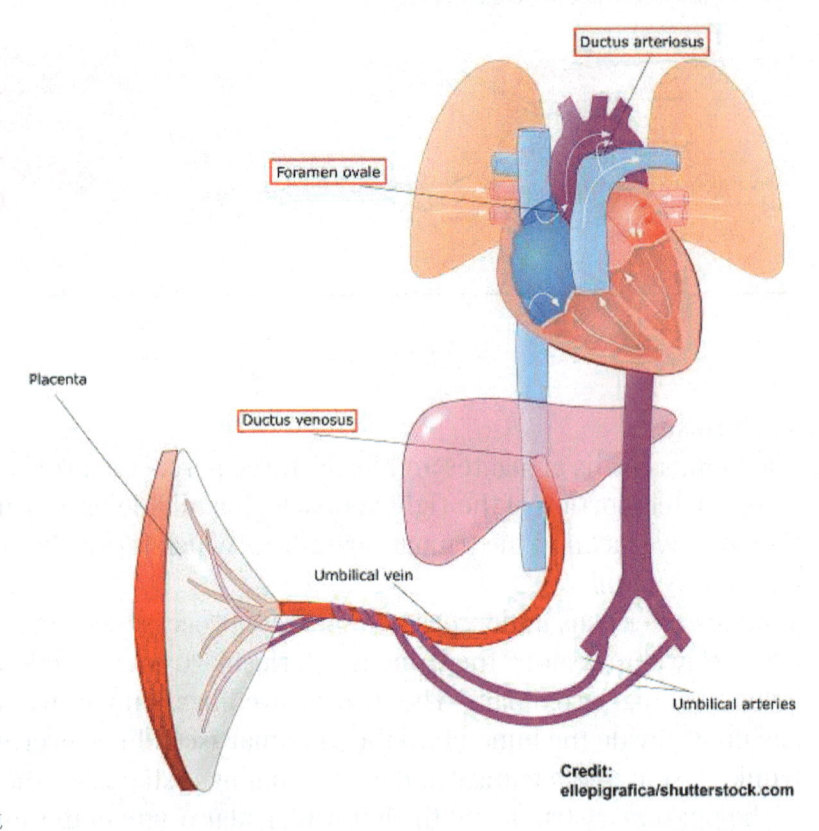

This less oxygenated blood is pumped from the right ventricle into the pulmonary artery. A small amount of the blood continues onto the lungs. Most of this blood is shunted through the ductus arteriosus to the descending aorta. This blood then enters the umbilical arteries and flows into the placenta. In the placenta, carbon dioxide and waste products are released into the mother's circulatory system. Oxygen and nutrients from the mother's blood are released into the fetus' blood.

Blood circulation after birth

The closure of the ductus arteriosus, ductus venosus, and foramen ovale completes the change of fetal circulation to newborn circulation.

The umbilical cord is clamped, and the baby no longer receives oxygen and nutrients from the mother. With the first breaths of air, the lungs start to expand, and the ductus arteriosus and the foramen ovale both close. The baby's circulation and blood flow through the heart now function like an adult's.

14

UNIT 2

The TTE

Chapter 3

Intro to the TTE

TTE = Transthoracic Echocardiogram
Definition: a test that uses ultrasound (sound waves) to create images of your heart

Transthoracic means across or over the chest wall.

Pros:
- Minimal staff
- Portable
- Noninvasive
- Immediate results available

The echo is used to look at heart structure and function.

Equipment:
- Ultrasound machine
- Probe
- 3 lead EKG wires
- Gel

As we dive deeper into the TTE, we will expand on this very basic introduction.

Basic Physics

Again, as we dive deeper into the TTE, we will expand on this very basic introduction. To start, however, there are some basic concepts to understand.

What exactly is ultrasound?

Ultrasound is sound with frequencies greater than 20kHz/s. The very upper limit of what humans can detect. The ultrasound image is produced based on the reflection of the waves off of the body structures. The waves travel from a transducer, through the body, back to the transducer, then onto the monitor.

An ultrasound transducer, which is attached to the machine, is made of specialized crystals called piezoelectric crystals. These materials are able to produce sound waves when an electric field is applied to them, but can also work in reverse, producing an electric field when a sound wave hits them. The transducer sends out a beam of sound waves or echoes into the body. The sound waves are reflected back to the transducer by boundaries between tissues in the path of the beam. Using the speed of sound and the time of each echo's return, the scanner calculates the distance from the transducer to the tissue boundary. These distances are then used to generate two-dimensional images of tissues and organs. There are three main types of transducers – convex/curvilinear, linear, and phased/sector transducers. In addition, there are many specialty transducers, such as endocavity, transesophageal, volume, and continuous wave (CW)/pencil transducers. Different types of transducers are used for different ultrasound exams and are ideally suited to image different structures.

A TTE uses a phased array probe that is 2-5mHz.

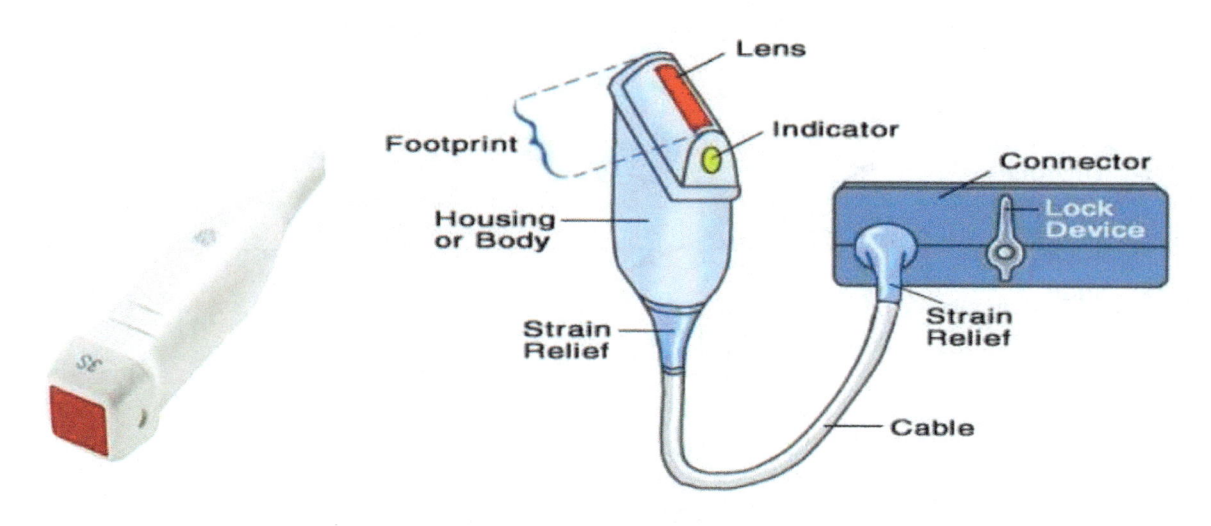

1. Head
    a. Location of PZT
2. Indicator
    a. Beam orientation.
3. Cord
    a. Electric supply
    b. Connection to machine

Ultrasound gel is used to grab the air barrier, as air is not a good conductor.

Transducer manipulation - scanning lingo

Direction of probe movement refers to the head

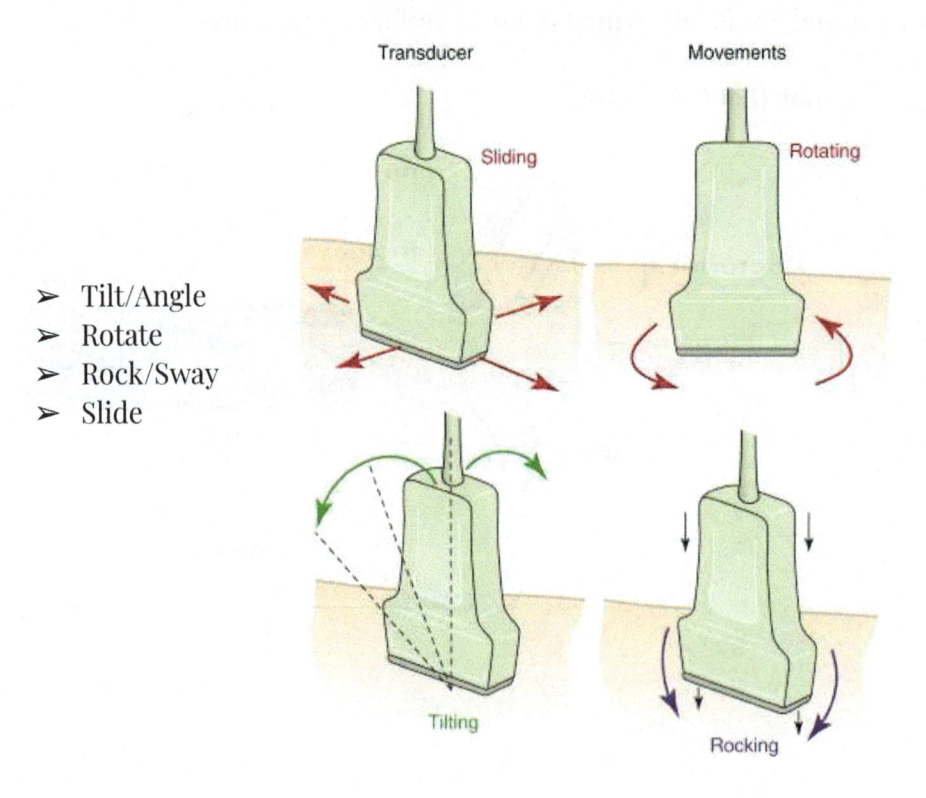

- Tilt/Angle
- Rotate
- Rock/Sway
- Slide

Image quality

To understand how to use the image, make it better and maneuver the beam, we must first touch on more basics of US physics & instrumentation.

Frame rate: the measurement of how quickly a number of frames appear within a second. The higher the frame rate, the better the image quality.
Adjustments to maximize frame rate:
- Decrease depth.
- Use smaller sectors.
- Use smaller ROIs.
- Use preprocessing Zoom.

Sector size:
- The size of the sector projected on the monitor.

Depth:
- Changes the ultrasound beam penetration.

Preprocessing zoom:
- Preprocessing refers to the manipulations that occur during data collection before scan data are stored in the computer memory.
- This is done by using the zoom control after a picture is taken.

Zoom vs Depth:

- The zoom is used for magnifying the area of interest.
- Unlike the depth which magnifies by moving the area of interest closer, the zoom actually magnifies by making the region of interest appear bigger.
- The depth determines how "deeply" into the body one wishes to image.

Focus Position / Focus Depth:

- The focal position tells the ultrasound the depth at which you'd like the highest resolution.
- The image resolution improves in the area of the selected focal position.

Gain:
- Refers to the amount of amplification of the returning echoes.
- The image on the screen is whitened by a uniform margin, as though the returning signal is stronger than it is, to make it easier to see.

TGG - Time Gain Compensation:
- Equalizes differences in received reflection amplitudes because of the reflector depth. Reflectors with equal reflector coefficients will not result in equal amplitude reflections arriving at the transducer if their travel distances are different.
- TGC allows you to adjust the amplitude to compensate for the path length differences.
- The longer the path length the higher the amplitude. The TGC is located on the right upper-hand corner of the monitor and is displayed graphically.
- The goal of TGC is to make the entire image look evenly lit from top to bottom.

Gain vs TGC

Unlike TGC, overall gain alters the amount of amplification applied to signals from any depth. This is used to increase or decrease the overall brightness of the image. Overall gain amplifies the return signal and has no effect on the transmitted pulse. Therefore, gain cannot compensate for inadequate penetration.

Grayscale:
- The image gray scale can be changed by adjusting the Grey Scale Map (Grey Map/Map).
- This permits the brightness of the B-Mode dots to be displayed in various shades of gray to represent different echo amplitudes.
- This is one of the first changes to make with optimizing a custom preset.
- Adjusting gray maps on your image has a similar effect on an ultrasound image as changing the dynamic range, but they are different.

Dynamic Range (also known as Compression):
- Allows you to tell the ultrasound machine how you want the echo intensity displayed as shades of gray.
- A broad/wide range will display more shades of gray and an overall smoother image.

Frequency:
- Number of waves passing by a specific point per second

Harmonics:
- Is a wave or signal whose frequency is an integral (whole number) multiple of the frequency of the same reference signal or wave.
- As part of the harmonic series, the term can also refer to the ratio of the frequency of such a signal or wave to the frequency of the reference signal or wave.

Image orientation

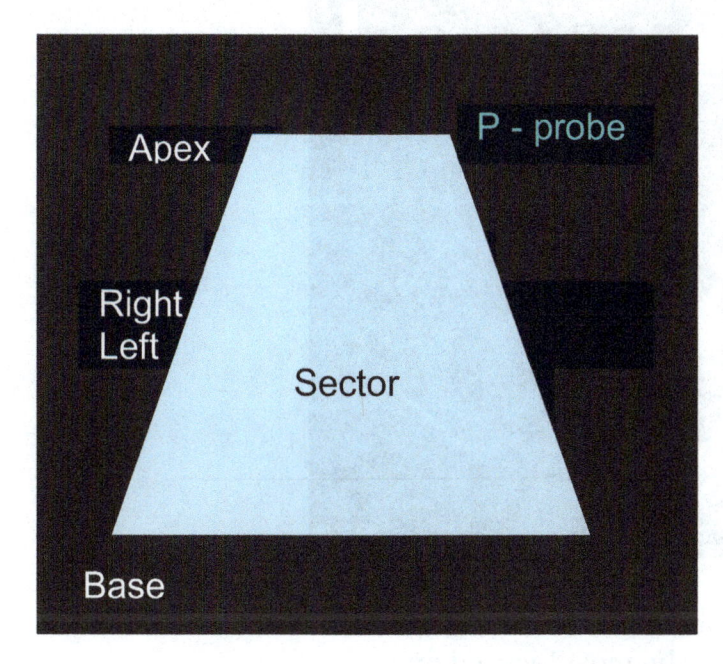

The heart appears on the screen flipped both vertically and horizontally.

The "P" represents the probe position.

Zones/Fields

Near: closest to the probe
Focal: within the focal zone
Far: furthest from the probe

Near, Focal and Far Zones

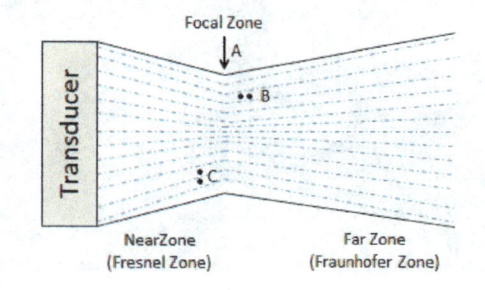

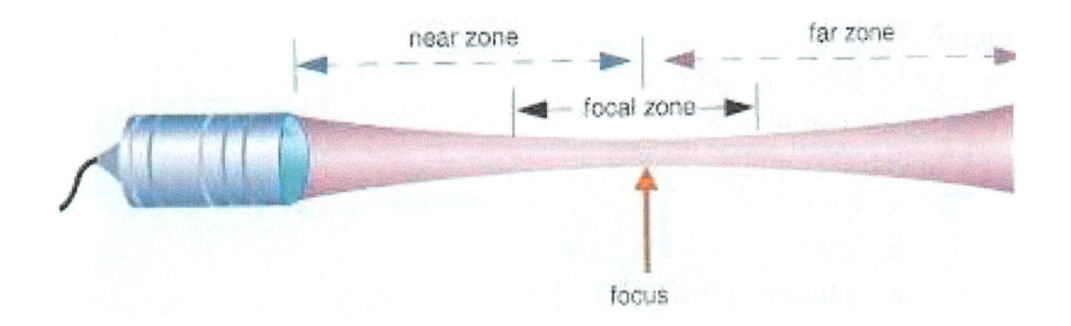

21

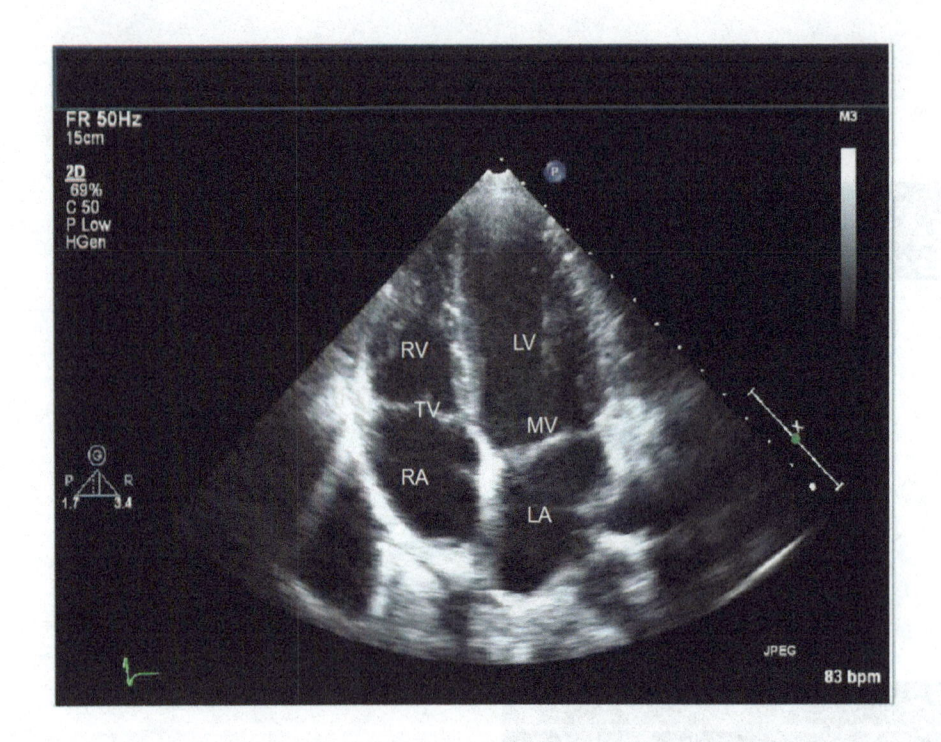

All zones depend on where the focal point is set. The focal point should be set at the point of which structure needs to be the most focused on.

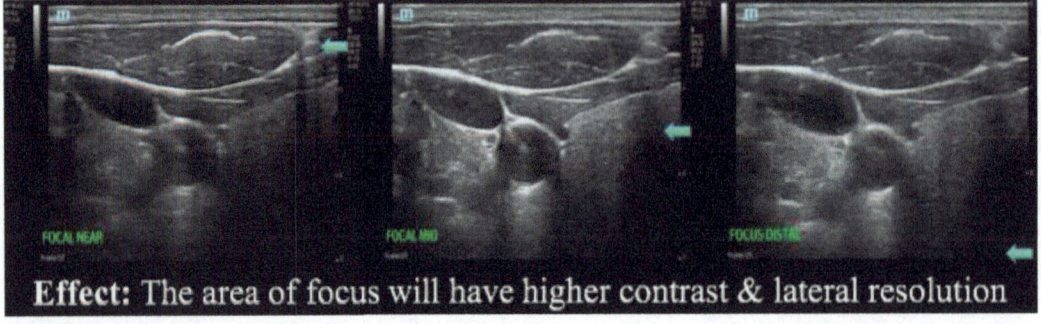

Effect: The area of focus will have higher contrast & lateral resolution

Modes
- 2D / B-mode
- M-mode
- Doppler
    - Color Flow Doppler
    - Tissue Doppler
    - Spectral Doppler
        - CWD
        - PWD
        - non-imaging CWD
- Strain

2D / B-mode

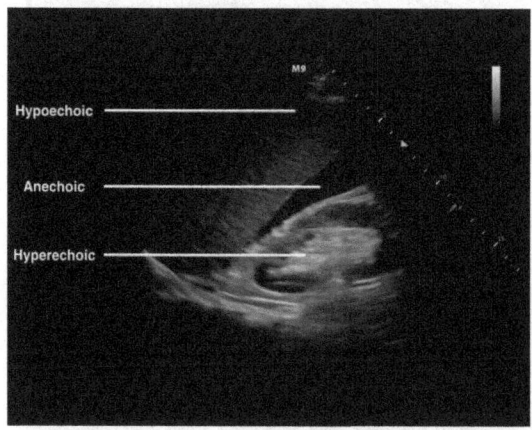

B-mode or 'brightness mode' provides structural information utilizing different shades of gray (or different 'brightness') in a two-dimensional image.

Brightness is determined by the amplitude of returning echoes.

Anechoic/Echolucent – Complete or near absence of returning sound waves, area is black.

Hypoechoic - Structure has very few echoes and appears darker than the surrounding tissue.

Hyperechoic/Echogenic – Large amplitude of returning echoes appears brighter than surrounding tissue.

B-mode adjustments:
- Gain
- TGC
- Gray map

M-mode

M-mode (motion mode) captures returning echoes in only one line of the B-mode image displayed over time

- The movement of structures positioned in that line can now be visualized.
- Often M-mode and B-mode are displayed together in real-time on the ultrasound monitor.

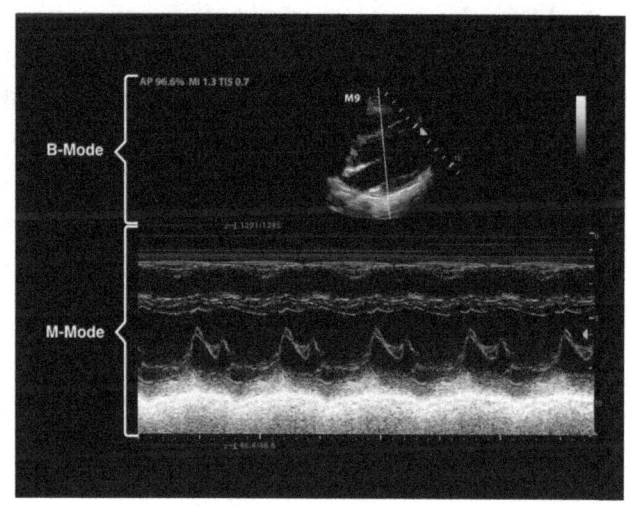

Doppler: Examines the characteristics of direction and speed of tissue motion and blood flow and presents it in audible, color or spectral displays.

Color flow Doppler - CFD
- It is used to show blood flow or tissue motion in a selected two-dimensional area
- Direction and velocity of tissue motion and blood flow are color-coded and superimposed on the corresponding B-mode image
- Typically, red depicts movement towards the transducer, while blue depicts movement away from the transducer

BART

Blue moves away from the probe
Red moves toward the probe

When the color has a mosaic pattern, this means the velocity is aliasing and above the Nyquist limit.

Nyquist limit.:
Represents the maximum Doppler shift frequency that can be correctly measured without resulting in aliasing in color or pulsed wave ultrasound.

If the blood flow velocity exceeds this limit the device will incorrectly register the direction and velocity of the flow, resulting in color or spectral Doppler aliasing artifacts.
Spectral Doppler is a term used to describe pulsed wave (PW) Doppler and continuous wave (CW) Doppler imaging. In these forms of Doppler imaging, a range of frequencies returning to the transducer over a particular period undergo machine-automated Fast Fourier Transform functions. These functions allow averaging of the returned frequencies, which are converted to velocity and plotted as a function of time.

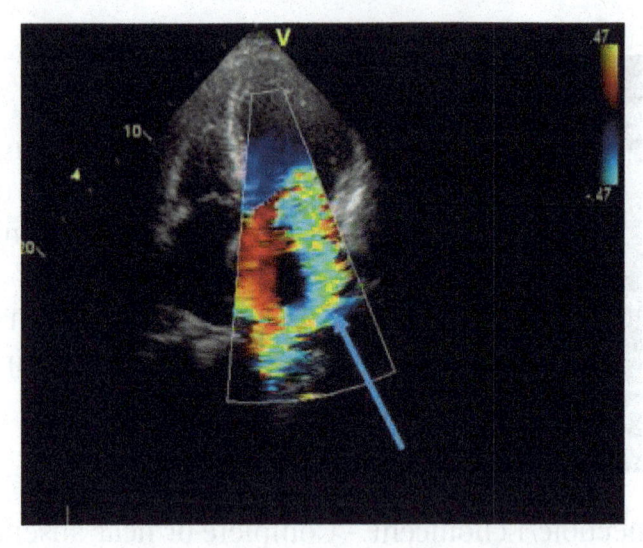

Continuous wave Doppler

- Transducer continuously sends and receives signals
- This allows for the detection of very high-frequency signals
- Velocities along the entire line of interrogation are measured and not localizable
- Cursor in middle of valve

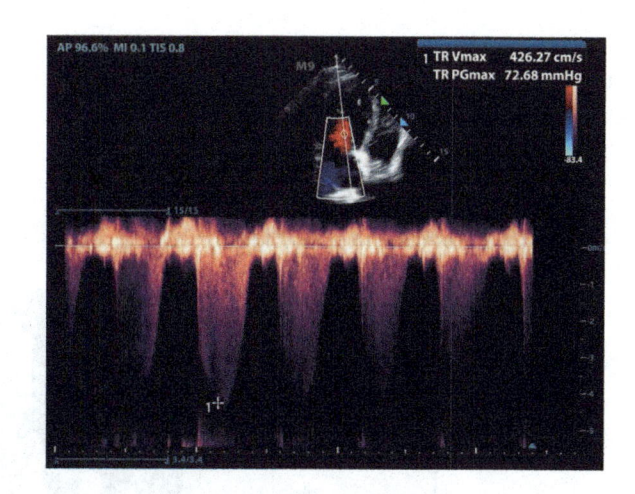

Pulsed-wave spectral Doppler

- Transducer sends pulses of ultrasounds to a predetermined depth
- Transducer then listens for returning echoes to determine flow velocities at that given location
- The "spectrum" of the returned Doppler frequencies is plotted in a characteristic two-dimensional display
- Sample volume (=) at tip of structure

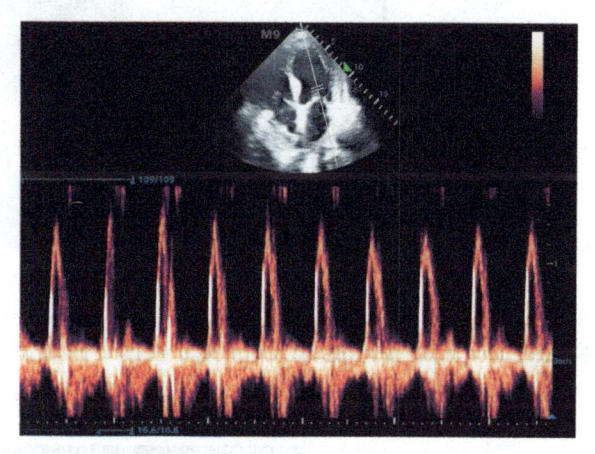

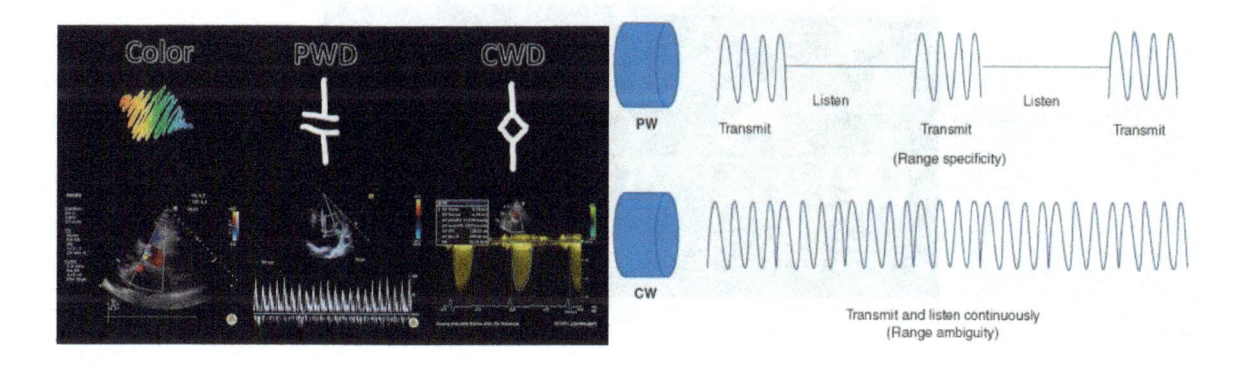

Non-imaging CWD - Looks like CW waves, just no image
- pencil probe
- PEDOF
- blind, stand-alone Doppler probe
- improved Doppler recordings

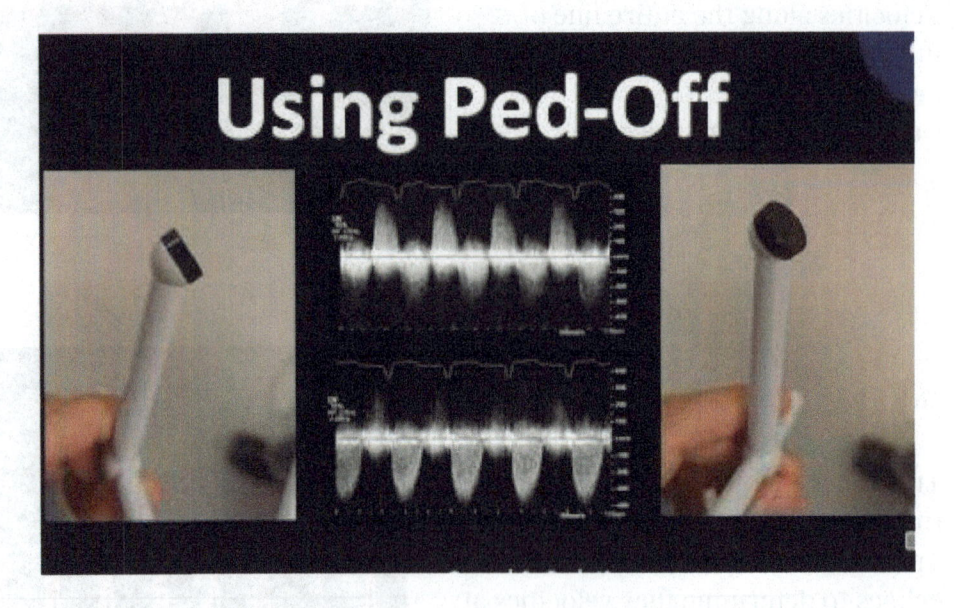

Tissue Doppler imaging (TDI) is a relatively new echocardiographic technique that uses Doppler principles to measure the velocity of myocardial motion.

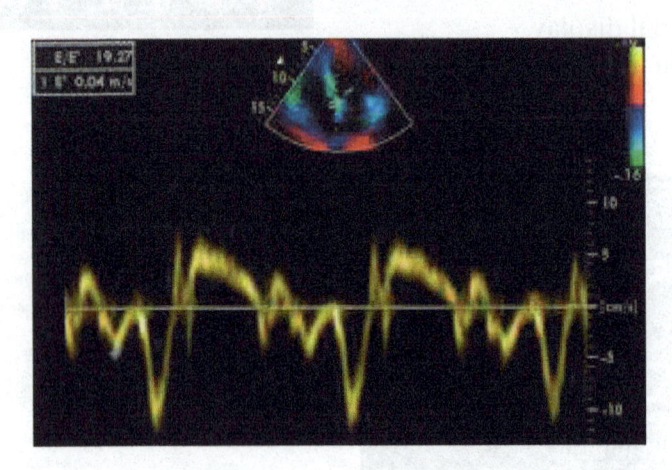

Strain imaging

In echocardiography, the term strain indicates the degree of deformation of the myocardium during the phase of contraction and relaxation. For its measurement, the speckle tracking method is used, which is a non-invasive method independent of the limits of the Doppler signal. The speckles are acoustic markers generated by the myocardium, which can be followed in their displacement during the cardiac cycle. Negative strain values are indicative of a shortening or compression of the object under examination, while positive values indicate elongation of the same. By averaging the various regional strains, it is possible to calculate the global strain or global longitudinal strain (GLS), a parameter that can accurately identify the damage of the sub-endocardial longitudinal fibers early, for example, after ischemic injury.

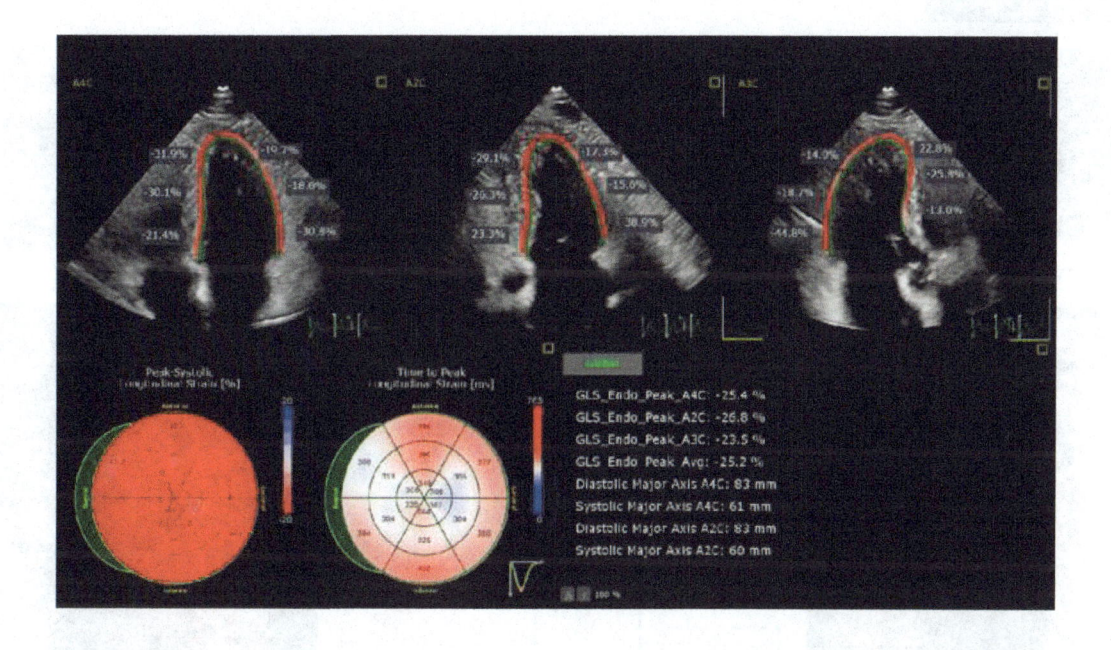

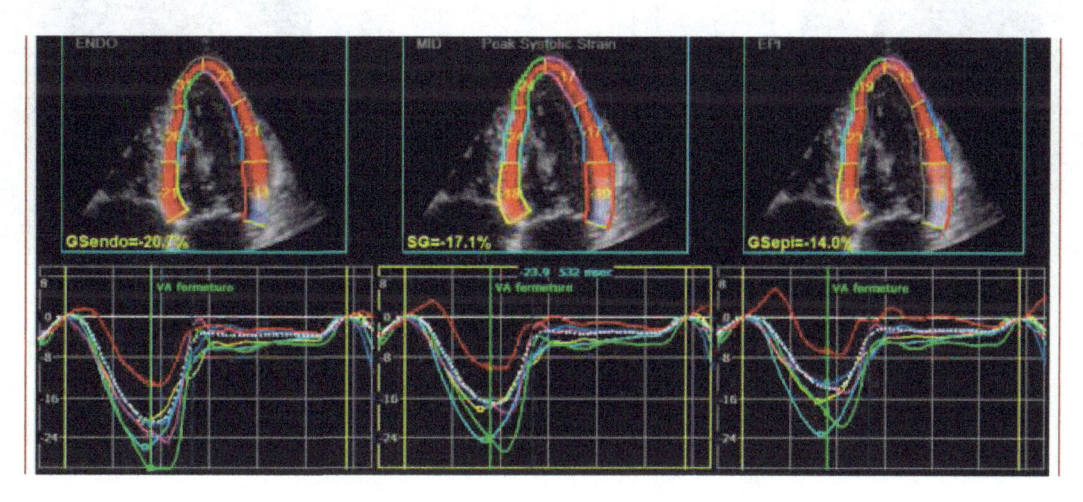

Speckle tracking echocardiography: In the fields of cardiology and medical imaging, speckle tracking echocardiography is an echocardiographic imaging technique. It analyzes the motion of tissues in the heart by using the naturally occurring speckle pattern in the myocardium.

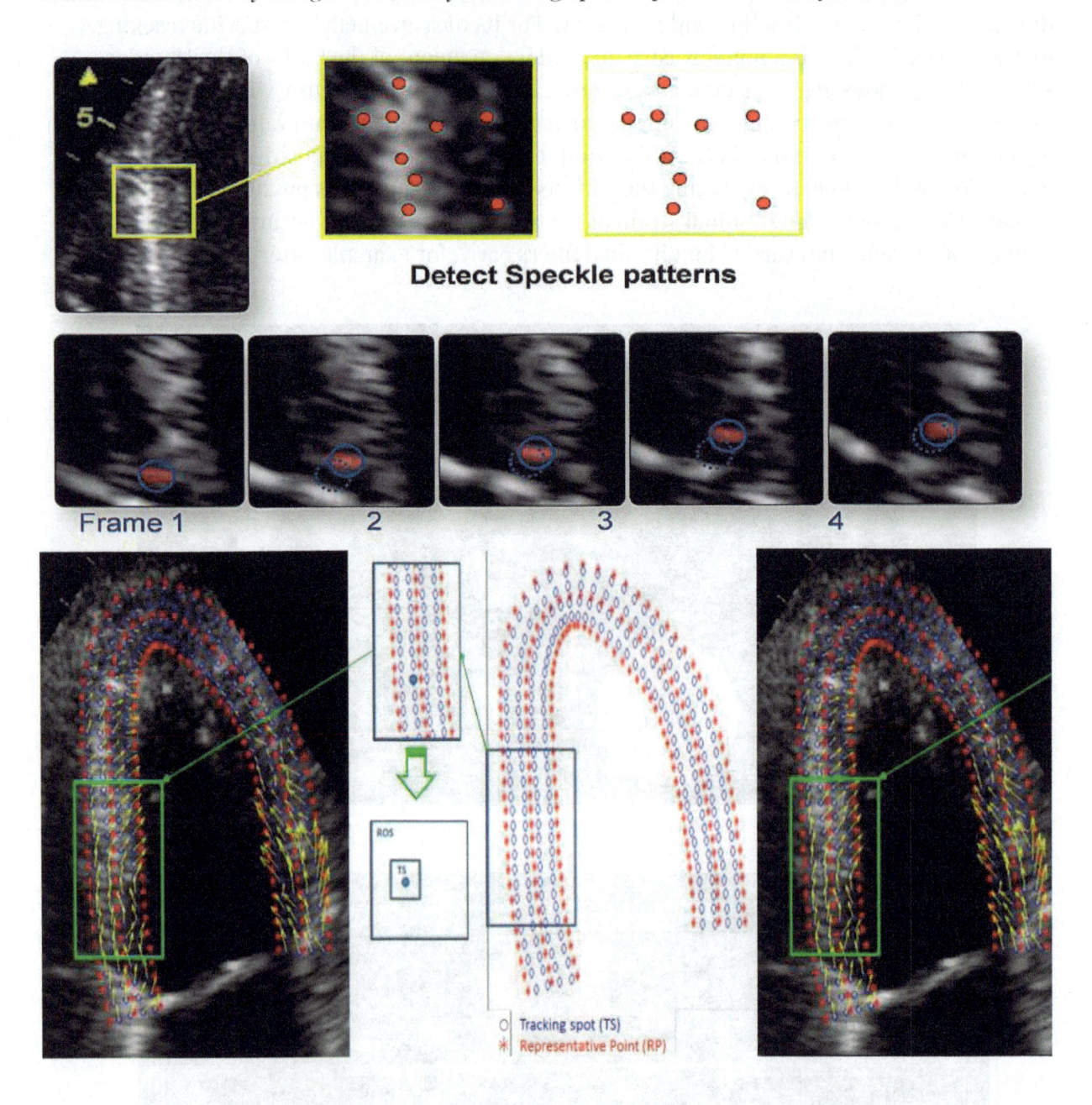

Chapter 4

Windows & Views

In echocardiography, we have windows, views and planes. The acoustic windows are named for the location of where the probe is penetrating through the chest wall. A view or plane are different images made by manipulating the probe within the same window.

There are 4 windows:
1. Parasternal
2. Apical
3. Subcostal
4. Suprasternal notch

Parasternal = Adjacent to the sternum - Start off by placing the probe on the sternum around the 3rd or 4th intercostal space.

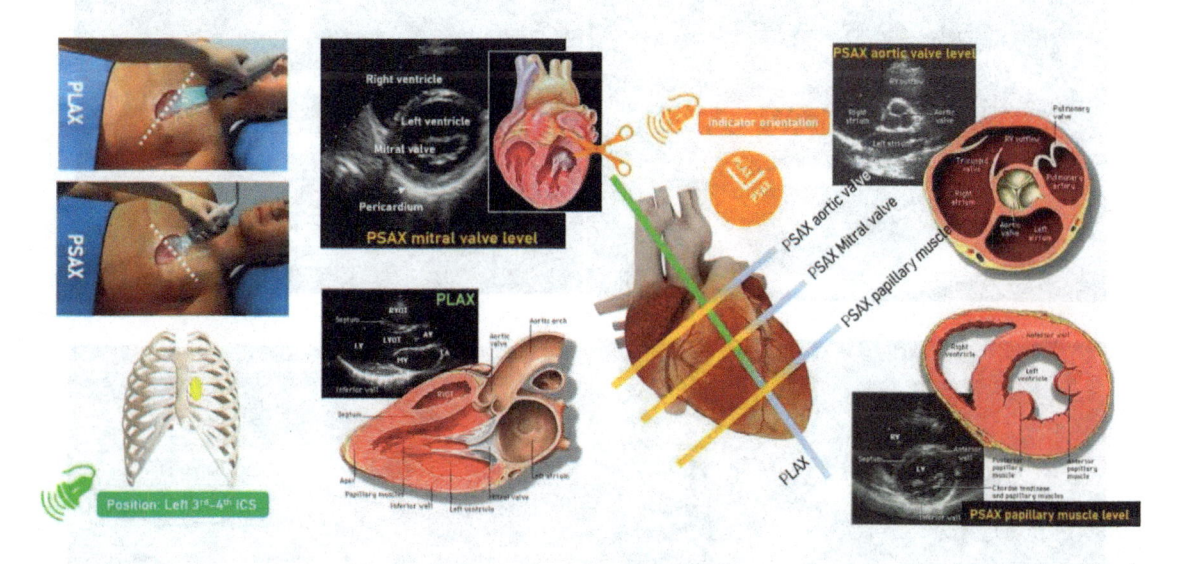

Parasternal views
Long axis - PLAX - Indicator towards the right shoulder
RVIT - tilt the probe down slightly
Short axis - SAX - rotate the prob approximately 45° clockwise
    AoV level
    MV level
    Mid papillary level   *to switch between short access views
    Apex level   tilt probe in an up/down motion*

Parasternal echo images (in order)

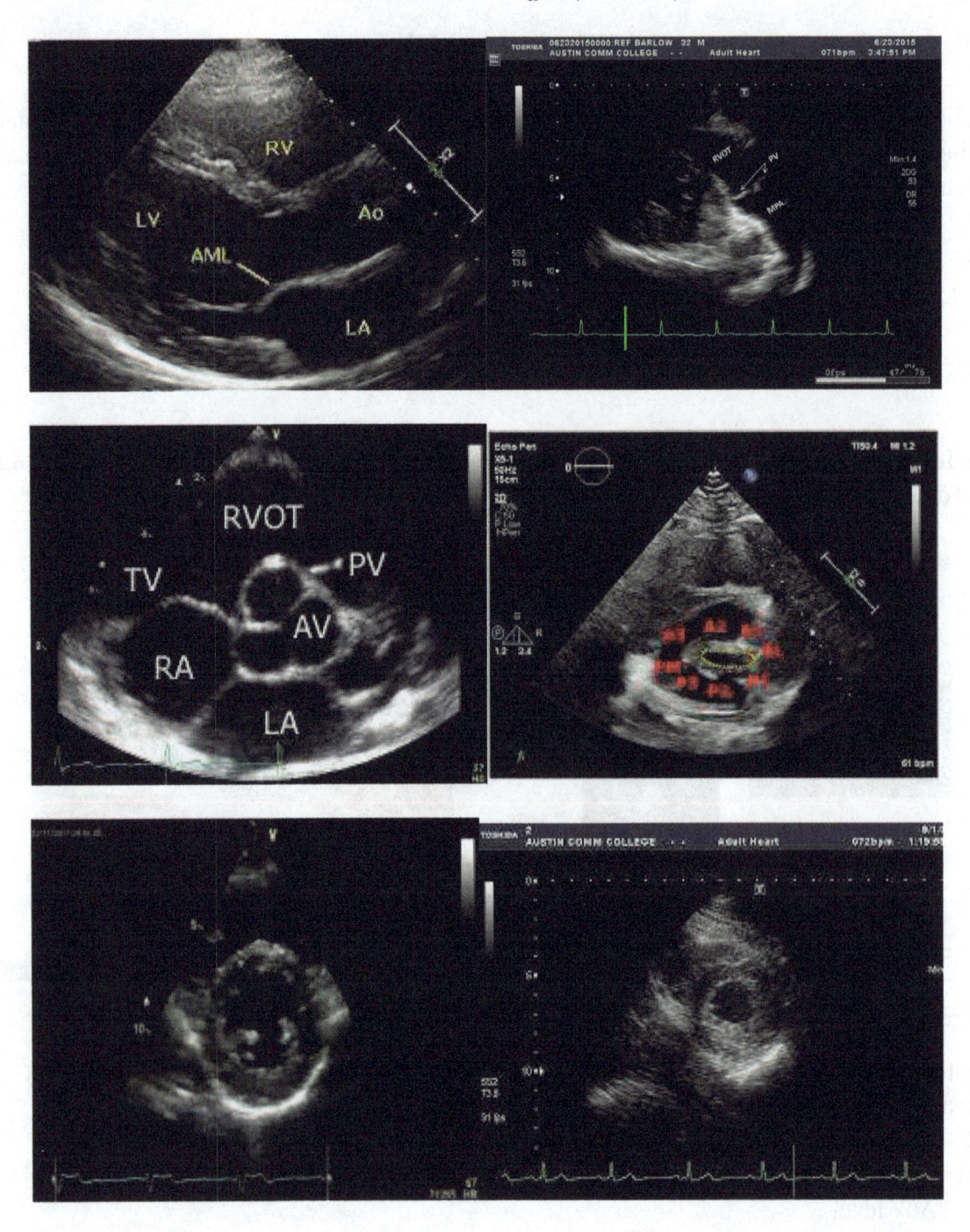

Apical window - The transducer is placed at the 4th-5th rib space and the patient's mid axilla with the image marker toward the bed.

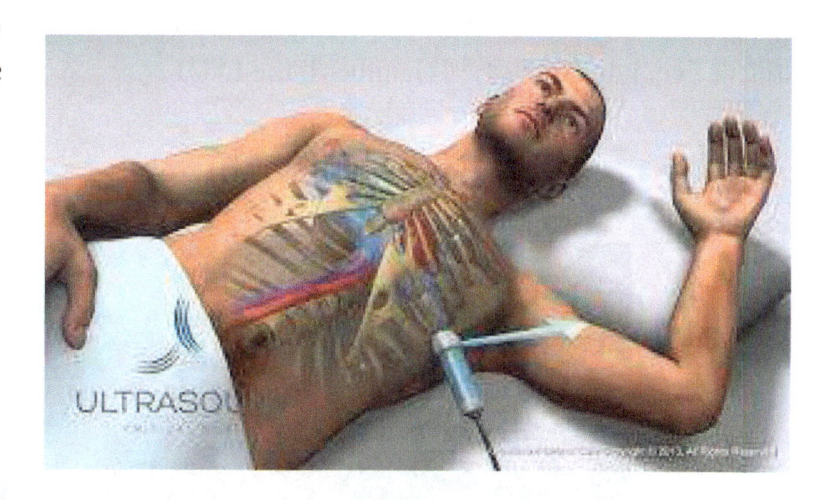

Apical views
4 chamber - starting position
5 chamber - Tilt probe very slightly superior along with a very slight clockwise rotation
2 chamber - When starting out, it's best to get the two chambers by going back to your four-chamber and then rotating the probe 45° counterclockwise
Apical long / 3 chamber

Apical 4

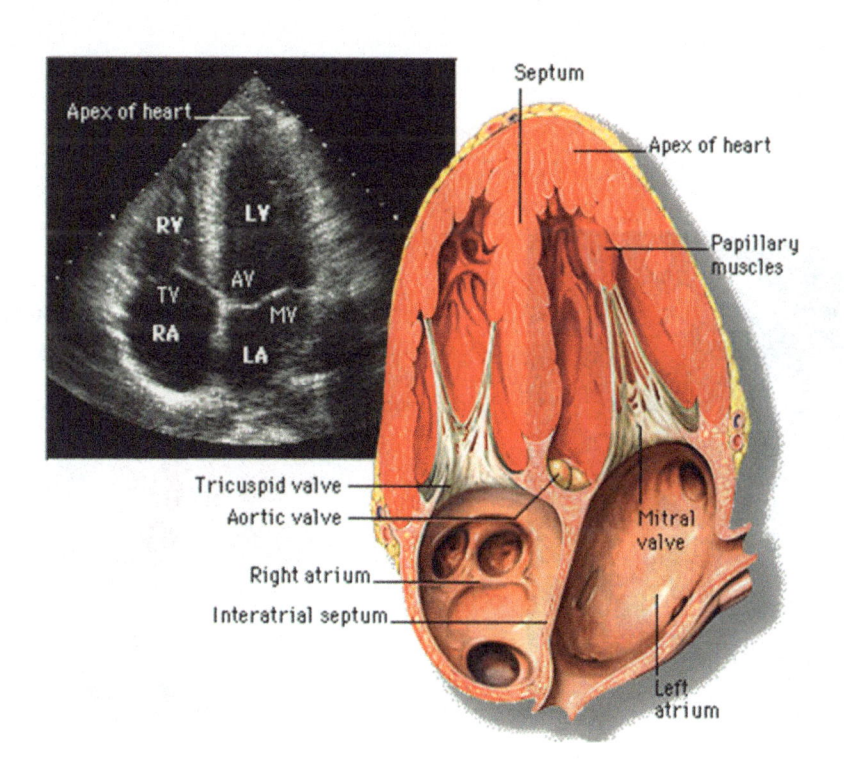

Apical 5
Still all 4 chambers, the "5th" chamber ii the LVOT

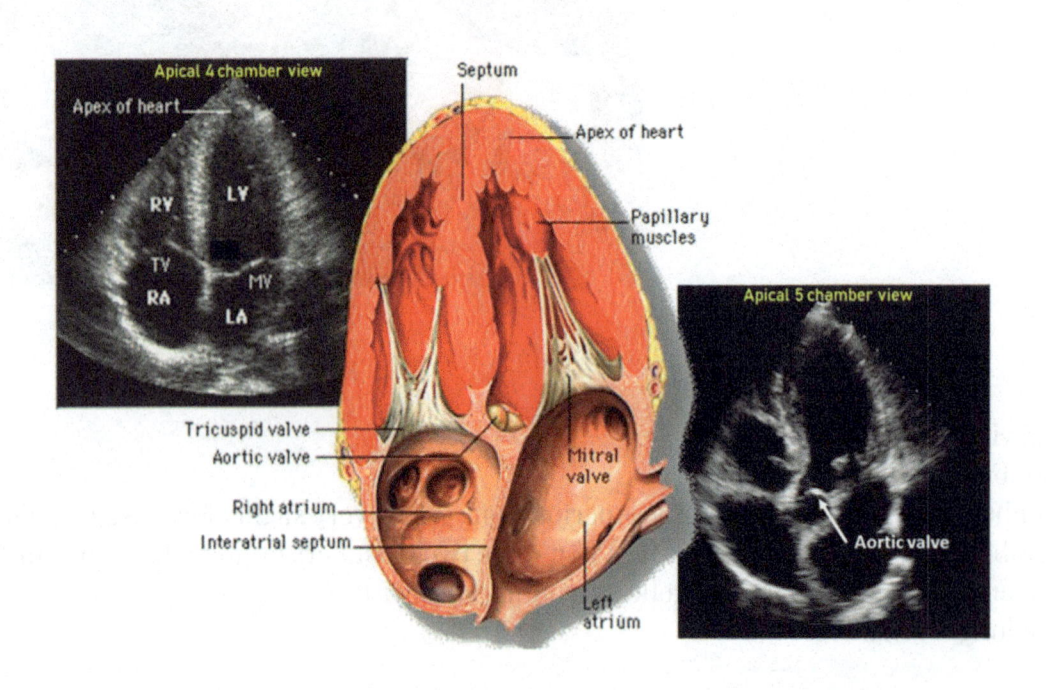

Apical 2

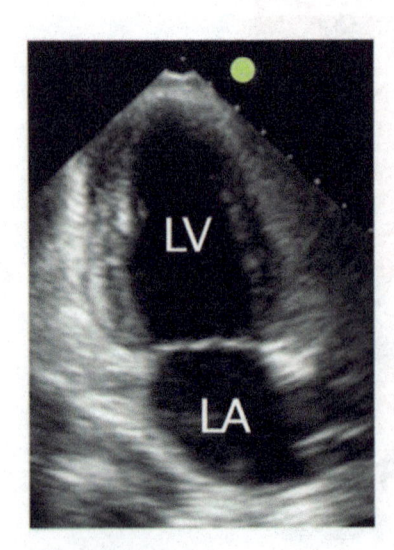

LV = left ventricle
LA = Left atrium

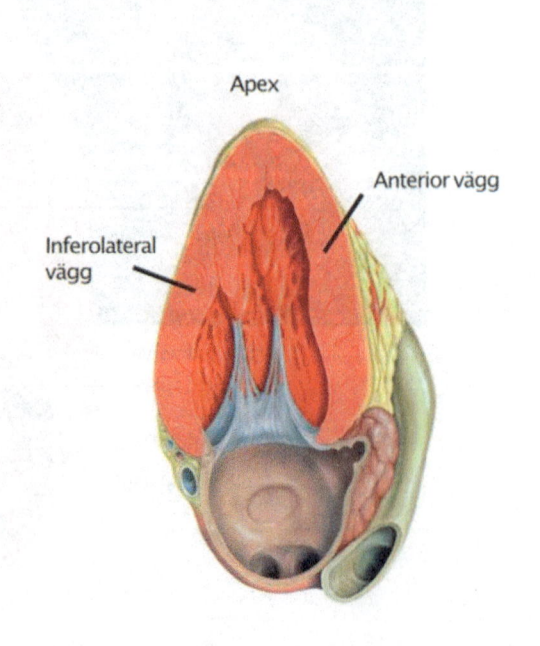

Apical 3/Long

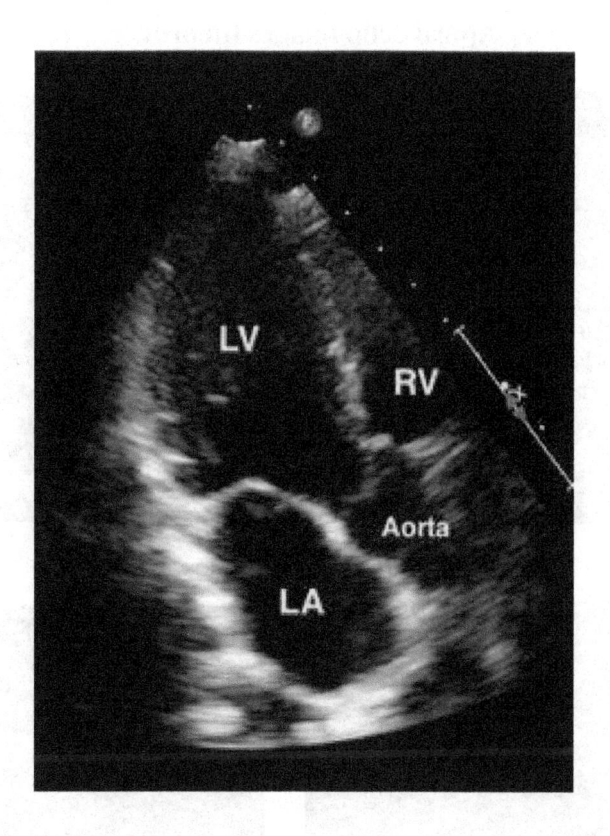

Some apical tips & tricks:
- ★ Remember that starting points are just an approximation, every patient is different. you may have to move up space or down a space, or even rotate and tilt a little more with each patient
- ★ The order in which you acquire these views is not of equal importance as getting the views themselves. As a beginner, if you happen to get the apical five first go ahead and continue on with the apical five and then move to your apical four.

Apical window - steps:
1. Started your April 4 around the 4th to 5th intercostal space and the indicator to the patients left towards the bed
2. to move to the apical five tilt the probe slightly superior and slightly twist clockwise
3. go back to your apical four, rotate your probe approximately 45° to get your apical too
4. rotate approximately another 45° for your apical 3/long

Apical echo images (in order)

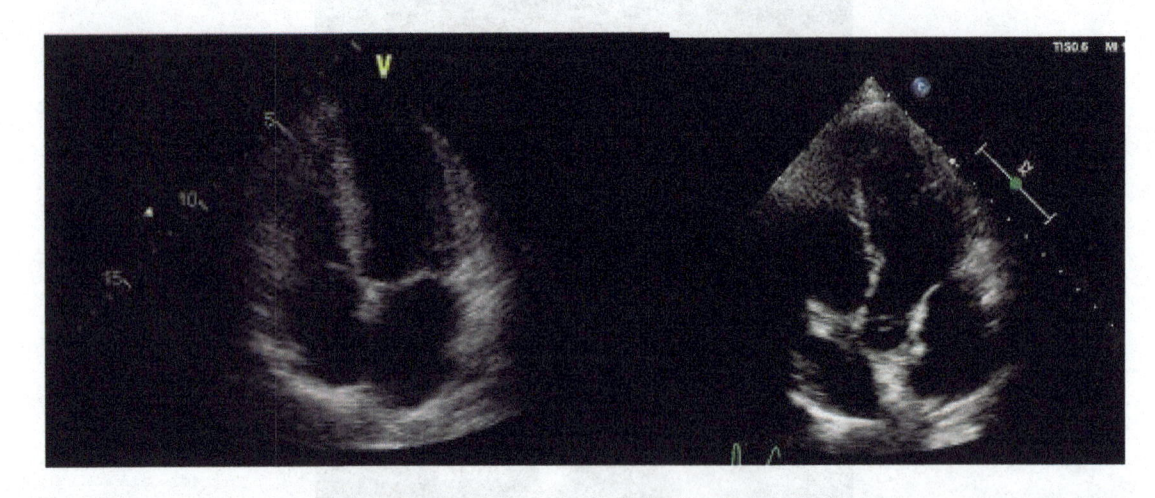

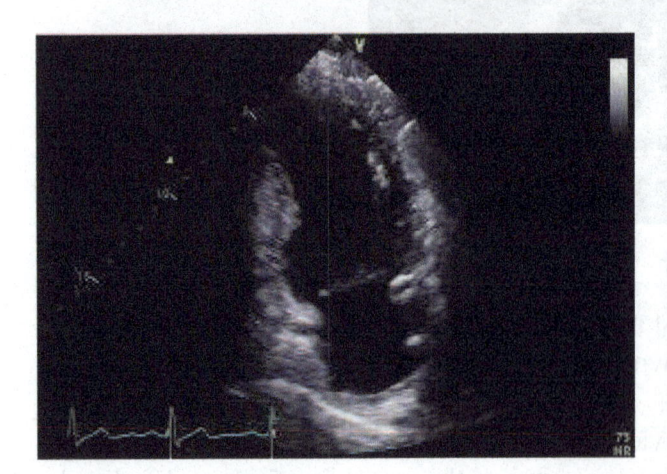

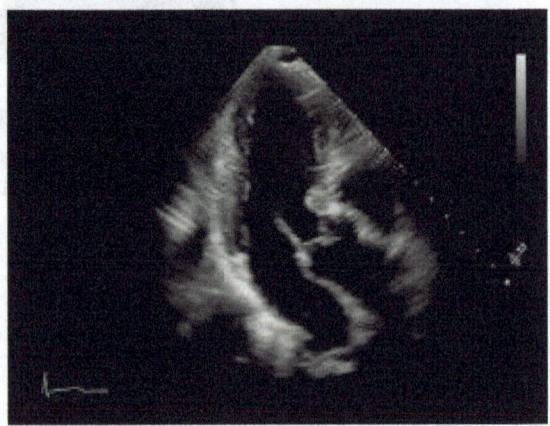

Subcostal window Images are taken below the rib cage just under the end of the sternum. indicator is to the left side of the patient. The transducer is parallel to the chest wall. This window is sometimes to the right or to the left of the sternum and not always directly underneath.

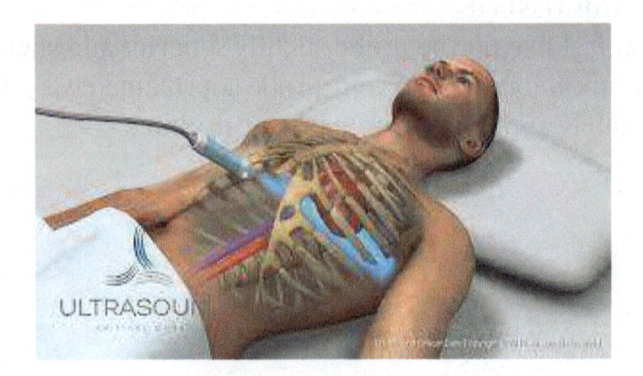

Subcostal views:
- SubC4
- SubC SAX
- SubC IVC/hepatic

SubC 4 - starting point

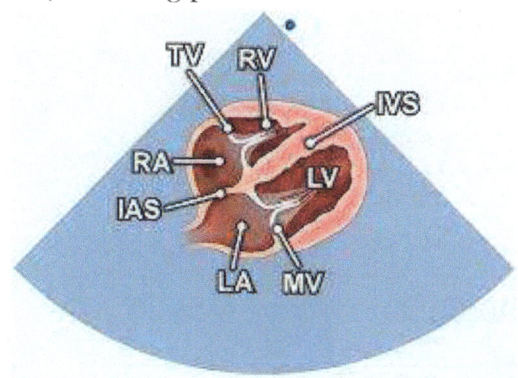

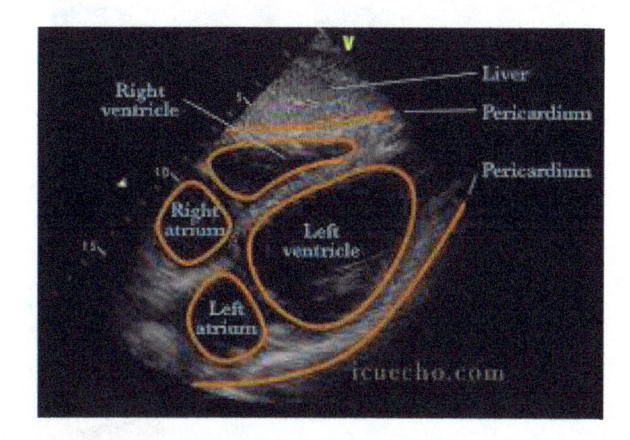

SubC SAX

This is the same structure as the short access in the parasternal view. While it is not ideal to use it for your short access it is available to you if parasternal windows are unable to be obtained.

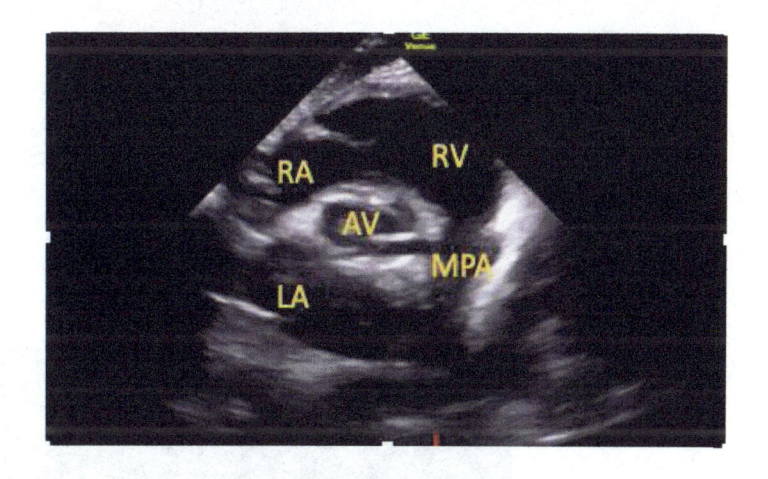

SubC IVC/hepatic - Rotate probe approximately 45° counterclockwise

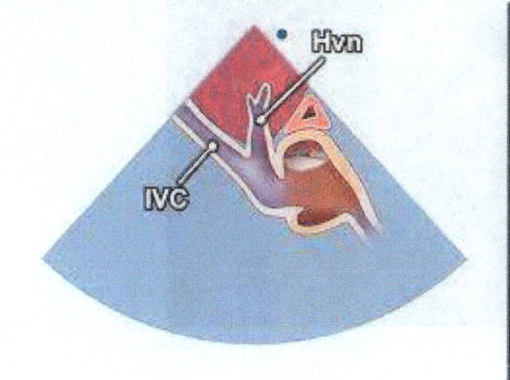

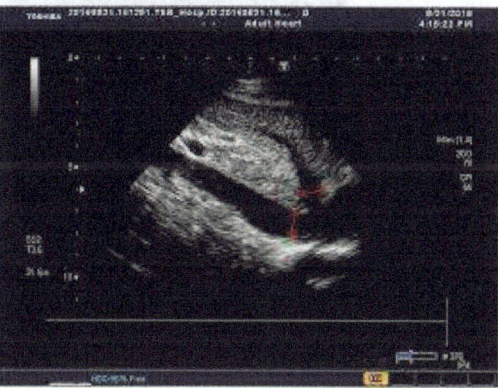

Suprasternal notch - indicator up towards the patient's chin

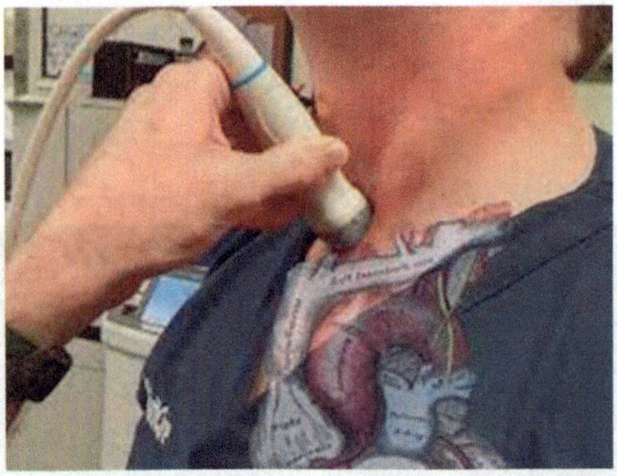

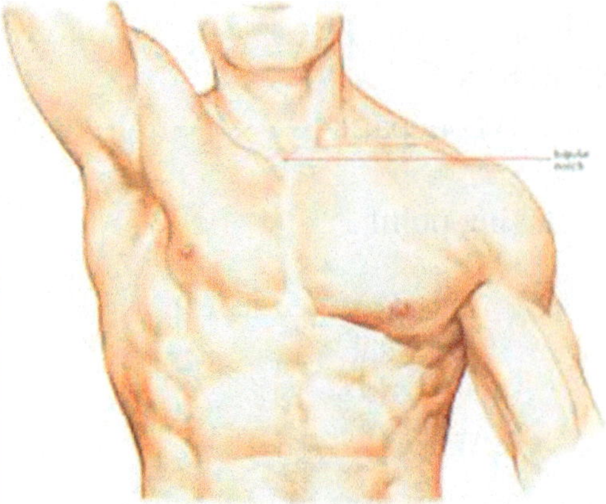

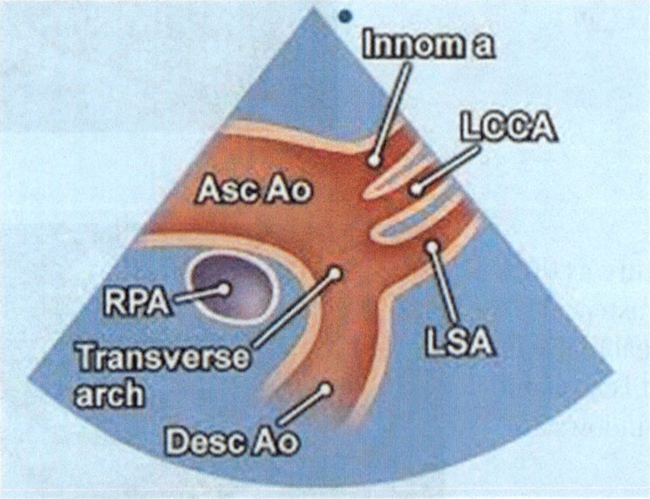
Innom a
LCCA
Asc Ao
RPA
Transverse
arch
LSA
Desc Ao

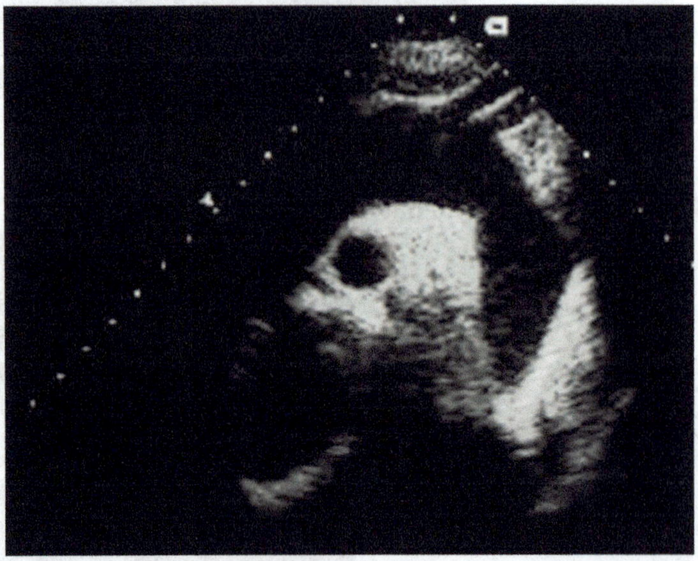

TTE windows and views

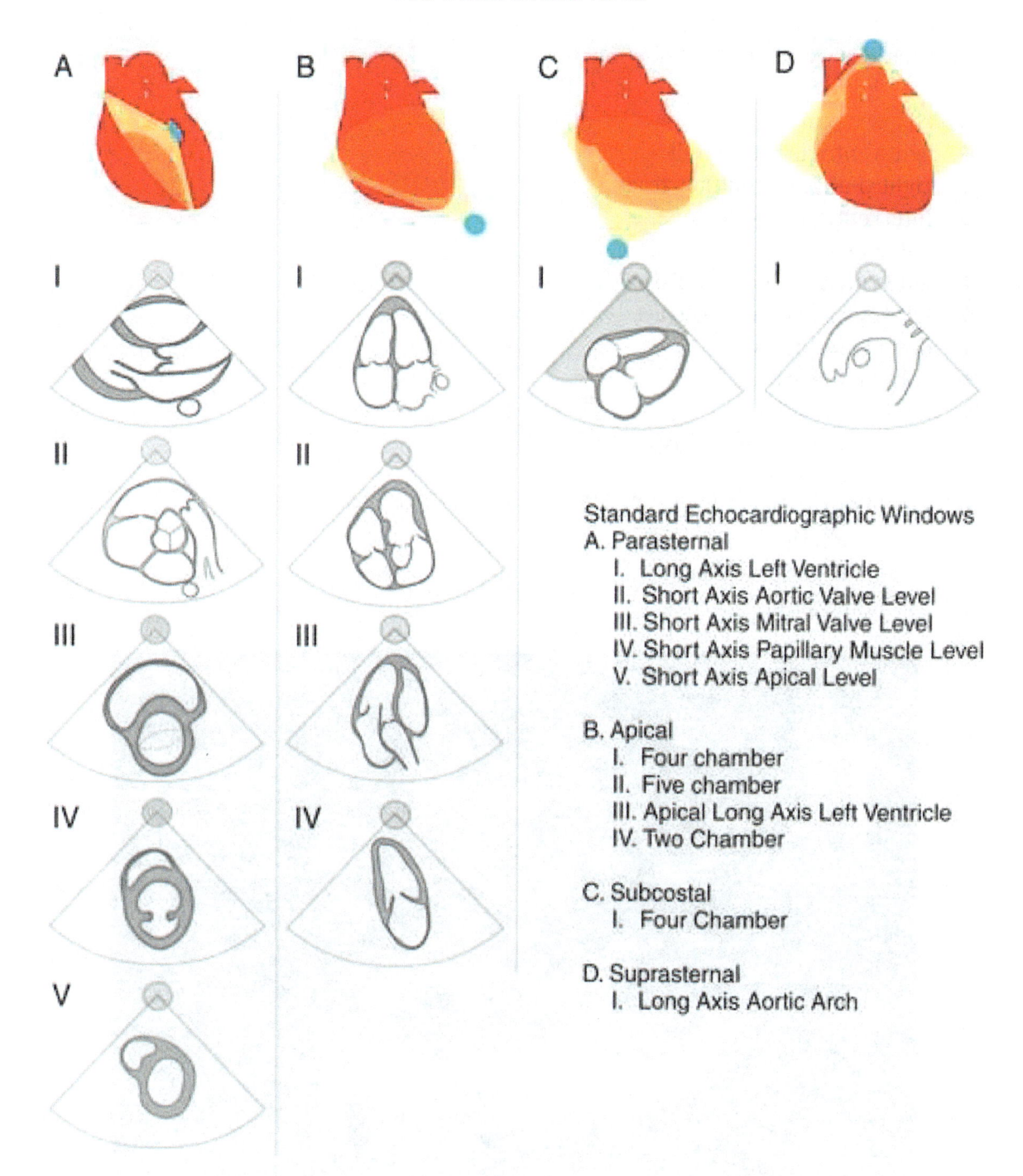

Standard Echocardiographic Windows

A. Parasternal
  I. Long Axis Left Ventricle
  II. Short Axis Aortic Valve Level
  III. Short Axis Mitral Valve Level
  IV. Short Axis Papillary Muscle Level
  V. Short Axis Apical Level

B. Apical
  I. Four chamber
  II. Five chamber
  III. Apical Long Axis Left Ventricle
  IV. Two Chamber

C. Subcostal
  I. Four Chamber

D. Suprasternal
  I. Long Axis Aortic Arch

Now that we have learned what the different windows, planes and views are, let's talk about exactly what it is we are looking at.

PLAX
- right ventricular free wall
- right ventricular outflow tract
- interventricular septum
- left ventricle
- left ventricular posterior wall
- left ventricular outflow tract
- descending aorta
- coronary sinus
- aortic valve
  - right coronary cusp
  - left coronary cusp
- mitral valve
  - anterior leaflet
  - posterior leaflet
- ascending aorta

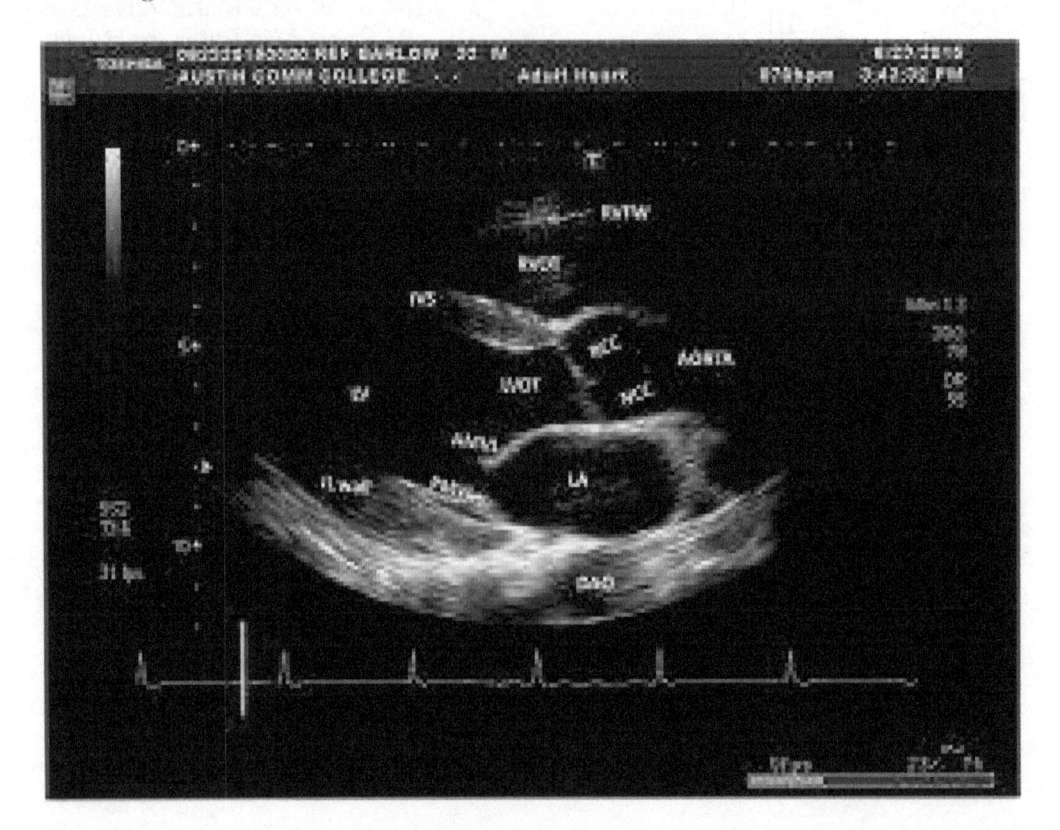

38

The left ventricular outflow tract is made up of five separate structures.
1. L V O T
2. aortic analysis
3. sinus of Valsalva
4. sinotubular junction
5. ascending aorta

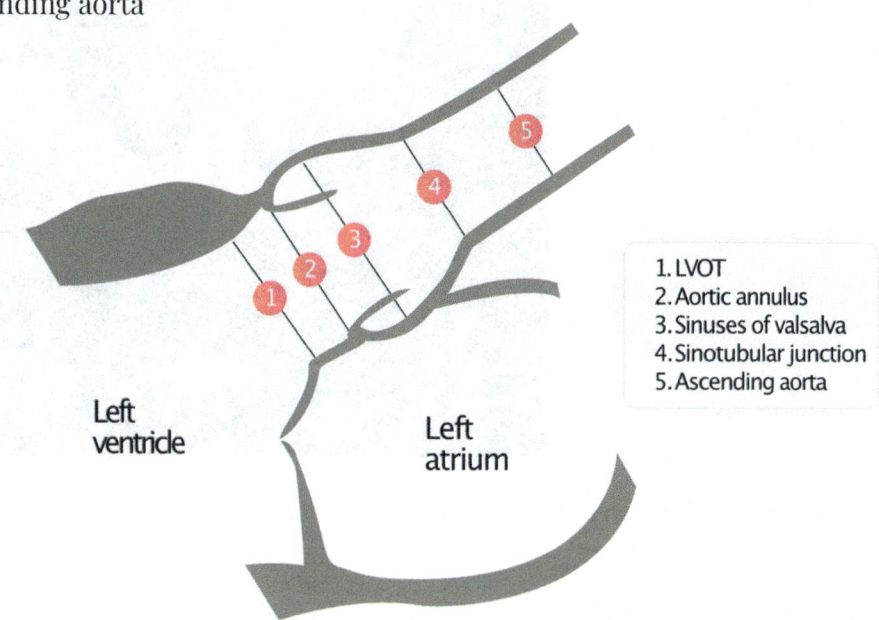

RVIT-right ventricular outflow tract
1. right ventricle
2. right atrium
3. tricuspid valve
    a. posterior leaflet
    b. anterior leaflet

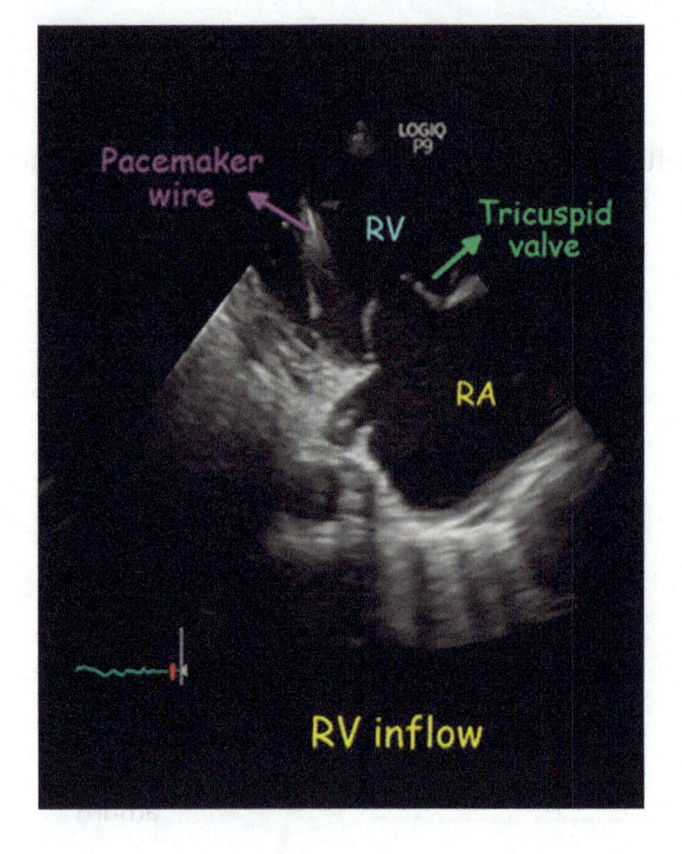

SAX apex –is the very tip of the heart

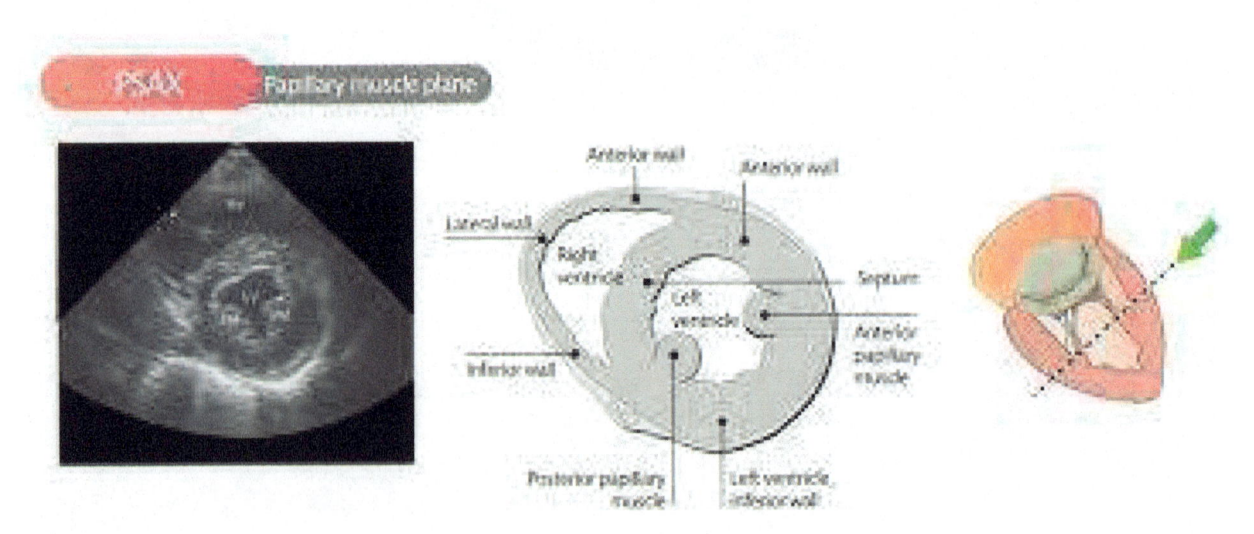

PSAX — Mitral plane

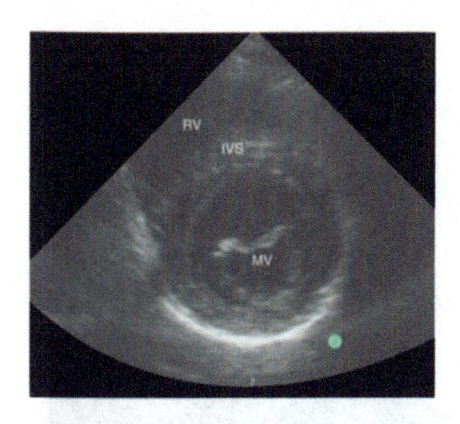

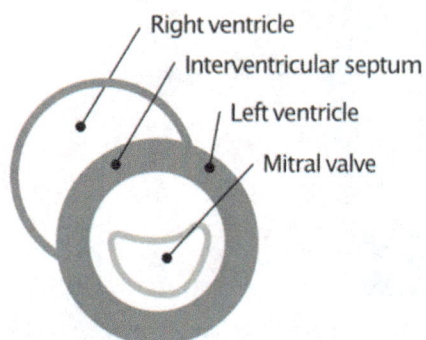

- Right ventricle
- Interventricular septum
- Left ventricle
- Mitral valve

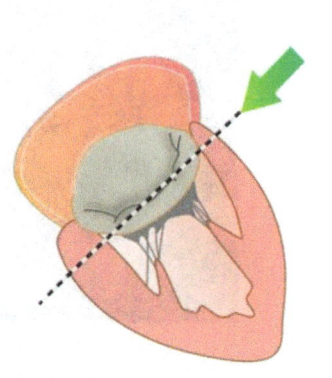

PSAX — Aortic plane

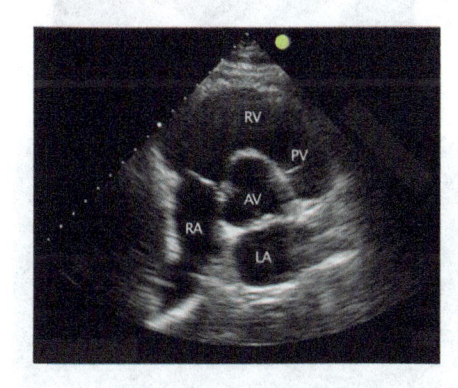

- Anterior cusp
- Septal cusp

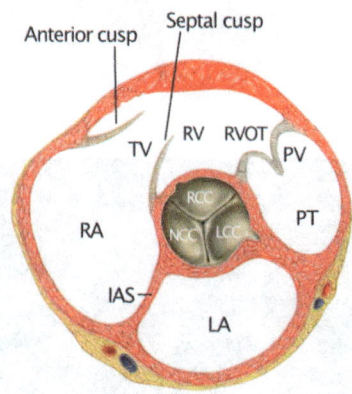

RV = Right ventricle
RVOT = Right ventricular outflow tract
AV = Aortic valve
　RCC = right coronary cusp
　NCC = non coronary cusp
　LCC = left coronary cusp
PV = Pulmonary valve
LA = Left atrium
RA = Right atrium
PT = Pulmonary trunk
TV = Tricuspid valve
IAS = Interatrial septum
PV = Pulmonary valve

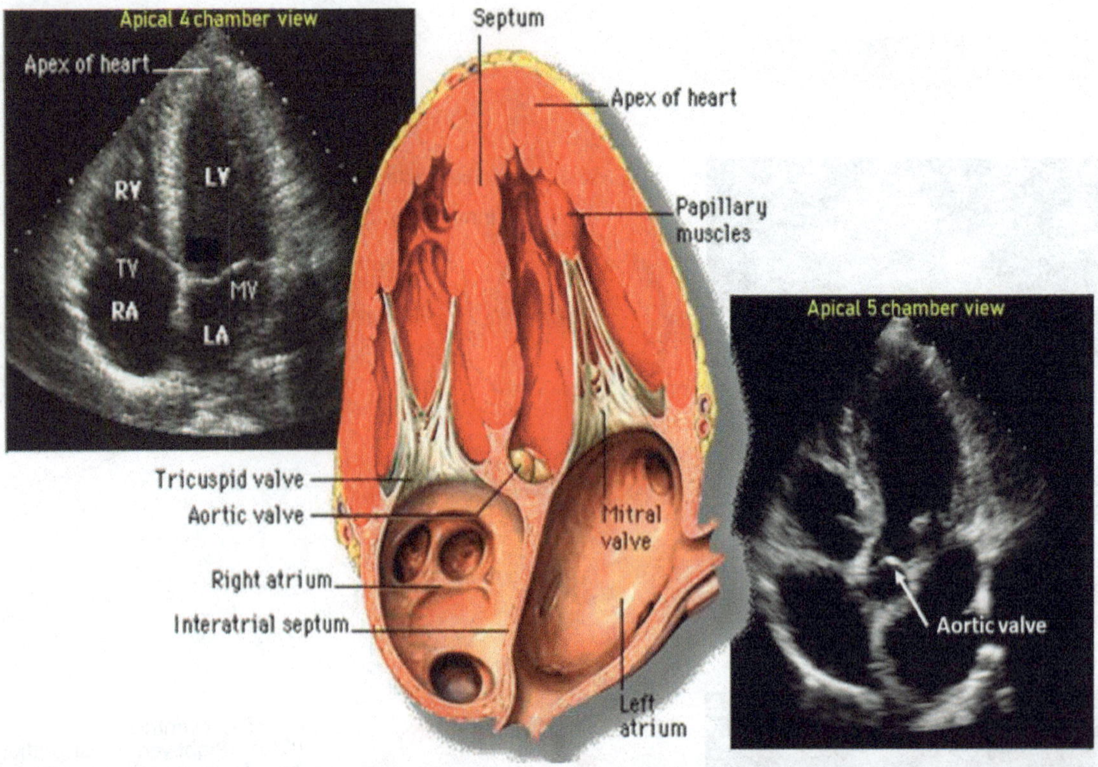
Apical 4 chamber view
Apex of heart
RV
LV
TV
MV
RA
LA
Septum
Apex of heart
Papillary muscles
Tricuspid valve
Aortic valve
Mitral valve
Right atrium
Interatrial septum
Left atrium
Apical 5 chamber view
Aortic valve

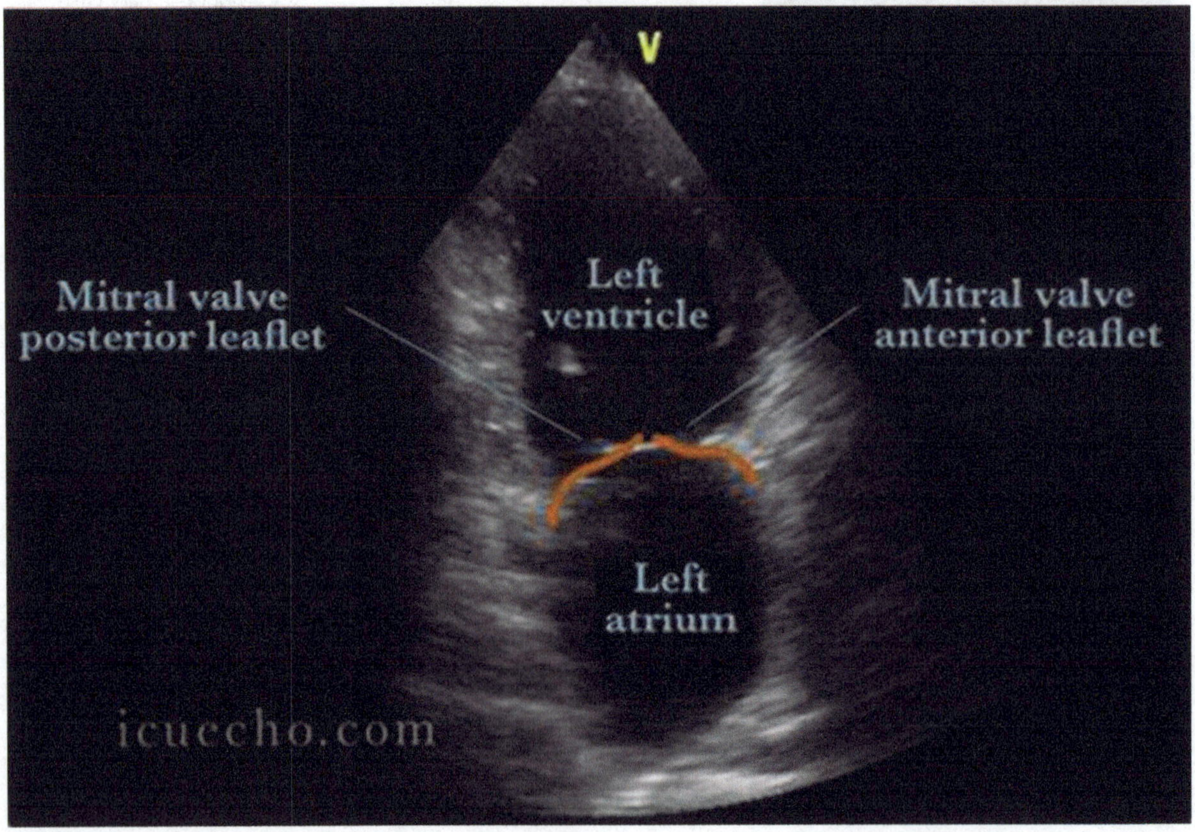
V
Mitral valve posterior leaflet
Left ventricle
Mitral valve anterior leaflet
Left atrium
icuecho.com

43

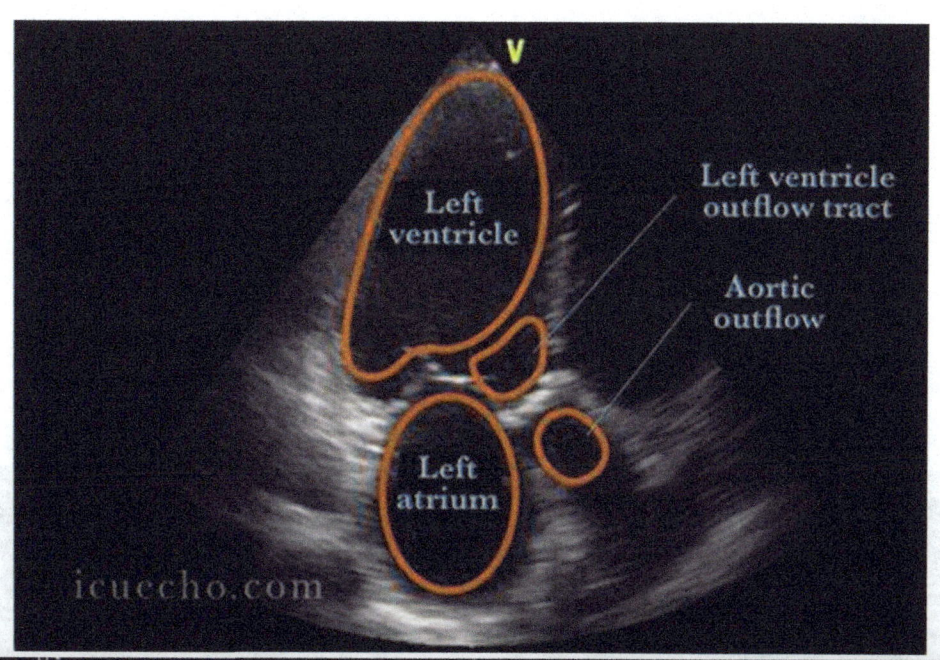

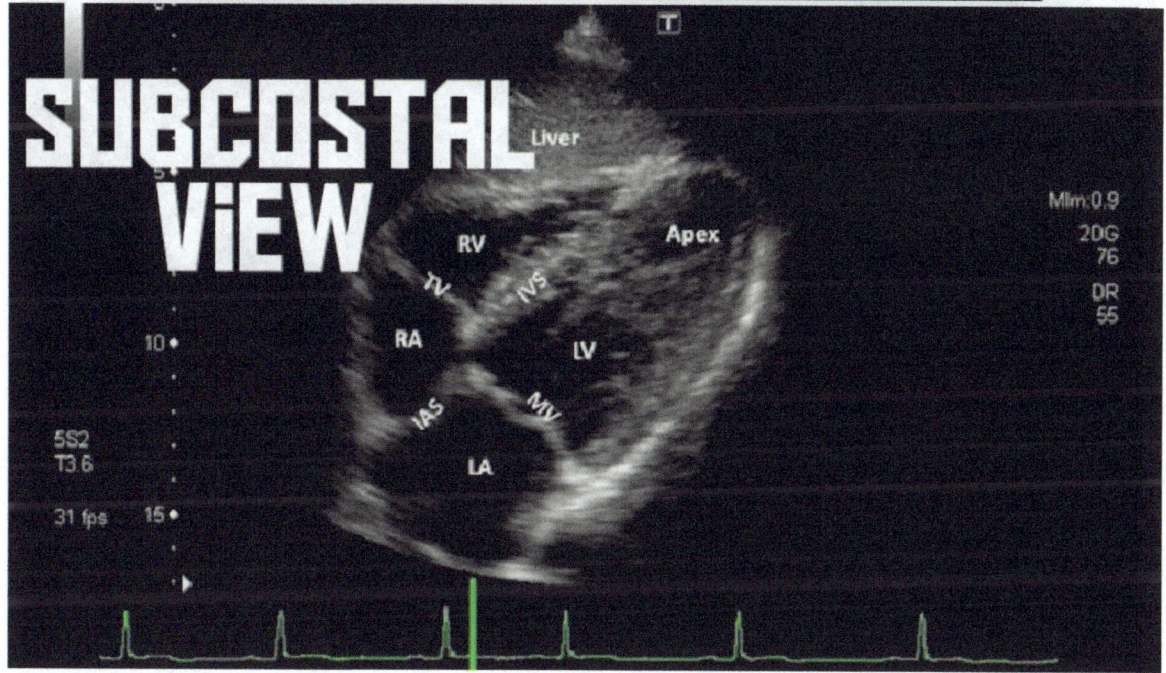

44

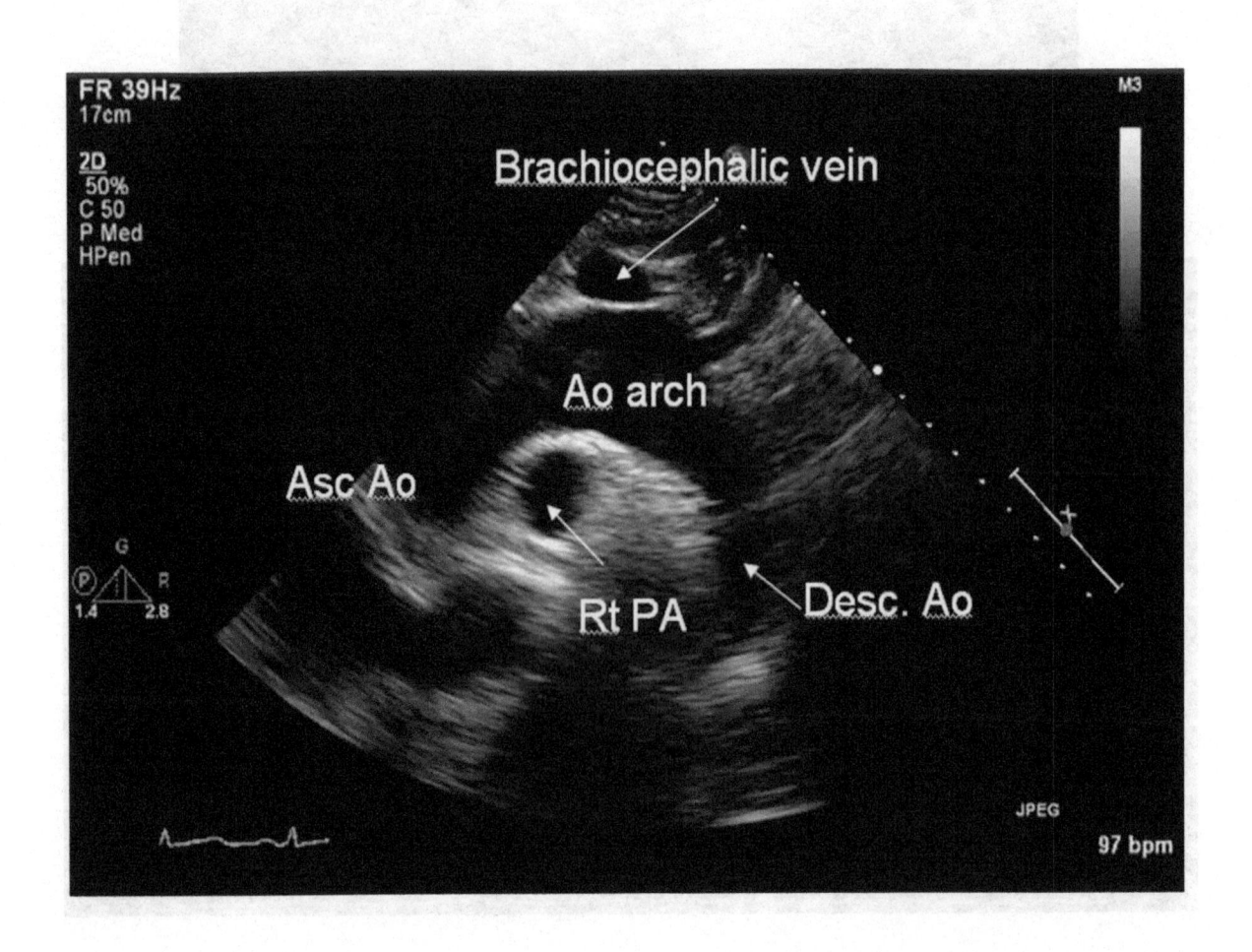

Chapter 5

Protocol & Measurements

Now that we have the different windows, views and what's inside of them down. Let's start the talk about what we do with them and in what order. The majority of echo labs in the United States use the protocol from the Intersocietal Accreditation Committee (IAC) and the American Society of Echocardiography (ASE). Protocols can and will differ depending on the facility and the facility's policies. however, any echo lab in the United States that is accredited by the IAC must obtain specific views. I refer to this as a basic protocol. The basic protocol is done on every single patient no matter, the reason or pathologies they may have. As we start to learn about the different pathologies of the heart we will add on to the basic protocol. it's important to remember, especially as a beginner, that it is more important to acquire every image of the protocol than it is in which order you acquire them.

Standard patient positioning for a transthoracic echocardiogram is left lateral recumbent.

Left Lateral Recumbent

From the IAC website:

Adult Echocardiography Protocol for Adult TTE
PROCEDURES AND PROTOCOL

Getting Started

A. Check previous studies and review key elements.
B. Optimize instrument settings prior to starting the study.
C. Verify indication for the exam.
D. Review the order and understand the physician's request.

Procedure Preparation

A. Review the order for the type of study to be performed. A verbal order may be used for stat echocardiography and a written order will be obtained as soon as possible.
B. Enter patient information into the ultrasound system (pick from list or manually).
C. Enter demographics, height, weight, BP, sonographer's name, all other information as needed.

Patient Preparation

A. Explain the procedure to the patient.
B. Verify patient ID.
C. Instruct the patient to lie on the left side.
D. Apply electrodes and attach leads.

Digital Capture

A. Make sure that you have an adequate ECG signal.
B. Patients in sinus rhythm, 2 beat captures are used.
C. Patients in Afib or any irregular rhythm, 3-5 beat captures should be used as needed.
D. When capturing a bubble contrast study use 5-10 second loops.

If images are suboptimal (when two or more LV segments cannot be visualized adequately for the assessment of LV function and regional wall motion assessment, and/or in settings in which the study indication requires accurate analysis of regional wall motion.) consider the use of an ultrasound-enhancing agent. Basic Exam (note: obtain a 2D image of the view first, followed by color/spectral Doppler in order to provide anatomic orientation). In general, spectral Doppler and M-mode should be captured at a sweep speed of 50 mm/s speed. Use 25-50 mm/s speed to demonstrate respirophasic changes that require documentation of changes across several cardiac cycles and 100 mm/s speed when making timing measurements. Optimization of Doppler signals. The Doppler display occupies about 2/3 of the scale for each velocity.
Pay particular attention to:
- Narrow aiming sector to optimize color and frame rate.
- If 2D imaging is poor (esp. in apical views) or two or more LV segments are unable to be assessed, ultrasound-enhancing agents may be considered to enhance the image.
- Proper setting of the scale, gain, filter, compress and reject with CW & PW Doppler.

- Look at extracardiac structures.
- Use off-axis images when necessary.

IMAGING PROTOCOL

Parasternal Long-Axis View
  A. Rule out pericardial/pleural effusion and assess extracardiac structures by increasing and decreasing depth. Capture 2D view. Zoom aortic and mitral valve and capture a 2D view.
  B. Measure LV septal thickness, LV end-diastolic dimension and posterior wall thickness in end-diastole at the level of the mitral valve chordae.
  C. Measure LV end-systolic dimension in end-systole at the level of the mitral valve chordae.
  D. Measure the aorta at the level of the sinuses of Valsalva. Additional measurements of the diameters of the aortic annulus, sino-tubular junction and mid-ascending aorta are needed when an abnormal aorta is suspected. A separate ascending aorta image may be required.
  E. Measure the LA dimension in end-systole.
  F. Perform color Doppler of AV/MV/Ventricular septum (requires separate captures). AV and MV with zoom and color Doppler as needed.

RV Outflow Tract View

  A. Capture a 2D image
  B. Perform color Doppler of the PV
  C. PW RVOT
  D. CW PV

RV Inflow View

  A. Capture 2D images.
  B. Perform color Doppler of TV for TR.
  C. Measure peak TR velocity for calculation of RA/RV pressure gradient.

Parasternal Short-Axis View (Aortic Level)

  A. Capture a 2D image at the level of the AV (imaging AV, TV, PV, and LA), examine AV, PV and TV leaflets, structures with 2D, PW, CW, and color Doppler.

B. Aortic valve level:
C. 2D image.
D. Zoom aortic valve.
E. Perform color Doppler on the AV.
F. Perform color Doppler on the PV and PA.
G. Perform PW and CW Doppler across the PV.
H. Perform CW Doppler to obtain TR velocity to calculate PASP if TR is present.

Parasternal Short-Axis (Mitral valve)

A. Capture a 2D image

Parasternal Short-Axis (Left ventricle)

A. Capture 2D LV at basal, middle (papillary muscle) and apex levels.
B. Zoom the LV at the MV leaflet level and perform color Doppler in the presence of MV disease as needed.

Apical 4-Chamber View

A. Capture a 2D image to examine the structure and wall motion; avoid foreshortening of the LV. Use a narrow 2D sector and/or zoom to improve image quality to assess LV wall motion and look for a thrombus. Adjust depth, focal point, probe setting (frequency) and gains to optimize images.
B. Obtain a 2D image focused on the RV. Adjust transducer placement to ensure RV apex and free wall anatomy are the focus of the image. Use a narrow 2D sector and/or zoom to improve image quality as needed. Adjust depth, focal point, probe setting (frequency) and gains to optimize images.
C. Perform color Doppler of MV, TV and AV.
D. Perform PW Doppler of the MV with the sample volume at the leaflet tips, measure E/A waves velocities.
E. Perform tissue Doppler of lateral and septal mitral annulus to measure E', for E/E' ratio as needed.
F. Perform Color M-mode Doppler as needed.
G. Perform CW of MV, TV.
H. LV volumes are measured in diastole and systole to obtain an ejection fraction. During tracing, pay particular attention to apical foreshortening; including (not excluding) papillary muscle in tracing; apical alignment; mitral annulus. If calculated EF is

significantly discordant with a visual estimate, review, acquire and measure additional cardiac cycles.
I. Each of the above measurements will be frozen and then acquired.
J. Measure LA and RA areas as needed.
K. Perform PW Doppler of pulmonary veins (sample volume 3-4 mm) as needed.

Apical 5-Chamber View

A. Capture 2D images.
B. Perform Color Doppler, PW, and CW Doppler of LVOT; pay attention to the position of PW sample volume.

Apical 2-Chamber View

A. Capture 2D images, take care not to foreshorten the image.
B. Perform color Doppler of the MV.
C. Perform LA area and volume as needed.

Apical 3-Chamber View (Apical Long-Axis View)

A. Capture 2D images, take care not to foreshorten the image.
B. Perform color Doppler of the MV and the AV.
C. Perform PW/CW of LVOT/AV (in the presence or suspicion of aortic stenosis or calcification or LVOT obstruction). Pay attention to the position of the PW sample volume.

Subcostal View

A. Capture 2D images.
B. Perform color Doppler of the MV and TV and IAS and IVS to look for a shunt.
C. Perform CW for the TR velocity to calculate the pressure gradient as needed.
D. Capture 2D of the IVC and observe for collapse (set for 3-5 seconds to appropriately capture). Be sure to include inspiration/expiration and "sniff" if needed.
E. Perform color Doppler of HV/IVC.
F. Perform PW Doppler of the HV/IVC flow.
G. Capture 2D subcostal short-axis view as needed (if parasternal view is not optimal).

Suprasternal View

A. Capture a 2D image of aortic arch.
B. Perform color Doppler, PW and CW Doppler as needed

Once you have all of the required pictures taken you can then move on to your measurements. Most Echo technicians who have experience do measurements as they go. As a beginner it is recommended that you get all your pictures, focus on image optimization and ensure you have the required protocol acquired. You can then go back post-exam and do all of your measurements. Before we get into normal values look at the table below to help identify spectral Doppler measuring.

Measurement name	Unit	Measurement technique
Vmax	cm/sec	Max point
VTI	cm²	Trace
PHT	ms	Slope

PLAX Measurements & values (cm) - Mode: 2D

LVIDd	3.5 - 5.6	LAs	2.5-3.0
LVIDs	2.0 - 4.0	LVOTms	~2.0
IVSD	0.6 - 1.0	SoV	3.0 - 3.4
LVPWd	0.6 - 1.0	STJ	2.6 - 3.0
RVDd	0.7-2.3	ascAo	2.5 - 3.0

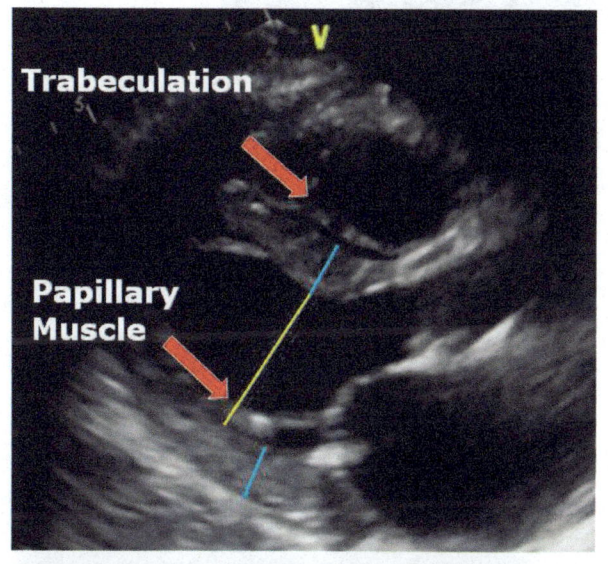

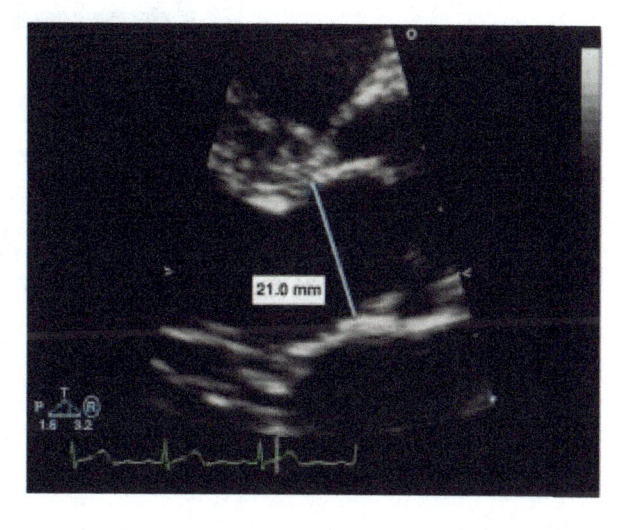

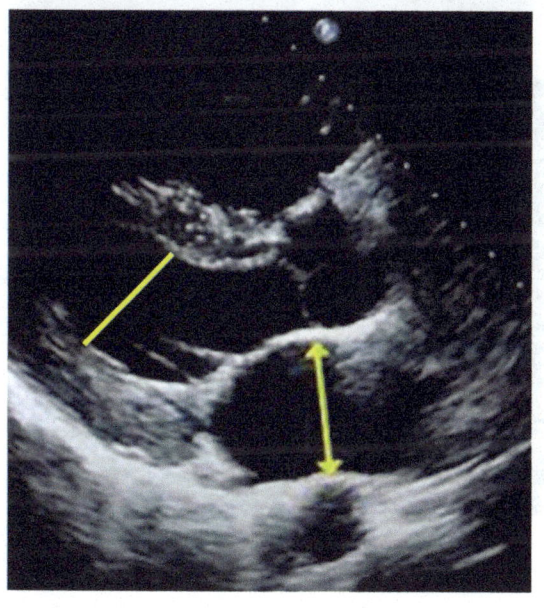

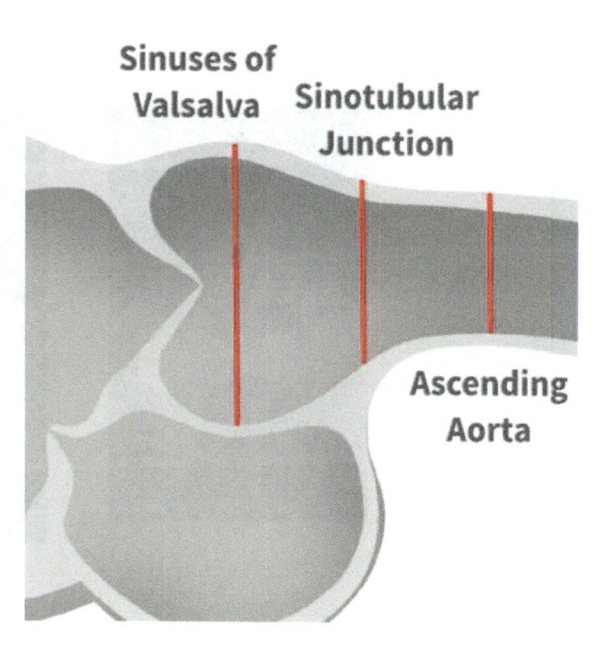

Apical 4
Mode: M-mode
TAPSE ~1.7

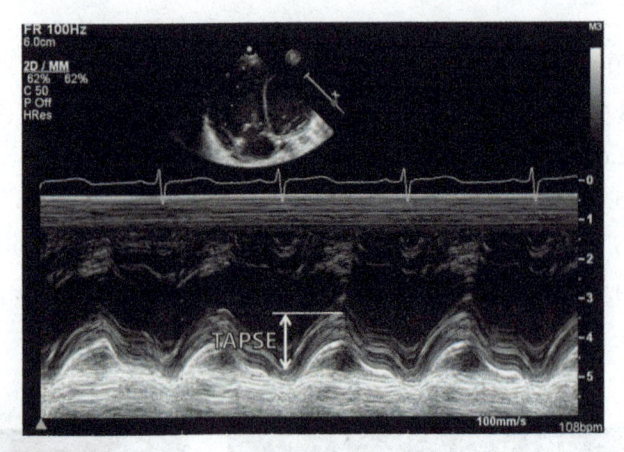

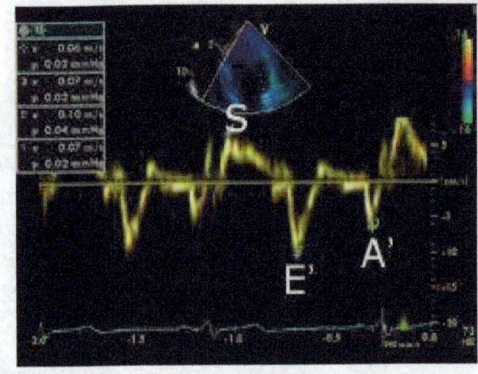

Mode: TDI
RVS`»~1.8
Med e`~ (needed for E/e` calculation)
Lat e`~ (needed for E/e` calculation)

Mode: CW

AoV VTI Vmax

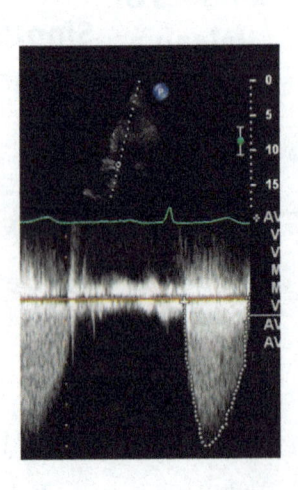

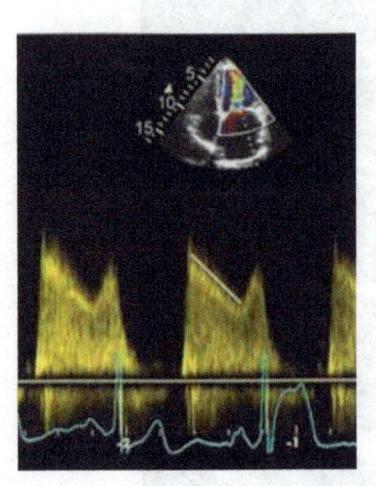

MV VTI & PHT

Mode: PW

MV E point, A point, Decel slope
Used for E/A ratio

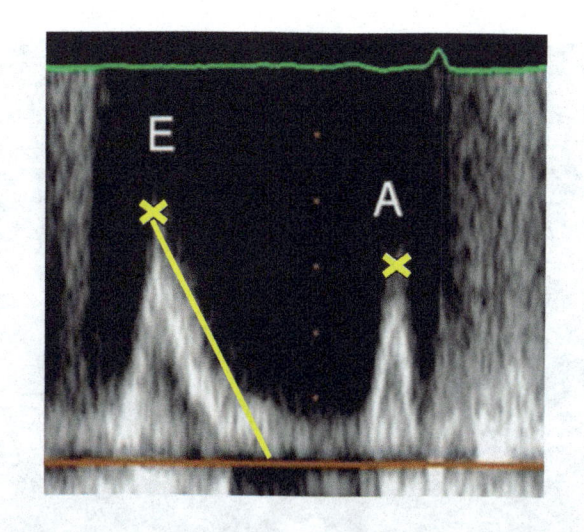

LVOT VTI & Vmax

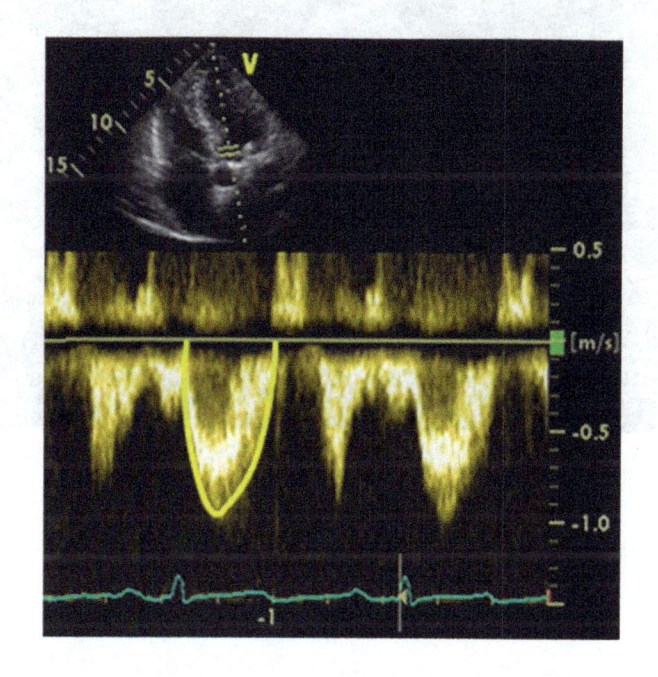

Mode: 2D
LAVIml/m²   34-38
- ★ Trace LA in systole
- ★ This is a biplane calculation, measurements from A4 & A2 are needed

LV EF (%)   55%-70%
- ★ Trace the LV in both diastole and systole
- ★ This is a biplane calculation, measurements from the A4 & A2 are needed
- ★ Measure from the edge of the endocardium around the entire left ventricle

54

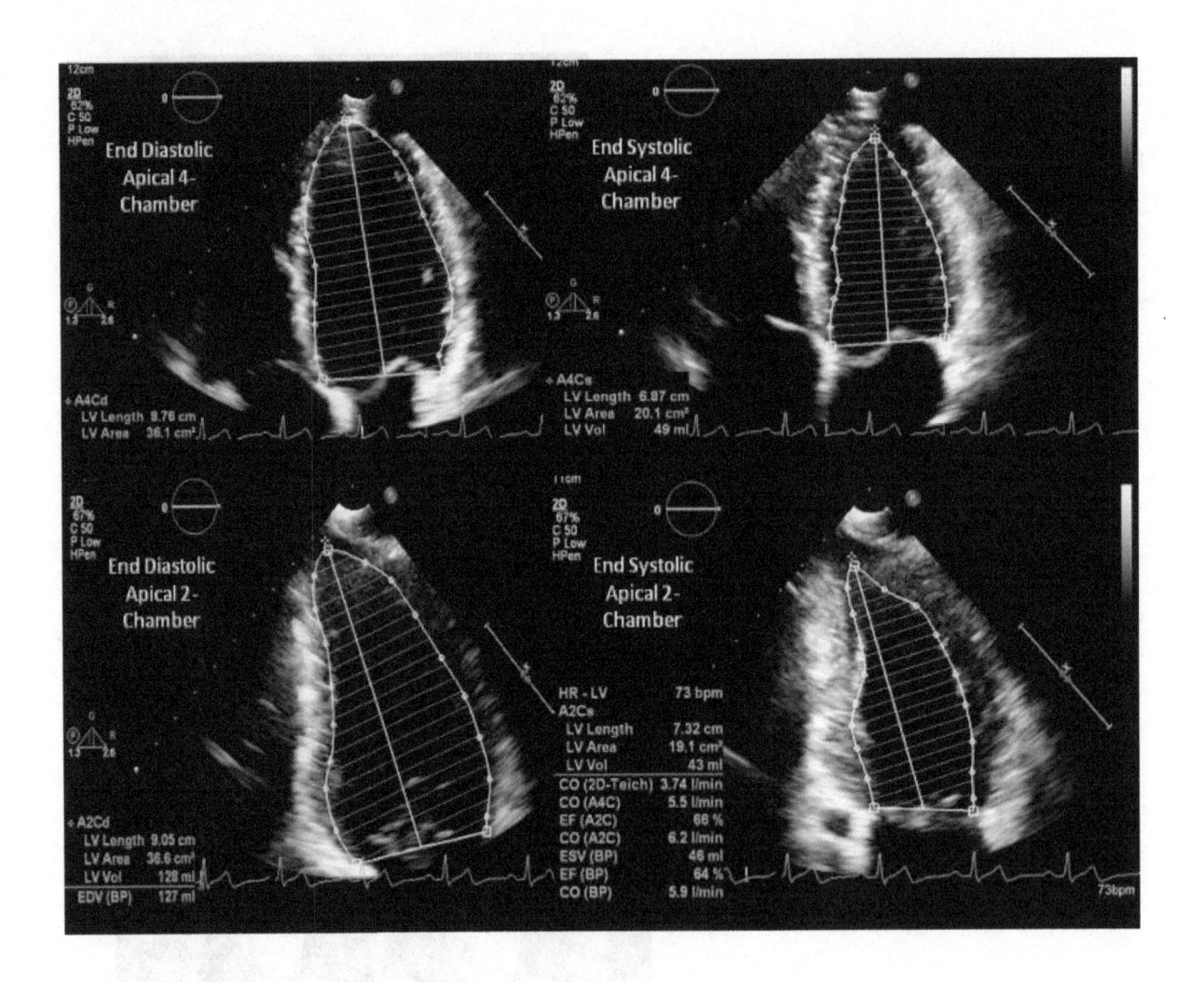

UNIT 3

Pathology

Chapter 6
Valvular Heart Disease

Valvular heart disease is when any valve in the heart has been damaged or is diseased. Heart valve disease may be present at birth(congenital), or it can also occur in adults due to many causes and conditions such as infections and other heart conditions. The four heart valves, which keep blood flowing in the right direction are the mitral, tricuspid, pulmonary and aortic valves. Each valve has flaps or leaflets that open and close once per heartbeat. If one or more of the valves fail to open or close properly, the blood flow through the heart to your body is disrupted. In order to fully understand valvular heart disease, you must ensure that you have a full understanding of blood flow and how the hemodynamics are throughout the valves. Like color flow Doppler, spectral Doppler shows the direction of flow. AV valves flow in the same direction, Towards the probe, while the semilunar valves also flow in the same direction which is away from the probe. From what we have learned already, if the AV valve flows towards the probe what direction will the waveform on the baseline? What about the semilunar valves? In the last unit when talking about measurements there were examples of spectral Doppler for the mitral and aortic valves. When trying to answer this, think about the blood flow, think about the direction it's moving throughout the heart. The correct answers are AV valves flow above the Baseline while your semilunar valves flow below. If the valvular disease is significant enough it can create an extra hard sound which clinically is called a murmur.

Valvular stenosis
Stenosis is the narrowing or restriction of a blood vessel or valve that reduces blood flow. The valve flaps become thick or stiff and possibly fuse together. This results in a narrowed valve opening and reduced blood flow through the valve. Stenosis causes pressure overload. The easiest way to imagine the change of velocity through a stenotic valve is to imagine water flowing through a hose. that would represent the normal velocity through the valves. Now imagine putting your thumb at the end of the hose, this represents a stenotic valve. that narrowing causes a significant increase in velocity.

Laminar Flow   Turbulent Flow

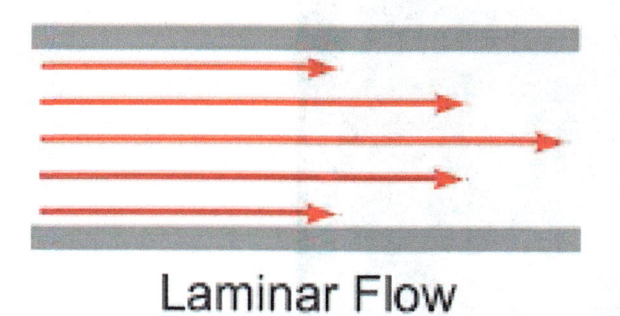

Critical Thinking

Consider what's happening...

First, we know
- Valve doesn't open as well
- Blood has a more difficult time passing through
- Causing the flow to increase in velocity

So, knowing that how will a stenotic valve look different in color mode?
- ➢ Color will have a mosaic appearance due to the velocity reaching the Nyquist limit and causing an aliasing artifact

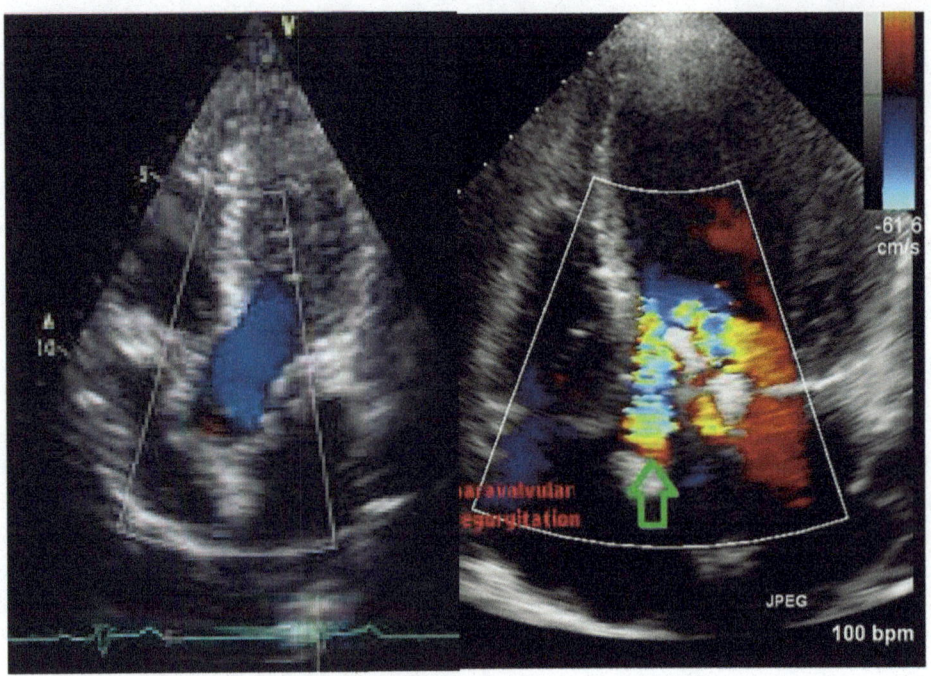

Normal flow   Stenotic flow

How will a stenotic valve look different in spectral Doppler mode?
- The Vmax or peak velocity Will be much greater than the non-stenotic waveform

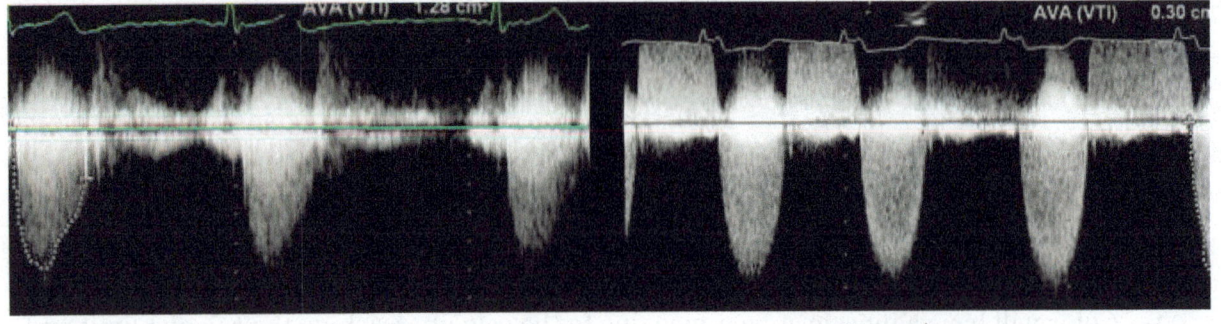

Normal   Stenotic

Stenosis

Causes	Risk Factors	Complications
infection	high cholesterol	heart failure
buildup of calcification	coronary artery disease	enlarged chambers
congenital	immunocompromised	weakened heart muscle
age	age	overload

| other | other | other |

Stenosis is measured by obtaining the VTI and continuous wave Doppler. To calculate the valve area most machines are already programmed with the continuity equation. This applies to all the valves while obtaining their area. There are four measurements that are needed in order for this calculation to produce the valve area.

Right side valves	Mode	Left side valves
RVOT diameter	2D	LVOT diameter
RVOT VTI	PW	LVOT VTI
Valve VTI	CW	Valve VTI

Valvular regurgitation/insufficiency

Regurgitation is the name for leaking heart valves. Sometimes the condition is minor and may not require treatment. At other times valve regurgitation places a strain on the heart. It can cause the heart to work harder, and it may not pump the same amount of blood. Blood flows back through the valves of the leaflets that are closing or the blood May leak through the leaflets that don't close properly. regurgitation causes volume overload.

Critical Thinking

Consider what's happening, first, we know
- Valve doesn't close as well
- blood leaks backward
- the regurgitation causes the flow to flow in the opposite direction

So, knowing that how will a leaky valve look different in color mode?
- ➤ Color will have a mosaic appearance due to the velocity reaching the Nyquist limit and causing an aliasing artifact

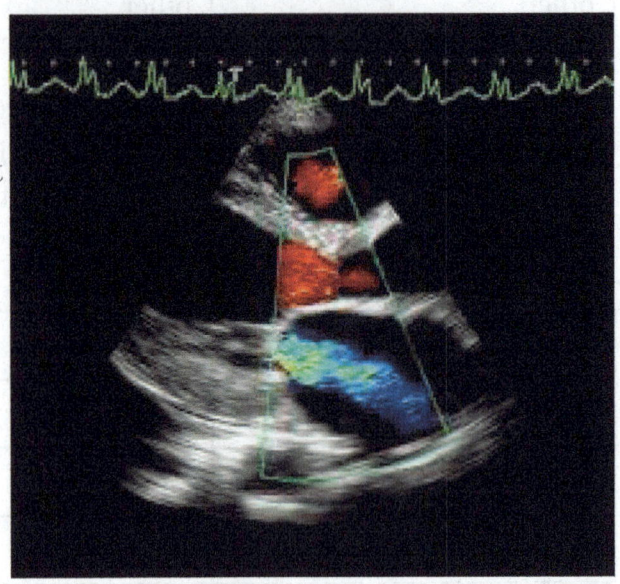

How will the valve look different in spectral Doppler mode?
- ➤ in addition to the normal flow of the corresponding valve there will be flow in the opposite direction due to the leak.

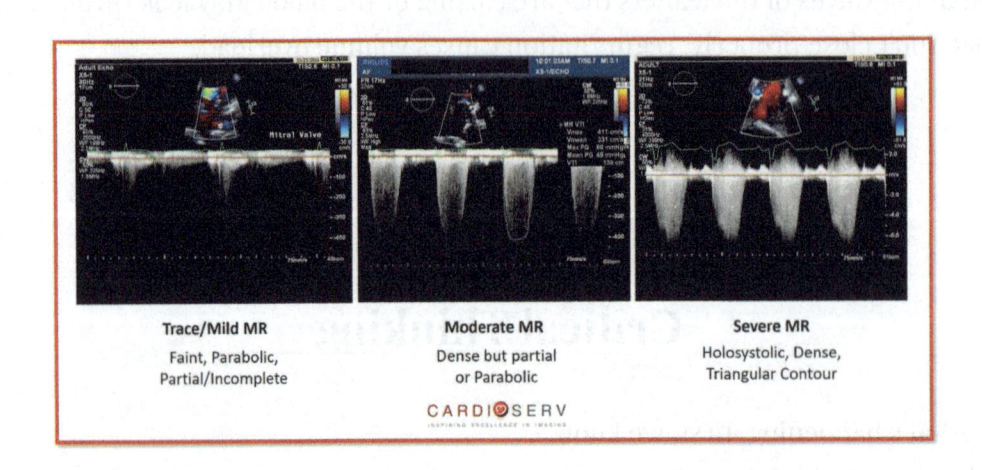

Learn to recognize signs
- ★ Velocity changes
- ★ Hyperechogenicity
- ★ High V Max
- ★ Other 2D & doppler changes

60

Causes	Risk Factors	Complications
infection	high cholesterol	heart failure
buildup of calcification	coronary artery disease	enlarged chambers
congenital	immunocompromised	weakened heart muscle
age	age	overload
other	other	other

Measuring regurgitation

All valvular regurgitation can be measured by the vena contra (VC). Vena contra is defined as the narrowest part of the jet, just distal to the regurgitant orifice.

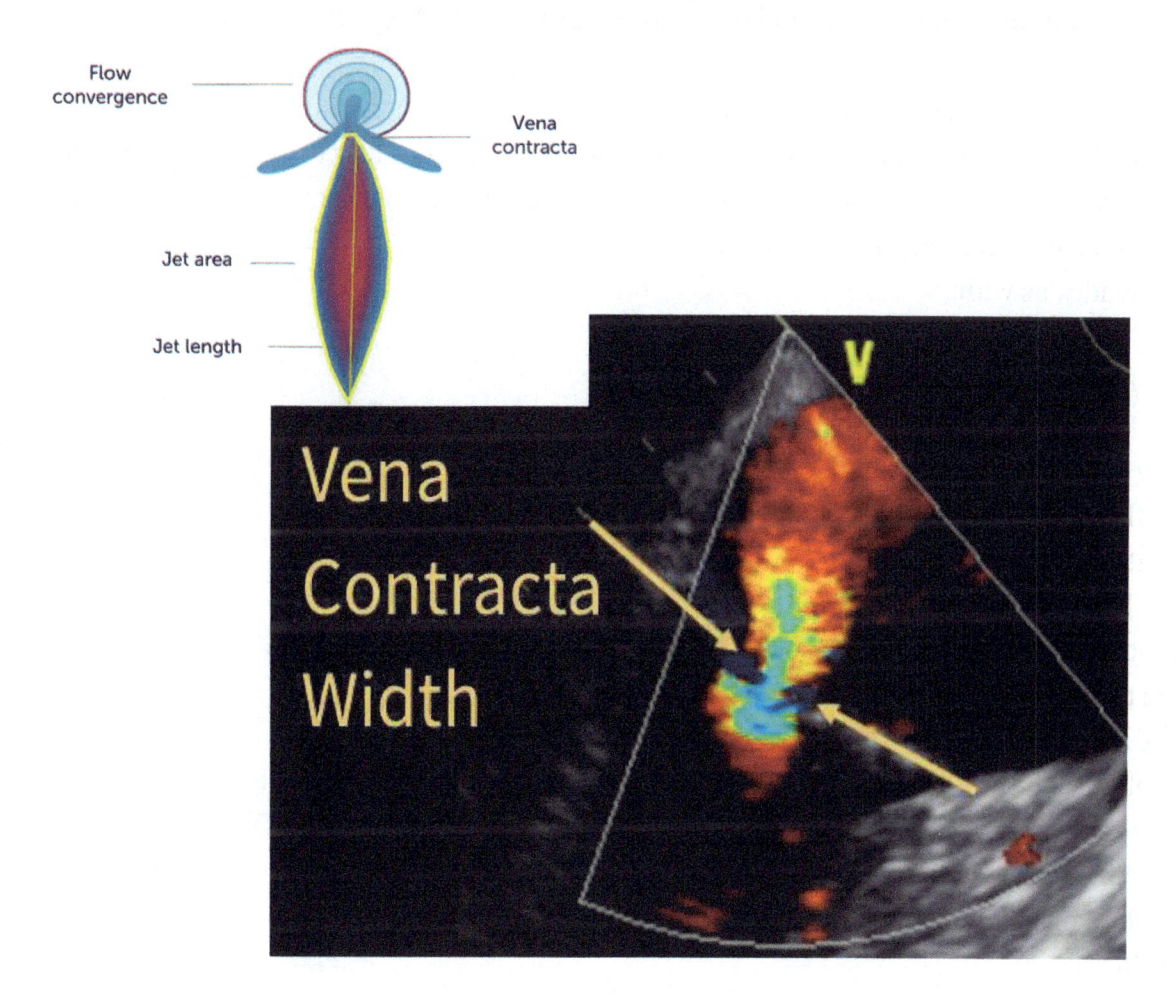

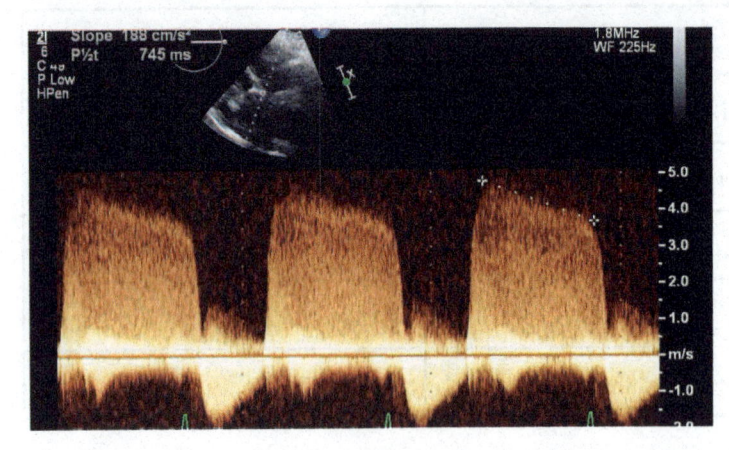

Semilunar valve regurgitation is also measured using the pressure half-time (PHT)

AV valve regurgitation has a few extra steps. The PISA method has proven to be the most accurate method of grading the severity of regurgitation. Other measurements that are helpful are the regurgitant volume (RVol) and the regurgitant fraction (RF).

Proximal Isovelocity Surface Area - PISA
PISA is a phenomenon that occurs when liquid flows through a circular orifice. The flow will converge and accelerate just proximal to the orifice. Used in echocardiography to estimate the area of an orifice through which blood flows.

PISA provides us with:
1. RF
2. EROA
3. RVol

The regurgitant flow rate is the amount of regurgitating flow per second being pushed back into the atrium. It's the product of the surface area of the hemisphere and the aliasing velocity.

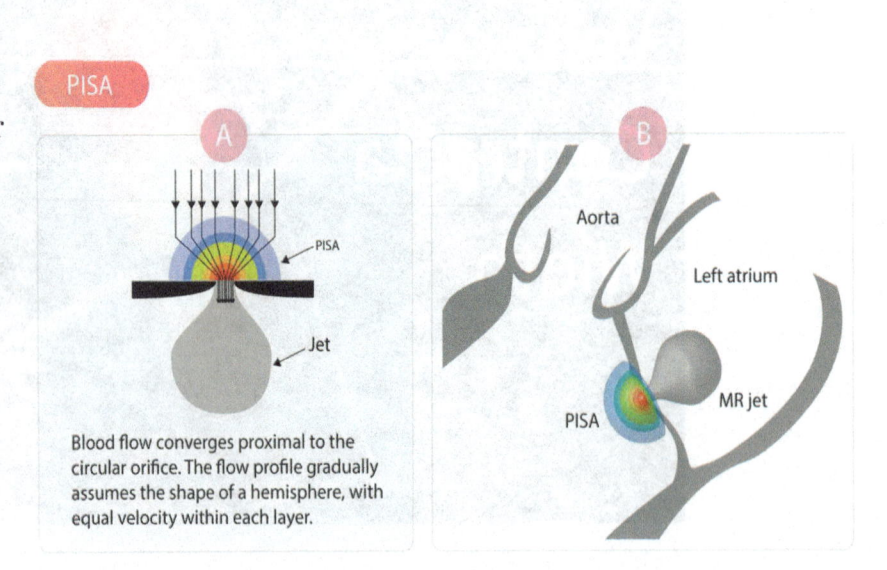

EROA -Effective regurgitant orifice area (EROA), calculated from the vena contracta width (VCW) as the narrowest portion of the proximal regurgitant jet, might be used to estimate the severity of mitral regurgitation.

62

Steps for PISA:
1. Adjust CFD baseline
    a. Bring down to the 30's
2. Measure the radius
3. Measure MV diameter
4. Measure MR jet

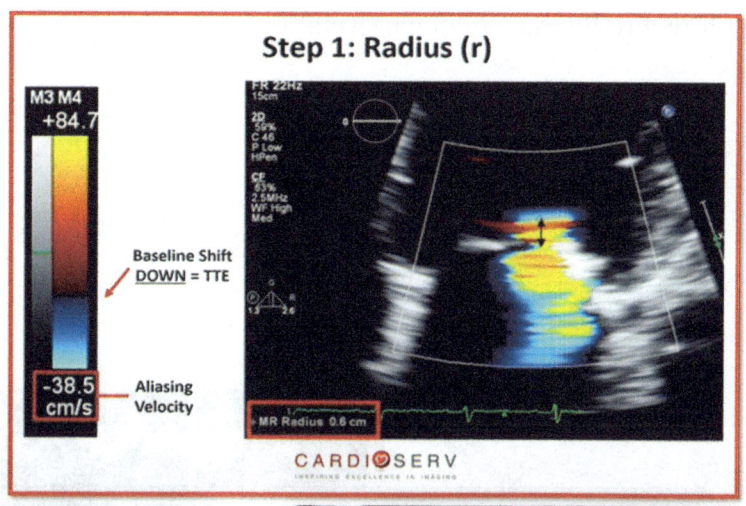

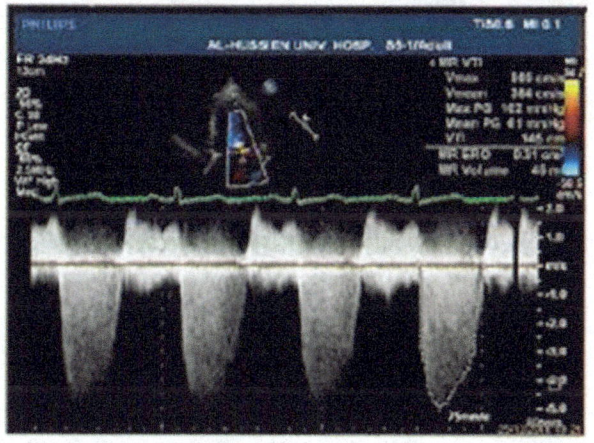

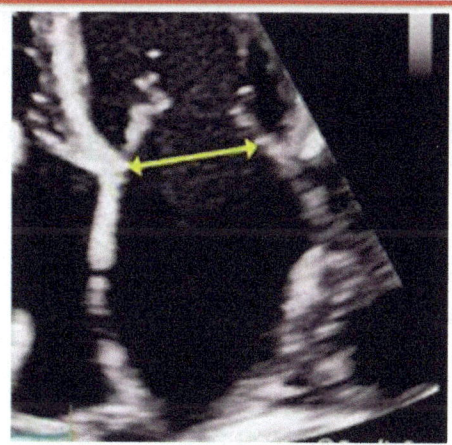

MR & MR grading

MR	MILD	MODERATE	SEVERE
VC – cm	< 0.3	0.3 – 0.7	> 0.7
PISA – cm	< 0.4	0.5 – 0.9	> 0.9
RV – ml	≤ 30	30 – 59	≥ 60
ERO – %	< 0.20	0.20 – 0.40	> 0.4

Don't forget to PW the pulmonary vein!!

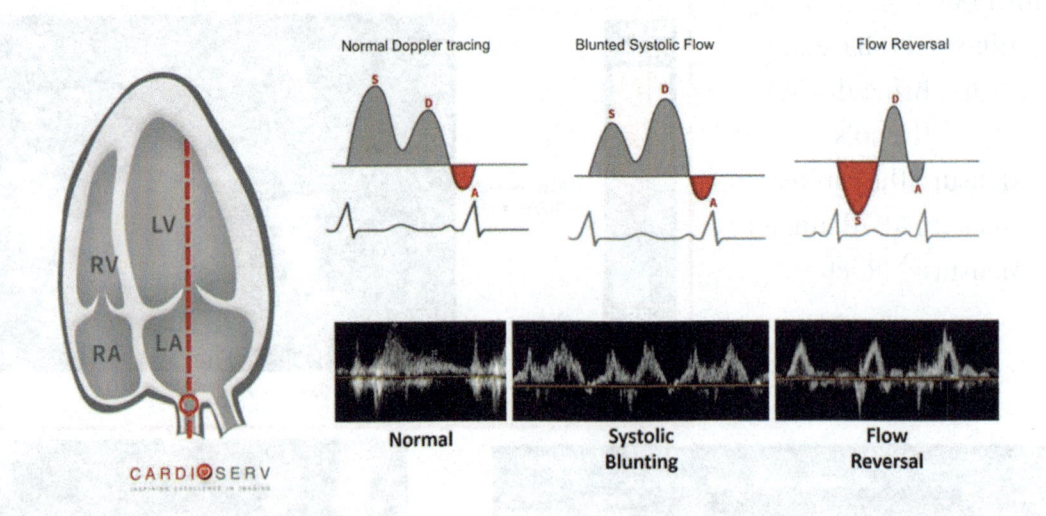

Measuring the LAVI is also imperative to the severity of regurgitation.

1. What all to measure
2. MR Jet - only if a full jet
3. MV diameter
4. LVOT dimension
5. LVOT VTI
6. Vena Contracta
7. PISA

MS & MS grading

There are three main causes of mitral valve stenosis:
1. Rheumatic fever: Rheumatic fever, a complication of strep throat or scarlet fever, is the most common cause of mitral valve stenosis.
2. Calcium deposits
3. Congenital heart defect: On rare occasions, babies are born with a defective valve, which may cause problems over time.

MS Assessment
- CFD
    - Turbulent flow
- CWD
    - PHT
    - MV VTI
- PWD
- M-Mode
- 2-D

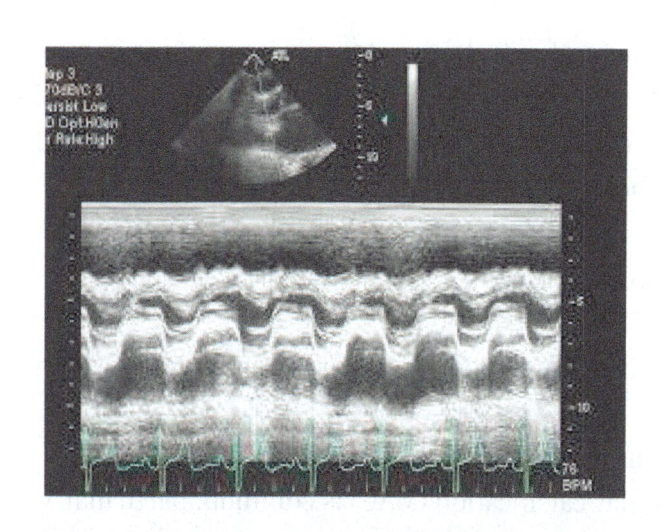

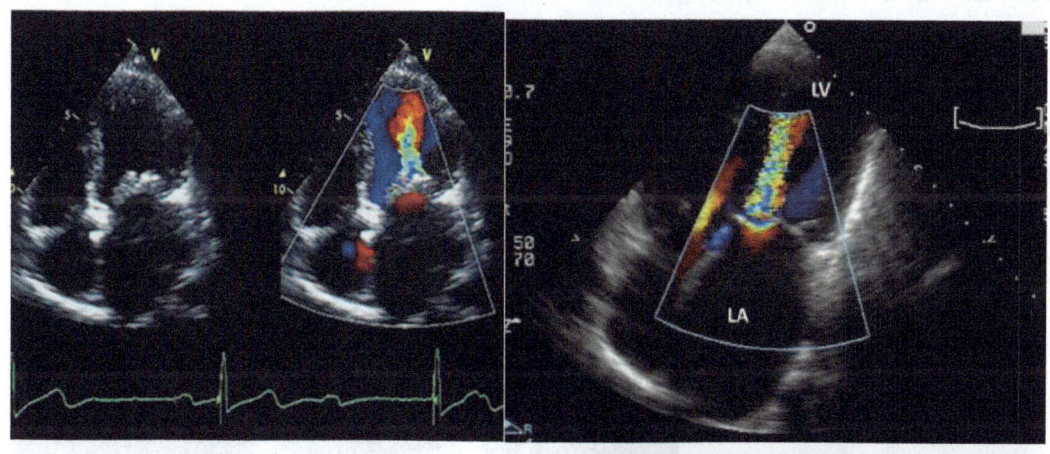

MS - Valve Area
Ways to calculate:
- MVA by PHT
    - MV VTI
    - MV PHT
- MVA by Continuity
    - MV VTI
    - LVOT VTI
    - LVOT diam
- MVA by Planimetry - trace in SAX

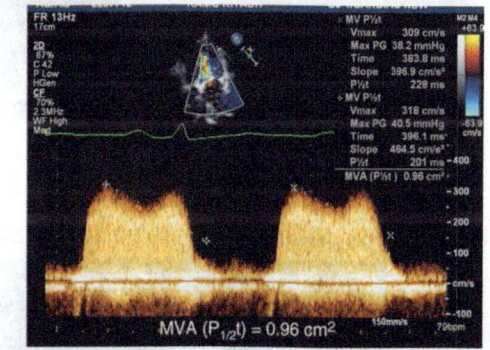

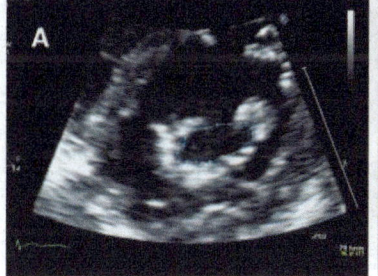

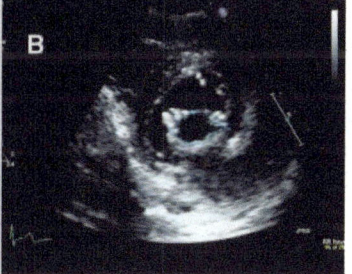

Rheumatic MS

The main cause of mitral valve stenosis is an infection called rheumatic fever, which is related to strep infections. Rheumatic fever — now rare in the United States, but still common in developing countries — can scar the mitral valve. Left untreated, mitral valve stenosis can lead to serious heart complications.

Non-Rheumatic Heart Disease

Stenosis caused by etiology outside of rheumatic fever.
Ex:
Myxomatous mitral valve disease
Mitral annular calcification (MAC) is common, particularly in the elderly. While thought to occasionally produce significant mitral regurgitation, it is considered a rare cause of mitral stenosis.

Rheumatic markers: such as typical tips and posterior leaflet involvement

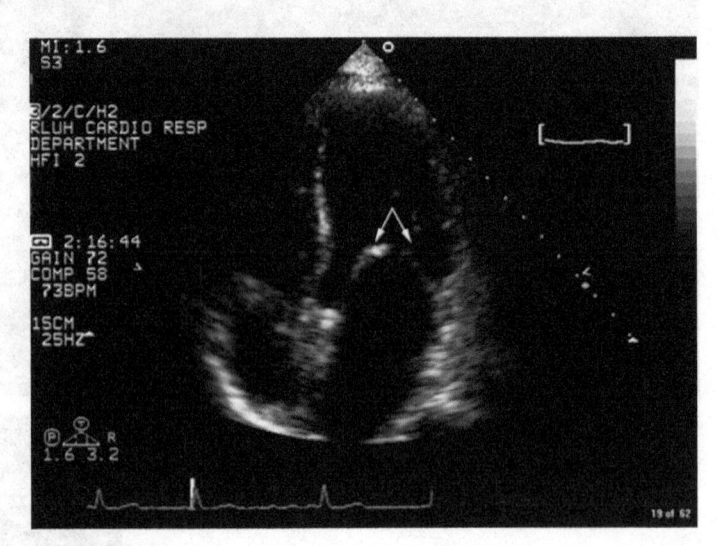

NRMS tends to be rather mild by both area and gradient measurements.

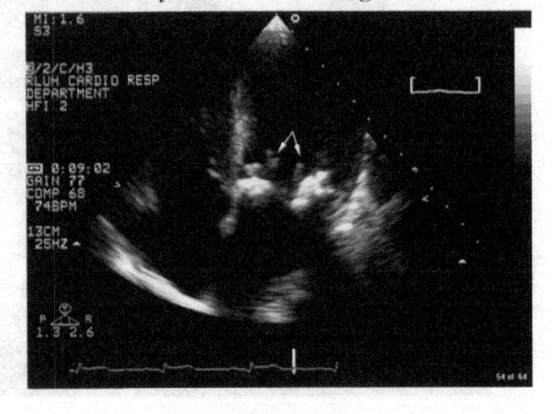

Mitral valve prolapse (Barlow's Syndrome) – MVP

A condition in which your mitral valve bows or flops back into your left atrium. That's why it's sometimes called "floppy valve syndrome." This floppiness may prevent your valve from closing as tightly as it should. Many people have no symptoms and don't even know they have it. That's because their valves can still function well.

Myxomatous mitral valve disease is degeneration of the valve, also known as "floppy valve" or mitral valve prolapse, and is the most common condition that requires mitral valve repair. It occurs when the mitral valve leaflets become floppy or loose and the valve does not open and close properly. The pathologic presentation of myxomatous mitral valve disease varies between valve thickness, degree of leaflet prolapse and the presence or absence of flail leaflets. The tissue of your mitral valve leaflets and chordae are abnormally stretch
Idiopathic

A & B show non-myxomatous prolapse, C&D show Myxomatous prolapse

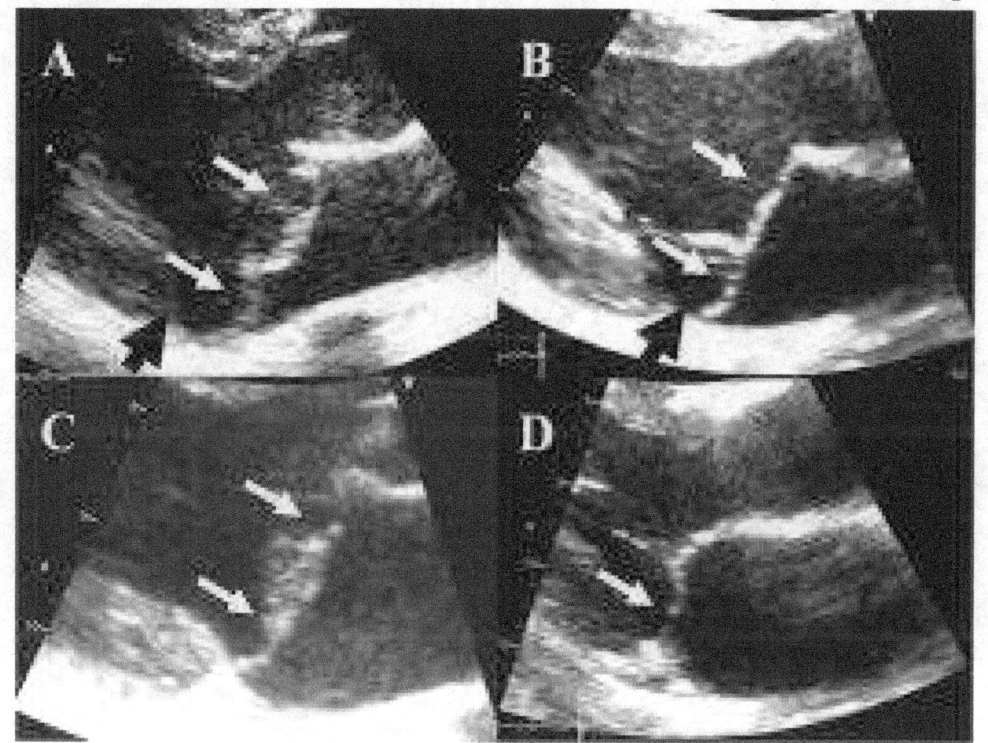

MVP should be diagnosed in the PLAX view only. B-mode & m-mode will show the prolapse.

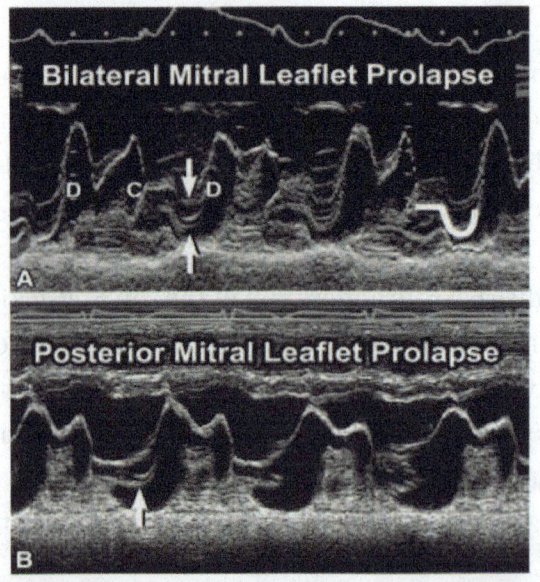

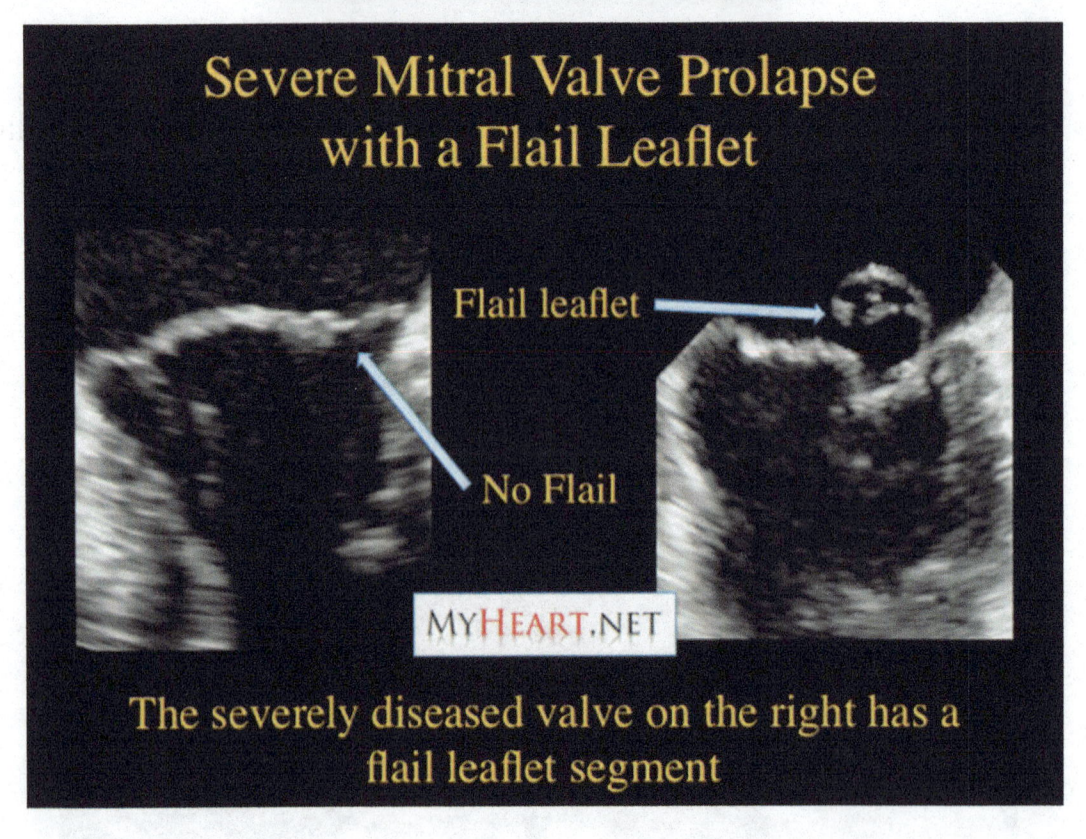

Severe Mitral Valve Prolapse with a Flail Leaflet

Flail leaflet

No Flail

The severely diseased valve on the right has a flail leaflet segment

Mitral annular calcification - MAC

A chronic, process in which there is deposition of calcium in the mitral valve annulus
The mitral annulus is typically flexible. In mitral annular calcification, it becomes less flexible and thicker. The posterior annulus is most commonly affected. In the majority of people, the amount of calcification is mild and therefore usually of no significance.

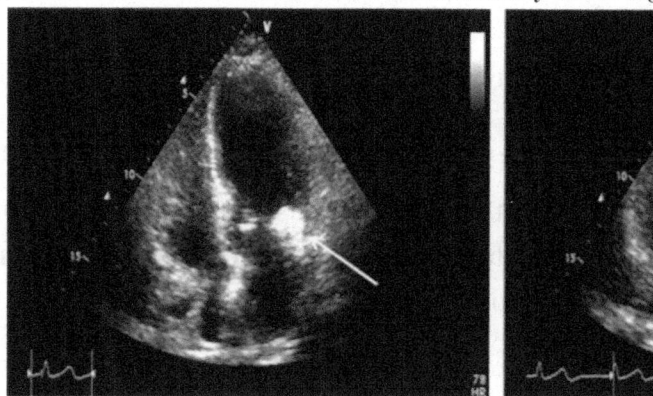

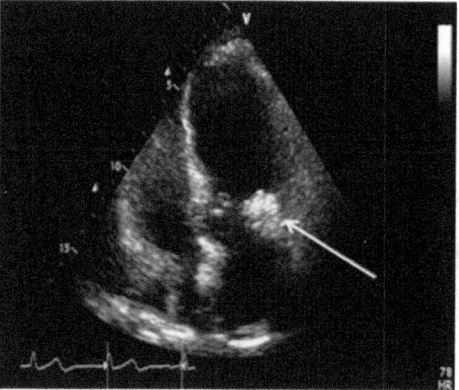

TR & TR grading

Measuring tricuspid regurgitation is very similar to measuring mitral regurgitation. However, instead of getting left-side measurements you want to get the right-side measurements. For example, instead of the LVOT diameter you want to grab the RVOT diameter. Also, in the presence of tricuspid regurgitation, it's imperative to check for pulmonary hypertension (PHTN). To do this you want to make sure you have optimal images in the subcostal window of the IVC. To correctly measure pulmonary hypertension you want to get the right ventricular systolic pressure (RSVP), to do this you must get the right atrial pressure(RAP). When assigning an RAP, use the chart below;

Both criteria normal	< 2.1cm & collapse >50%	3 mmHg
1 abnormal 1 normal	> 2.1cm & collapse >50%	8 mmHg
1 abnormal 1 normal	< 2.1cm & collapse <50%	8 mmHg
Both criteria abnormal	>2.1cm & collapse <50%	15 mmHg

Pulmonary Hypertension - PHTN

- High blood pressure that affects the arteries in the lungs and the right side of the heart
- Some common underlying causes
    - congenital heart disease
    - Cirrhosis
    - chronic lung diseases like emphysema
    - blood clots to the lungs

Pulmonary hypertension is a common cause of functional tricuspid regurgitation. While you're in the subcostal view of the IVC it's also important to pulse wave the hepatic vein to make sure the regurgitation isn't causing backflow of blood.

TS

TS Causes	TS Symptoms
Rheumatic fever	ascites
Epstein's abnormality	abdominal swelling
IV drug use	peripheral edema
infection	jaundice

To grade the severity of tricuspid stenosis you must obtain the right ventricular outflow tract diameter, the right ventricular outflow tract VTI and the tricuspid VTI.

PR/PI - FLOW ABOVE BASELINE!!!!!!! Measure the PHT

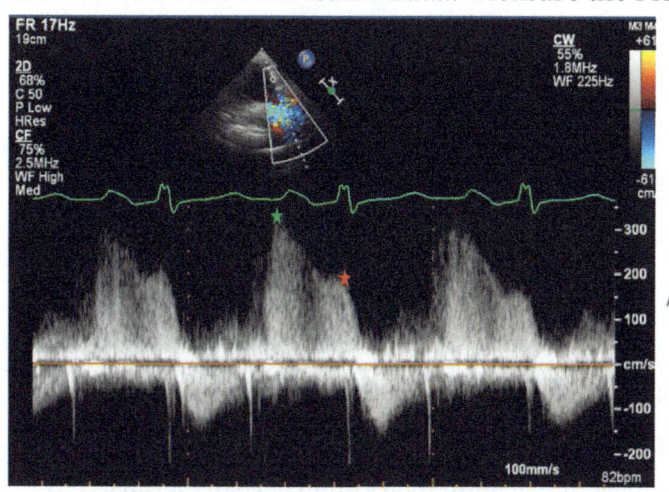

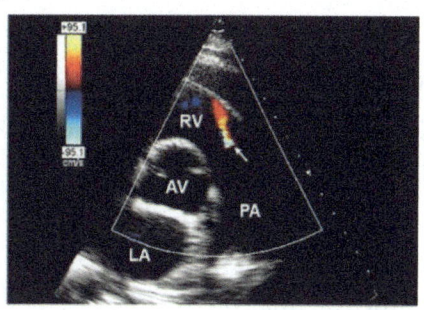

PS - Has a sharp dagger-like waveform and continuous wave. use the continuity equation substituting the right-side measurements for the left-side measurements.

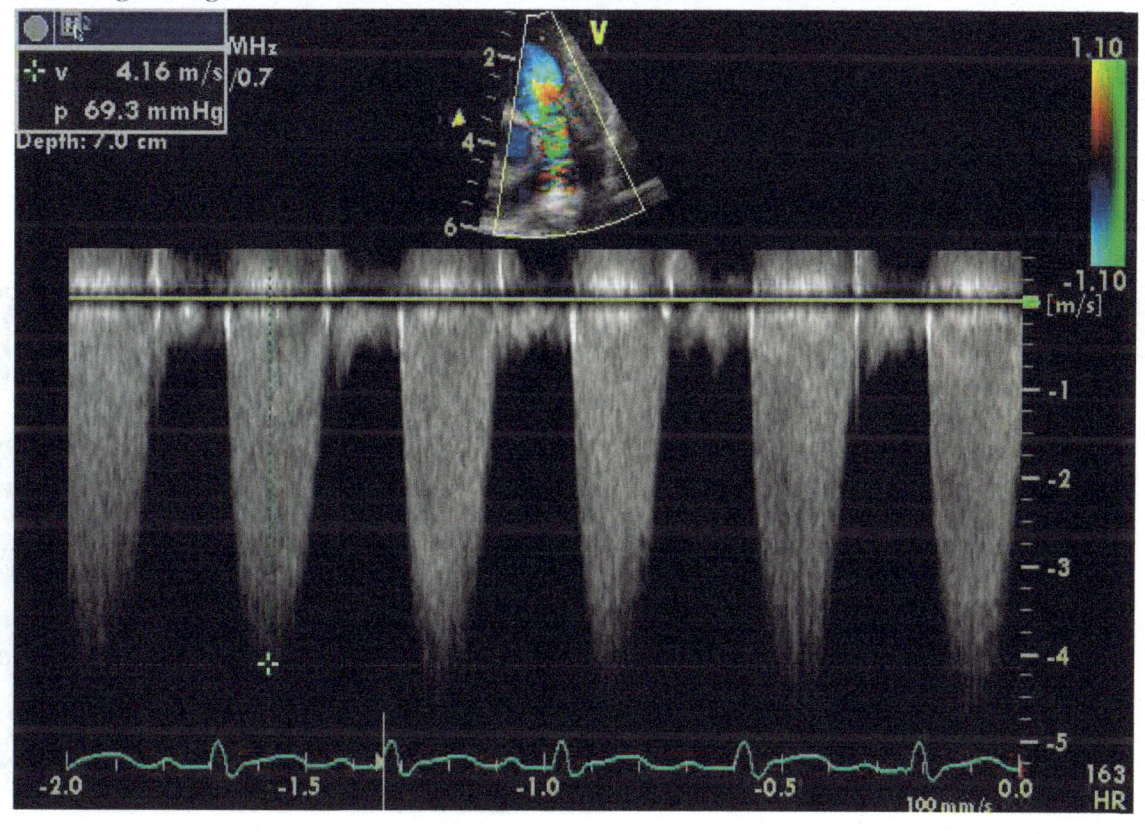

AoS

Aortic stenosis is most commonly caused by calcium buildup on the aortic valve over time. These calcium deposits that often come with age make the valve tissue stiff, narrow, and unyielding.

- Bicuspid valve
- Rheumatic
- Supravalvular AS
- Subvalvular AS

Aortic valve stenosis ranges from mild to severe. Symptoms generally occur when the narrowing of the valve is severe. Some people with aortic valve stenosis may not have symptoms for many years. Aortic valve stenosis may lead to heart failure. Heart failure symptoms include fatigue, shortness of breath, and swollen ankles and feet.

Symptoms of aortic valve stenosis may include:

- An irregular heart sound (heart murmur) heard through a stethoscope
- Chest pain (angina) or tightness with activity
- Feeling faint or dizzy or fainting with activity
- Shortness of breath, especially with activity
- Fatigue, especially during times of increased activity
- Rapid, fluttering heartbeat (palpitations)
- Not eating enough (mainly in children with aortic valve stenosis)
- Not gaining enough weight (mainly in children with aortic valve stenosis)

AoVS assessment:
1. CFD
    a. Turbulent flow
2. CWD
    a. PHT
    b. VTI
3. PWD
4. M-Mode
5. 2-D
6. Pedoff
    a. SSN
    b. RPS

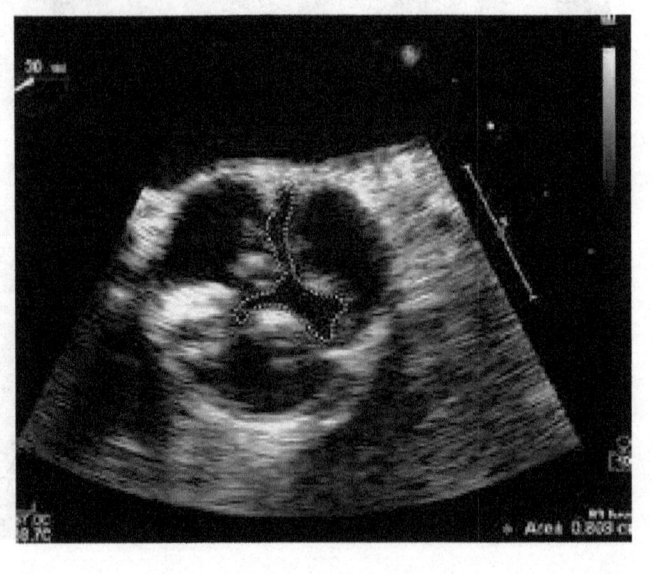

Severe AS M-mode

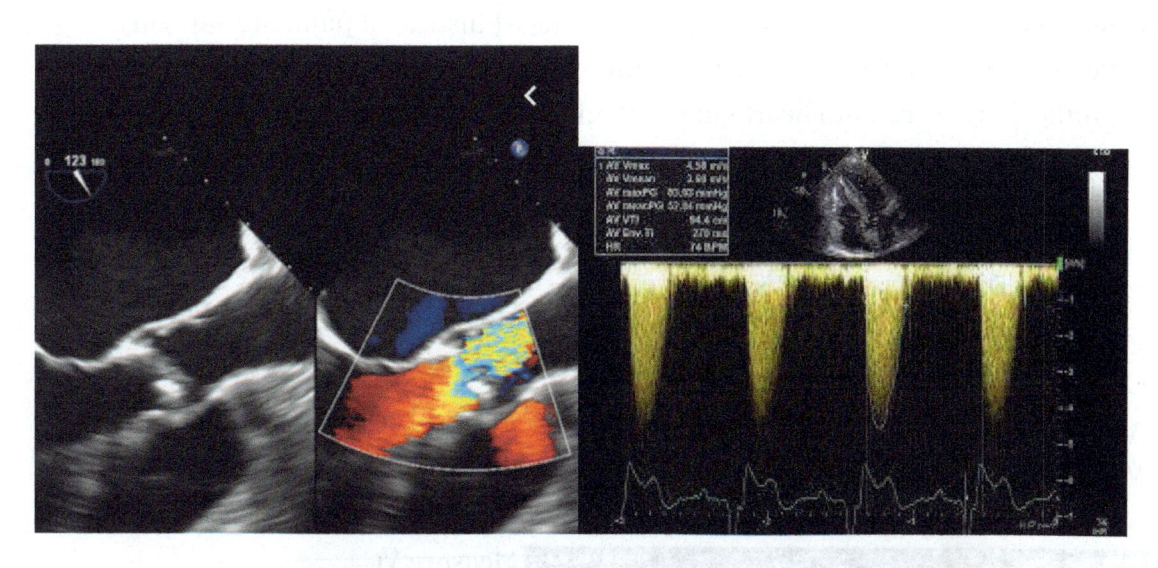

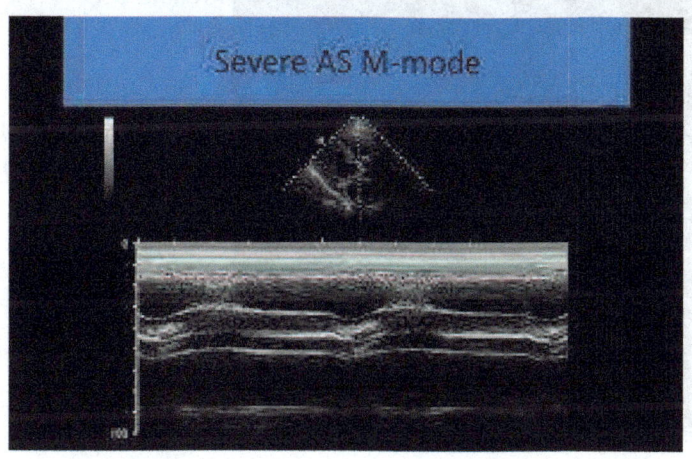

Table 3 Recommendations for grading of AS severity

	Aortic sclerosis	Mild	Moderate	Severe
Peak velocity (m/s)	≤2.5 m/s	2.6–2.9	3.0–4.0	≥4.0
Mean gradient (mmHg)	–	<20	20–40	≥40
AVA (cm^2)	–	>1.5	1.0–1.5	<1.0
Indexed AVA (cm^2/m^2)	–	>0.85	0.60–0.85	<0.6
Velocity ratio	–	>0.50	0.25–0.50	<0.25

AR / AI

In aortic insufficiency, blood flows backward into the heart instead of pumping out. This requires the heart to pump harder, which over time can lead to heart failure.
Symptoms often don't occur until heart failure develops. They include chest pain, shortness of breath, or fainting.

**** listen for that murmur ****

AR / AI - Extra steps
- Color M-Mode
- Adjust baseline to see AR (2 CWD images)
- Measure VC - PLAX
- SSN

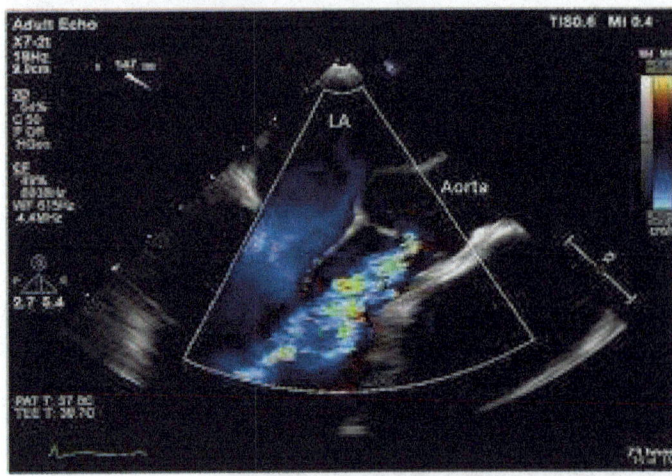

Measure VC

Vena Contracta - VC
The point in a fluid stream where the diameter of the stream is the least, and fluid velocity is at its maximum
Such as in the case of a stream issuing out of a nozzle (orifice).
It is a place where the cross-section area is minimal.

Measure PHT

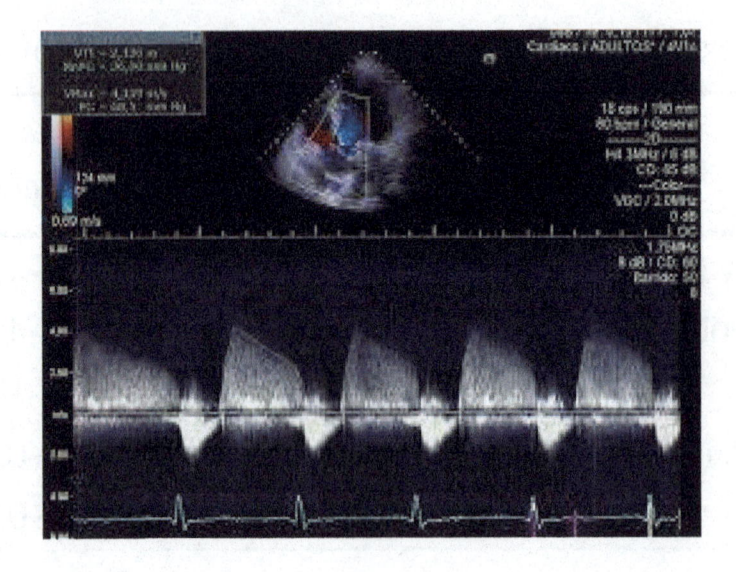

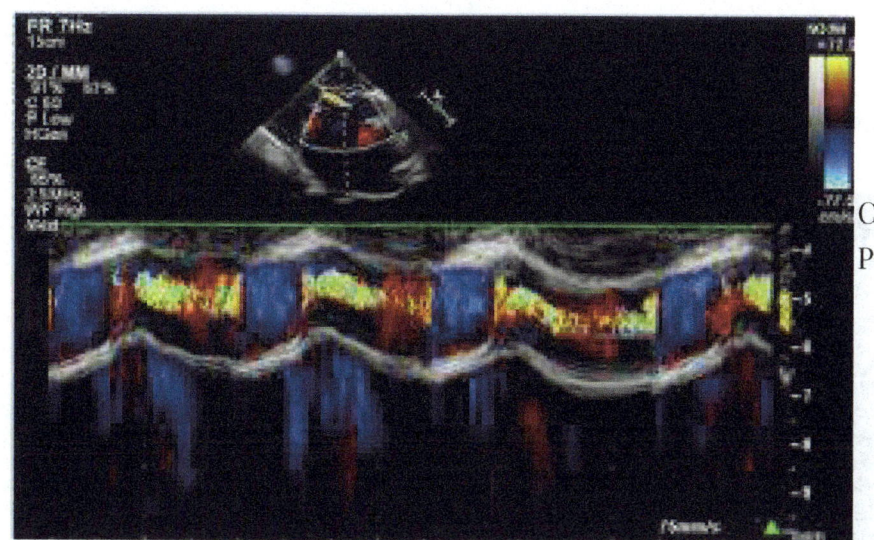

Color m-mode the AoV in PLAX

	Mild	Moderate	Severe
Colour Doppler width (%)	<25	25–65	>65%
Regurgitant volume (mls/beat)	<30	30–59	≥60
Vena contracta width	<3	—	>6
Regurgitant fraction (%)	<30	30–49	≥50
Pressure half time (ms)	>500*	250–450	<200*

Other valvular disease

Ruptured chordae tendineae can cause AV valve regurgitation.

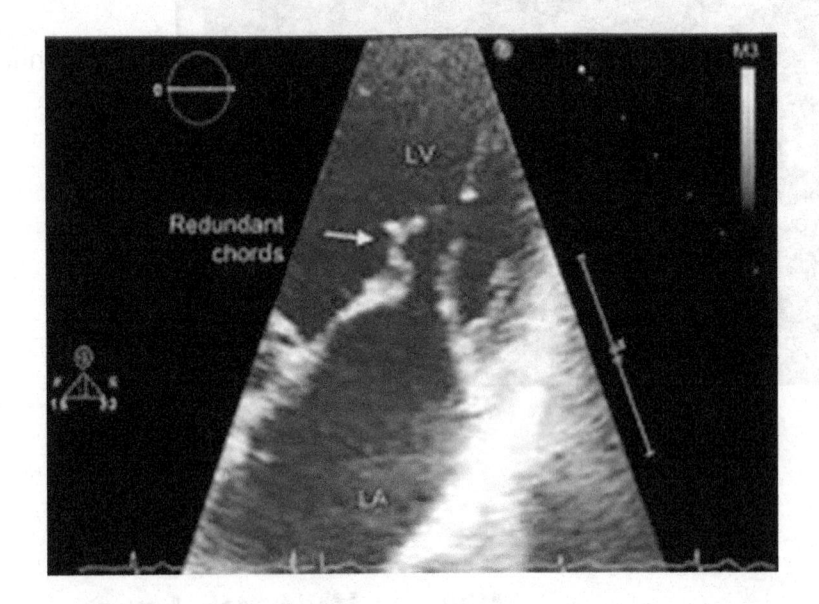

Mitral annular calcification - MAC

A chronic process in which there is deposition of calcium in the mitral valve annulus. The mitral annulus is typically flexible. In mitral annular calcification, it becomes less flexible and thicker. The posterior annulus is most commonly affected. In the majority of people, the amount of calcification is mild and therefore usually of no significance. The most common disease that causes mitral valve calcification is rheumatic valve disease

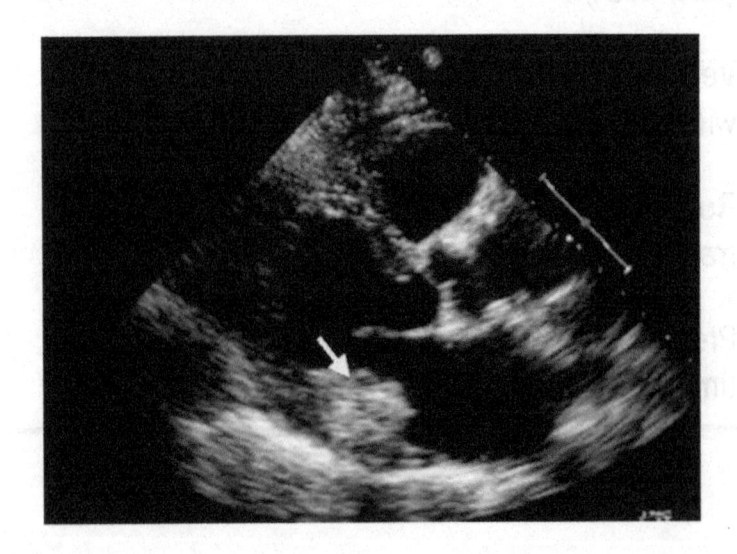

Prosthetic valves

When valve disease becomes hemodynamically significant, the valve may need to be replaced, depending on the patient's age, comorbidities and medical status. There are different types of prosthetic valves a physician can choose from, mechanical and bile prosthetic. Each type has its own pros and cons.

Type	Pro	Con
Bioprosthetic	No anticoagulation therapy	Last from 10 to 15 years
Mechanical	Lasts 30 + years	Anticoagulation therapy for life

Mechanical valves are made from metal and there are three main types: ball in cage, tilting disc(monoleaflet) and bileaflet.

Bileaflet   Monoleaflet   Caged Ball

There are also multiple types of bioprosthetic valves that differ between donor and type.
- Hetero - animal to human
    - Bovine - cow
    - Porcine - pig
- Auto - self to self
- Homo - human to human

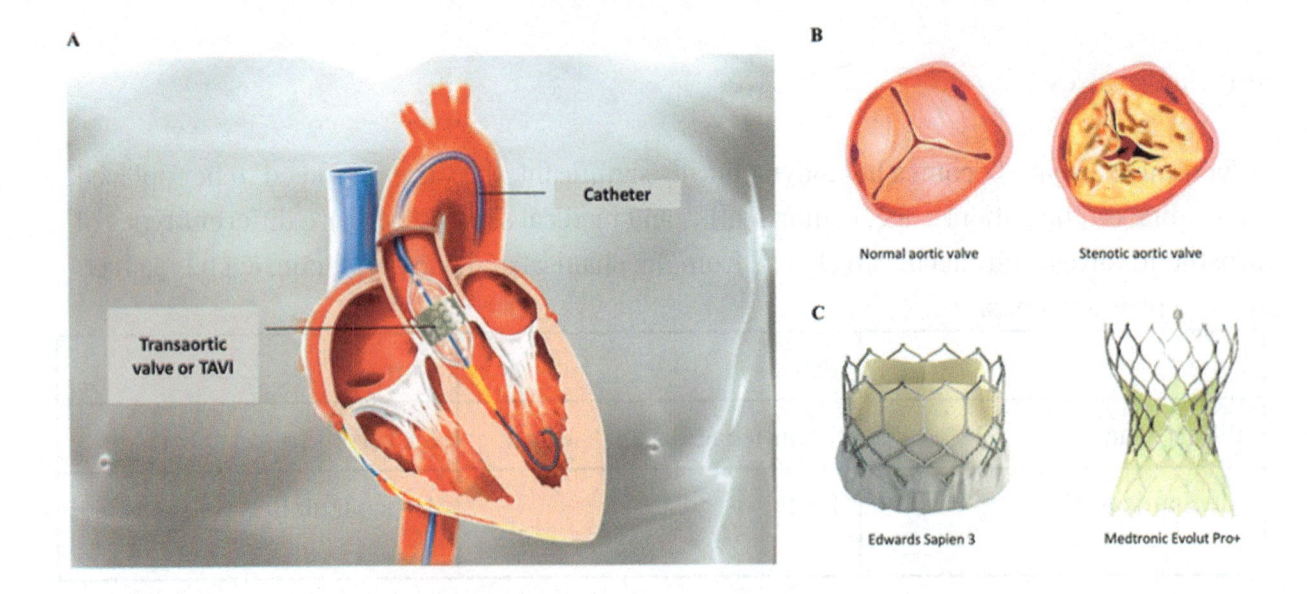

TAVR - transcatheter aortic valve replacement Is performed in the same way a cardiac angiogram is. The catheter wire is placed through the femoral or radial artery while the valve is in a closed position. Once in the correct position the prosthetic valve is inflated and secured in.

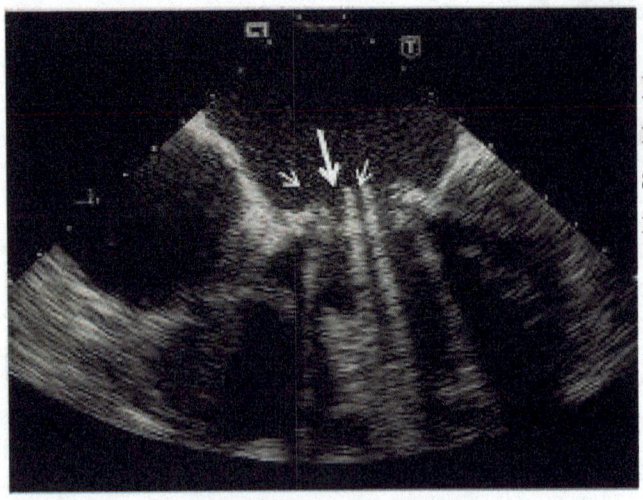

Prosthetic valves tend to produce a reflection artifact due to the that's either surrounding the bioprosthetic or because it's a mechanical valve.

78

Measurements
- Measurements are done with a stenosis protocol
- The same information is needed
    - VMAX
    - Mean G
    - Valve area

Protocol addition
1. Zoom in on the valve
2. CFD
    a. Drop color scale to the 30s

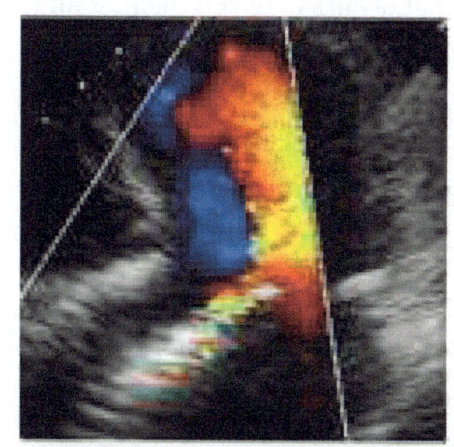

Paravalvular regurgitation: a leak caused by a space left between natural heart tissue and the valve replacement from a previous transcatheter aortic or mitral valve replacement.

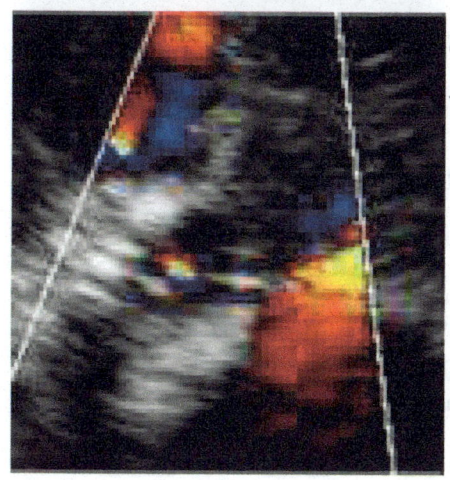

Transvalvular regurgitation: regurgitation through the valve.

Chapter 7
Cardiac Pathology

Chapter 7 is going to go over different non-congenital cardiac pathologies other than valvular disease. Well, the list is quite long we will go over most of them, but not in its entirety. Before we start the list of non-congenital cardiac pathologies there are a few terms to understand before moving forward.

Systole: a period of contraction of the ventricles of the heart that occurs between the first and second heart sounds of the cardiac cycle (the sequence of events in a single heartbeat).

Systolic Function: How well the heart functions in systole, how well the heart contracts.

Function calculated through ejection fraction, EF%
Normal is 55% -70% at rest
Above 70% is considered **hyperdynamic**
Below is considered hypodynamic
With lower EF usually comes wall motion abnormalities:
Akinetic - no movement
Hypokinetic - decreased movement
Dyskinetic - outward movement of the segment during systole

Diastolic Function: In clinical cardiology the term "diastolic function" is most commonly referred to as how the heart fills.
TDI e' & PW MV values give this information

Echocardiographic classification of diastolic dysfunction

	Normal diastolic function	Impaired relaxation Grade I	Pseudonormal Grade II	Reversible restricted Grade III	Fixed restricted Grade IV
	E/A 1.0 – 1.5 DT > 160 ms	E/A < 1.0 DT > 200 ms	E/A 0.8 – 1.5 DT 160-200 ms	E/A ≥ 2.0 DT < 160 ms	E/A ≥ 2.0 DT < 160 ms
Left atrial pressure	Normal	Normal	↑↑	↑↑↑	↑↑↑↑

There are certain heart diseases that prevent accurate diastolic function measures. When this occurs, calculating the IVRT (Isovolumic relaxation time) measures the period from the aortic valve closure to the mitral valve opening. IVRT is measured in apical 5 chamber view, using a pulsed doppler. place the sample volume in between the aortic valve in the mitral valve.

- When the mitral TDI doesn't form an "M", you will be unable to measure
- When the PW of mitral doesn't form an "M", you will be unable to measure the "Λ" point.

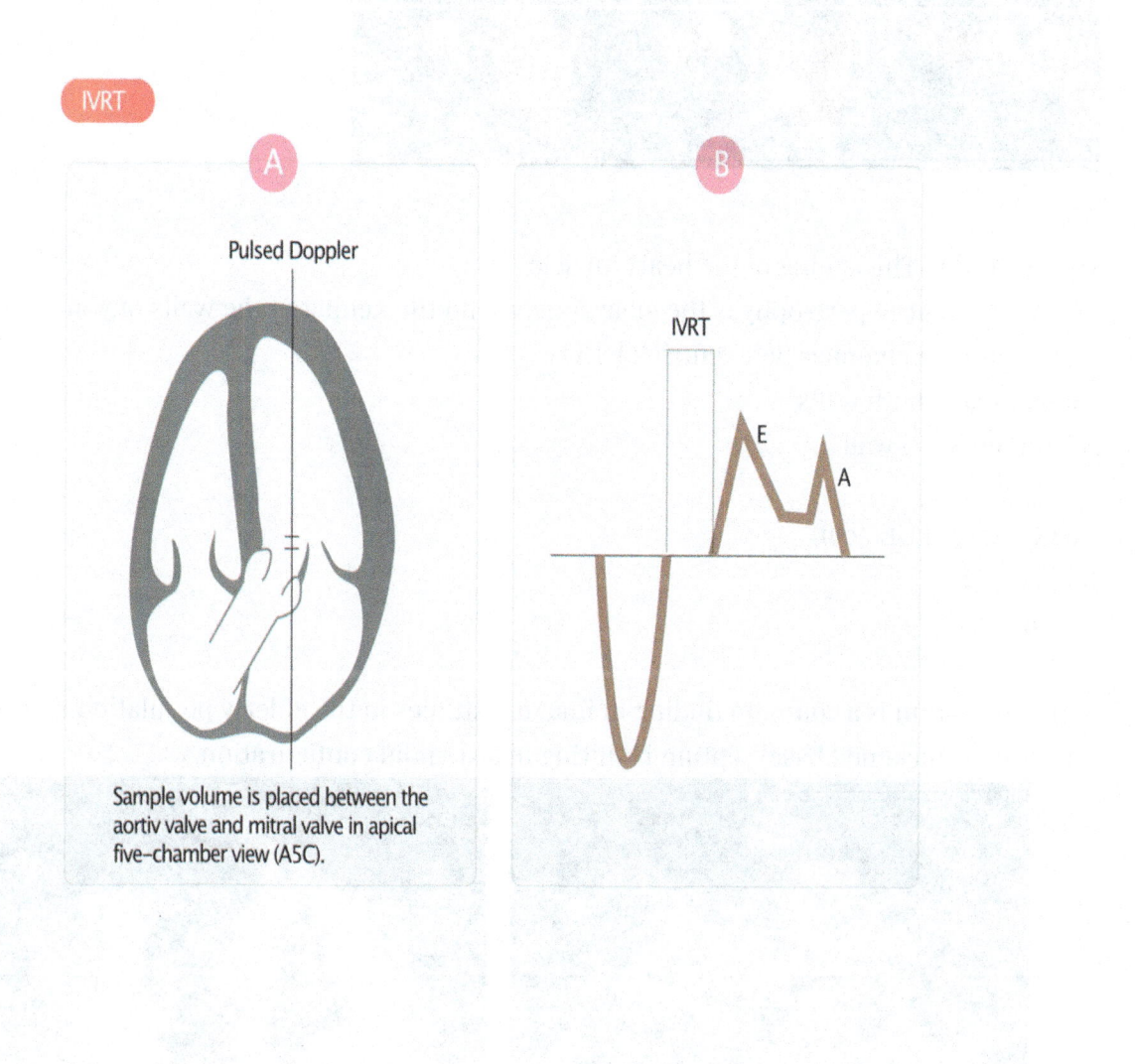

IVRT

A

Pulsed Doppler

Sample volume is placed between the aortiv valve and mitral valve in apical five-chamber view (A5C).

B

IVRT

E
A

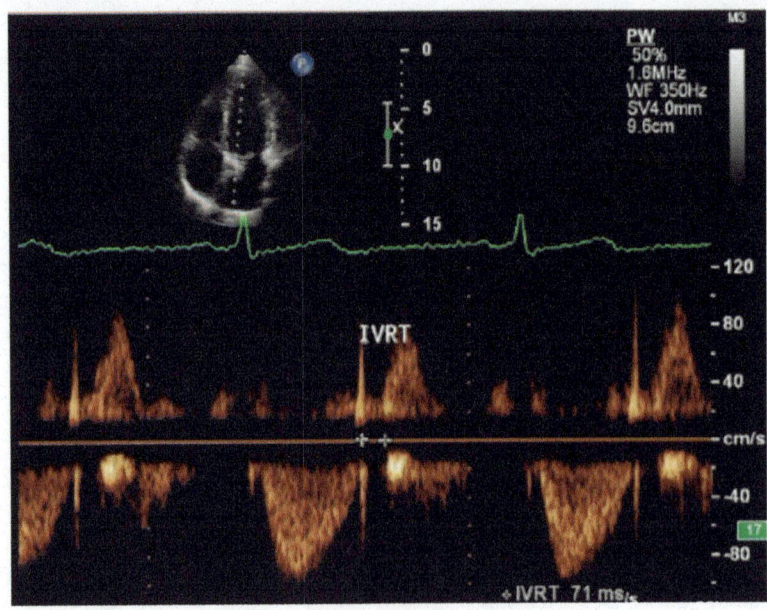

Tip:

When doing a PW for IVRT, change your PW speed to the fastest setting.

Doing this will make the waveforms larger & easier to measure.

Hypertrophy-Thickening of the heart muscle.
Left ventricular hypertrophy is the enlargement and thickening of the walls of your heart's main pumping chamber (left ventricle). LVH
Concentric = both walls
Asymmetric = 1 wall

NORMAL VALUES(cm)
M 0.6 - 1.0
F 0.6 - 0.9

Sigmoid septum is a common finding in imaging studies in the elderly population and refers to an isolated thickened basal septum resulting in a sigmoid configuration.

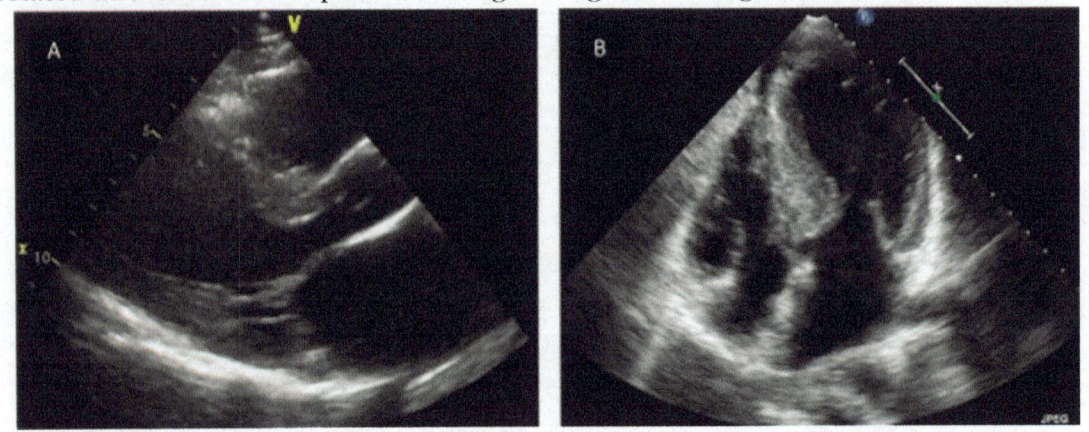

When measuring the walls in the PLAX view make sure to measure the sigmoid septum separately from the mid septum.

Infective endocarditis

Infective endocarditis is an infection caused by bacteria, fungus or a virus that enters the bloodstream and settles in the heart lining, a heart valve or a blood vessel
Infective endocarditis refers to infection in the lining of the heart but also affects the valves. It often affects the muscles of the heart.
- Bacterial endocarditis is most common
- Fungal endocarditis is the least common

Classic manifestation presents as a growth, which is called a vegetation
A vegetation is a mass-like structure that is a colony of the pathogen. A veg is usually attached to the leaflet on the side of the flow

Ex. AV = atria SL = ventricles

The infection can be caused by a pathogen introduced into the bloodstream. Infection can result from many sources, including poor dental hygiene, tooth brushing that causes minor injury to the lining of the mouth or gums, dental procedures, implanted cardiovascular medical devices, chronic skin disorders and infections, burns, infectious diseases and more.

Why does endocarditis pose more of a threat to the heart valves?

The heart valves are not supplied directly with blood. Therefore, the body's immune response system, including the infection-fighting white blood cells, can't directly reach the valves through the bloodstream.

There are two forms of infective endocarditis, also known as IE:
1. Acute IE — develops suddenly and may become life-threatening within days
   Highly powerful pathogen
   Sudden onset w/ rapid destruction of cardiac tissue
   Usually invades a normal valve
   #1 causing bacteria is staph

2. Subacute or chronic IE (or subacute bacterial endocarditis) — develops slowly over a period of weeks to several months.
- Sub-clinical: relating to or denoting a disease that is not severe enough to present definite or readily observable symptoms.
- Usually targets an abnormal valve
- #1 pathogen is strep

What are the symptoms of infective endocarditis?

ACUTE	SUBACUTE
Fever (102°–104°)	Mild Fever (99°–101°)
Chills	A Moderately Fast Heart Rate
Fast Heart Rate	Weight Loss
Fatigue	Sweating
Night Sweats	Low Red Blood Cell Count (Anemia).
Aching Joints and Muscles	
Persistent Cough	

Complications
- Embolism
- Aneurysm
- Flail leaflet
- Perforation
- Valve dehiscence (separation of sewing ring from the annular tissue of prosthetic aortic valve)
- Stenosis
- Regurg
- Heart failure

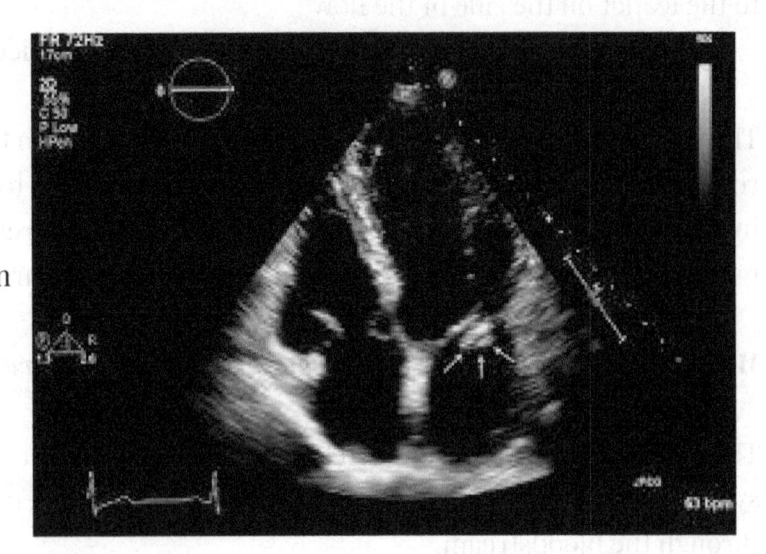

Rheumatic Heart Disease vs Infective Endocarditis

The key difference between the two diseases is, that unlike infective endocarditis, which is purely due to infectious causes, rheumatic heart disease has an autoimmune component in its pathogenesis.

Rheumatic heart disease, which is a complication of rheumatic fever, is characterized by deforming valvular fibrotic disease
Infective endocarditis is a microbial infection of the heart valves that leads to the formation of vegetations composed of thrombotic debris

Endocarditis = Vegetations

Ischemic heart disease

Ischemic heart disease is the most common type of heart disease and is caused by narrowed heart arteries.
- Aka CAD, Coronary Heart Disease
- OLD MI
- Acute MI
- Angina

The term ischemic heart disease (IHD) describes a group of clinical syndromes characterized by myocardial ischemia, an imbalance between myocardial blood supply and demand. Ischemic heart disease is a secondary cardiac pathology as it is caused by a pre-existing condition. As an echo technician, your main focus is wall motion abnormalities and ejection fraction.

Cardiomyopathies

A disease of the heart muscle that makes it harder for the heart to pump blood to the rest of the body
- HCM - Hypertrophic cardiomyopathy
  - Your heart muscle thickens.
- HOCM - Hypertrophic obstructive cardiomyopathy
  - The thickened muscle creates an LVOT obstruction
- Dilated cardiomyopathy
  - Your heart's blood-pumping chambers enlarge
- Restrictive cardiomyopathy
  - Your heart muscle scars, stiffens or both.

HCM - Hypertrophic cardiomyopathy

A disease in which the heart muscle becomes thickened (hypertrophied). The thickened heart muscle can make it harder for the heart to pump blood. Hypertrophic cardiomyopathy often goes undiagnosed because many people with the disease have few if any, symptoms. Clinical diagnosis of HCM when the wall thickness is >1.5 cm

*In certain situations, mild increases in LV wall thickness can be considered diagnostic (13-14 mm), including in relatives of patients with HCM

Typical causes:

- Hypertrophic cardiomyopathy is usually caused by changes in genes (gene mutations) that cause the heart muscle to thicken.
- People with hypertrophic cardiomyopathy also have a rearrangement of heart muscle cells (myofiber disarray). This can trigger arrhythmias in some people.

Typical complications:
- Atrial fibrillation.
- Mitral valve disease.
- Dilated cardiomyopathy.
- Heart failure.
- Fainting (syncope).
- Sudden cardiac death.

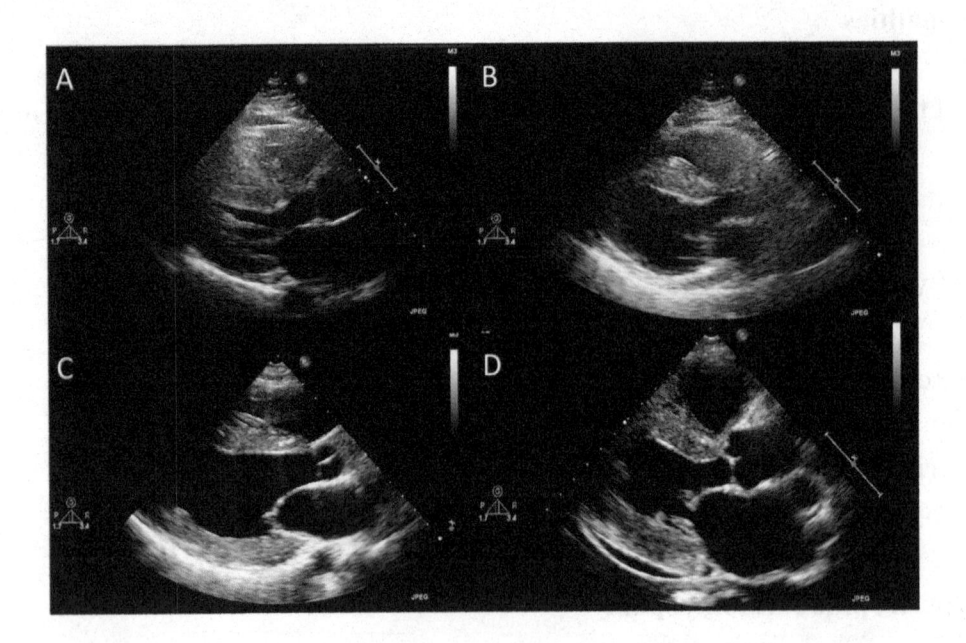

HOCM - Hypertrophic obstructive cardiomyopathy
Same as HCM but with an LVOT obstruction

Caused usually by:
- Sigmoid septum
- SAM

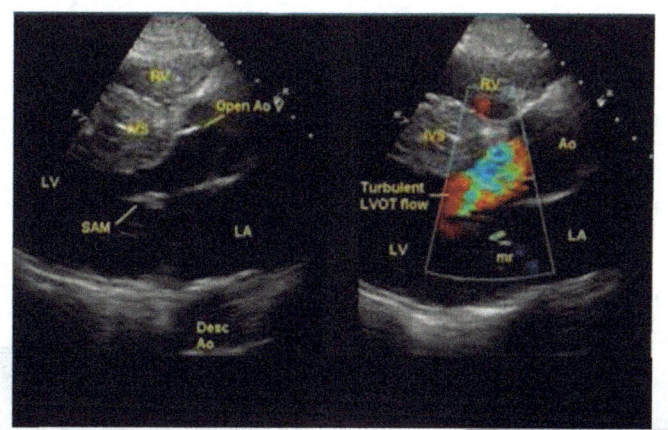

SAM - systolic anterior motion

- Evaluated by both the parasternal long-axis and the apical long-axis
- Dynamic movement of the mitral valve (MV) during systole anteriorly towards the LVOT
- Anterior motion of Mitral leaflets in systole resulting in movement of leaflets into the LVOT and thus impediment to EF

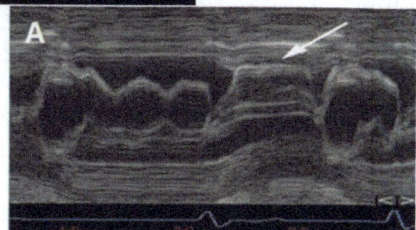

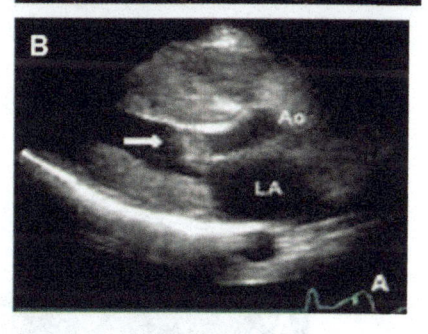

Systolic anterior motion (SAM) of the mitral valve with 2D (a)
- m-mode (b)
- causing LVOT obstruction

SAM-associated MR (c).
- A max instantaneous late peak gradient of 149 mmHg was measured with CW Doppler (d), indicative of severe LVOT obstruction

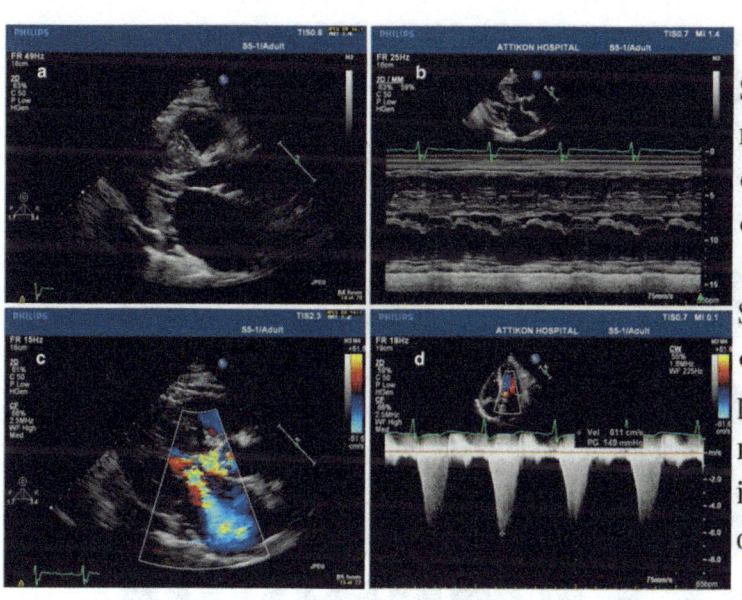

HCM & HOCM protocol addition:

When evaluating HCM & HOCM, always check the LVOT gradient.
Valsalva: via A5C or ALAX
- Label Valsalva
- Position the cursor through the LVOT
- CW - drop speed to the slowest setting
- Have the patient Valsalva in the middle of the CW
- Freeze, measure, record

When asking patients to Valsalva, have them bear down then QUICKLY release.

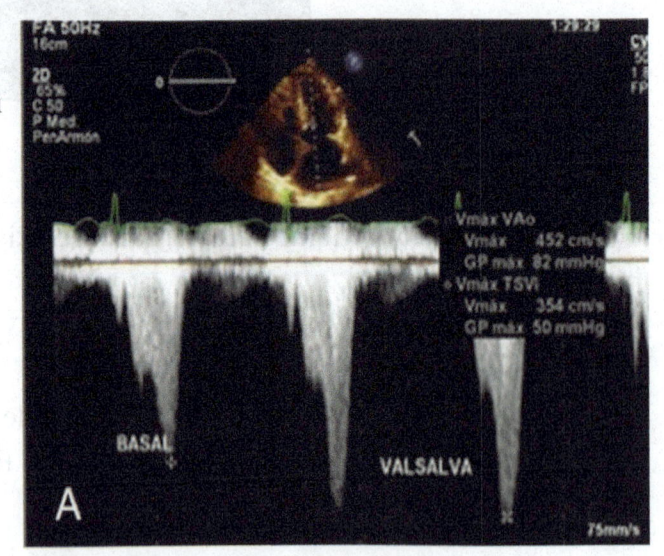

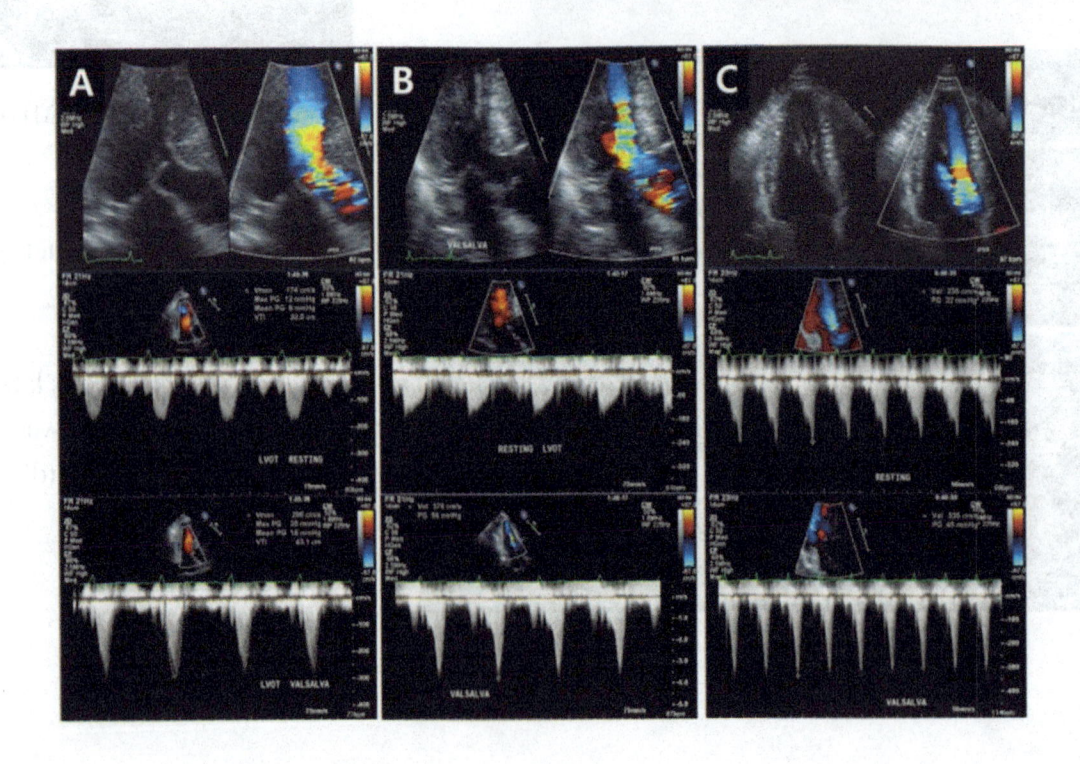

LVOT obstruction criteria

88

1. LVOT obstruction in HCM was defined as a resting LVOT gradient of ≥30 mm Hg
2. Resting Gradient <30 mmHg, Provocable Gradient > 30 mmHg
3. 50 mm Hg is generally recognized as the threshold at which LVOT obstruction becomes hemodynamically significant.

⭐ **ALWAYS VALSALVA** ⭐

Dilated cardiomyopathy
A type of heart muscle disease that causes the ventricles to thin and stretch, growing larger.

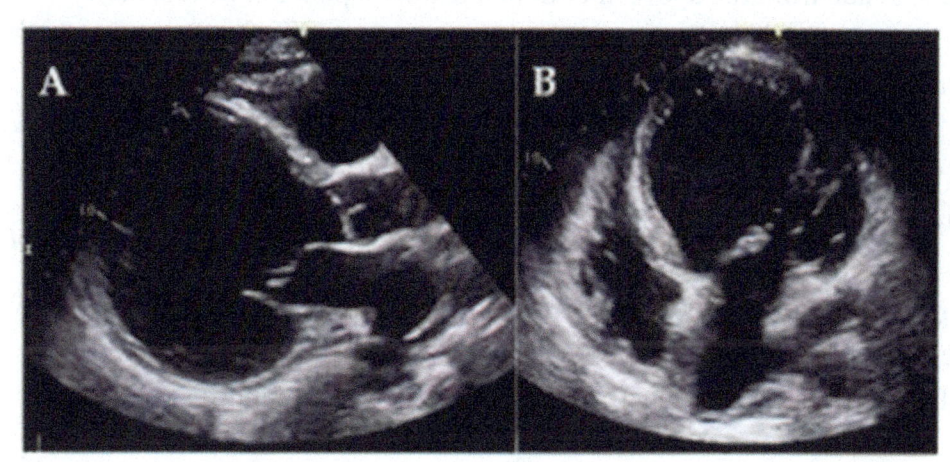

LV normal values
M: 4.2 - 5.8
F: 3.8 - 5.2

Typical causes:
- Coronary heart disease
- Infections, especially viral infections that inflame the heart muscle
- Alcohol, especially if you also have a poor diet
- Complications during the last month of pregnancy or within five months of birth
- Certain toxins such as cobalt
- HTN
- Idiopathic
- Comorbidities
- Certain drugs (such as cocaine and methamphetamines) and two medicines that treat cancer (doxorubicin and daunorubicin)

Typical complications:
- Abnormal heart rhythms (arrhythmia).
- Angina (chest pain).
- Blood clots in your heart.

- Heart attack.
- Heart valve disease.
- Stroke.
- Sudden cardiac arrest.
- Heart failure

Contractile dysfunction and impaired left ventricular ejection fraction are hallmarks of dilated cardiomyopathy. Dilatation of the ventricle is a compensatory mechanism to maintain an adequate stroke volume. Aside from the above-mentioned features, patients with dilated cardiomyopathy may have several other abnormalities.
Assessment of left ventricular function, ejection fraction & wall motion is essential

stroke volume is the volume of blood pumped out of the left ventricle of the heart during each systolic cardiac contraction

Postpartum cardiomyopathy known as peripartum cardiomyopathy (PPCM), is defined as new onset heart failure between the last month of pregnancy and 5 months post-delivery with no determinable cause. Postpartum cardiomyopathy is a rare cause of heart failure.
- 50% recover
- PPCM is considered a DCM

Restrictive cardiomyopathy
Restrictive cardiomyopathy refers to a set of changes in how the heart muscle functions. These changes cause the heart to fill poorly or squeeze poorly. Sometimes, both problems are present. Restrictive cardiomyopathy tends to affect older adults. The heart's ventricles become rigid because of abnormal tissue, such as scar tissue. As an echo technician we have no way of knowing exactly what type is presented in our image, further blood work and or biopsies are required for diagnosis. The technician's main function is to capture all pathologies and corresponding measurements for structure and function analysis.

Types:
- Amyloidosis
- Sarcoidosis
- Hemochromatosis
- Endomyocardial Fibrosis

Amyloidosis -a rare disease that occurs when a protein called amyloid builds up in organs

- Stiffins heart muscle
- Common to also have effusion
- Can mimic constrictive pericarditis

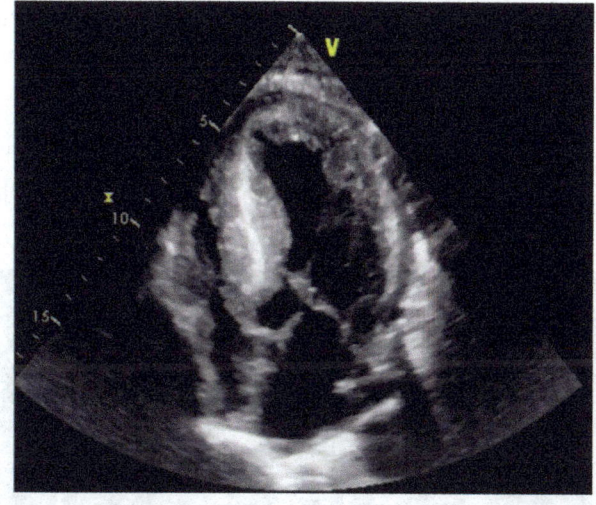

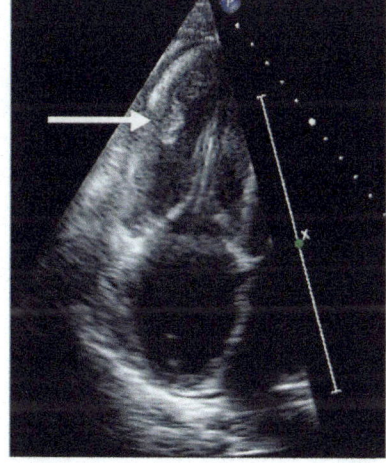

Sarcoidosis - a rare condition that causes small patches of swollen tissue, called granulomas, to develop in the organs of the body

Hemochromatosis- an inherited condition where excessive levels of iron in the body get absorbed, leading to iron overload. Iron overload can cause various symptoms and can cause damage to the body's organs. Where hemochromatosis causes a buildup of iron in the heart it can cause cardiomyopathy.
-Either HCM or DM

Endomyocardial Fibrosis - is principally an endemic disease of the equatorial tropics. It is exceedingly rare in Europe and North America characterized by fibrosis of the apical endocardium of the right ventricle (RV), left ventricle (LV), or both. Usually involves valves leading to severe regur and apical dilation.

Takotsubo cardiomyopathy - Broken heart syndrome
Brought on by an extremely stressful physical or emotional event.
- It occurs almost exclusively in women.
- Weakening of the left ventricle
- Typically, the patients present with akinesia of the apical and mid-ventricular segment while the basal segments are hypercontractile. The apex is more or less dilated (apical ballooning). The degree of left ventricular dysfunction may vary.

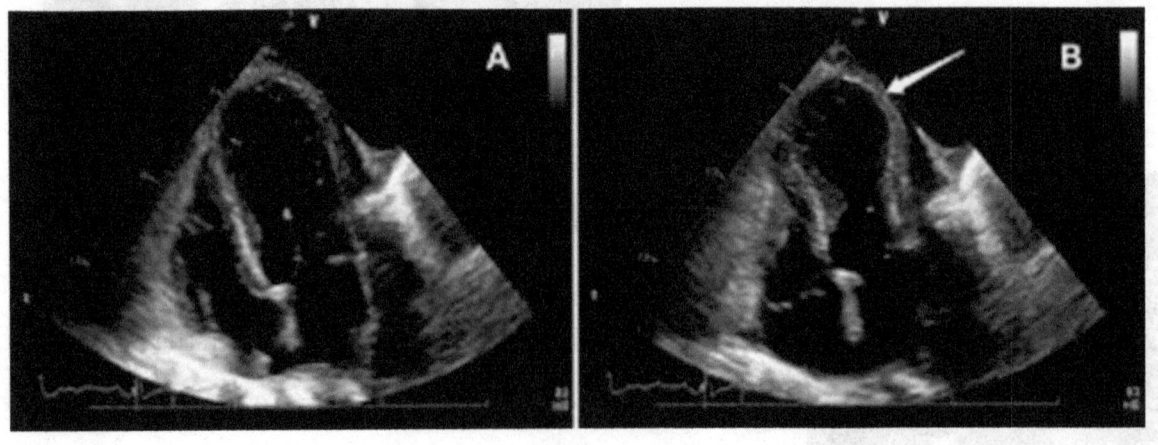

Heart failure

A chronic condition in which the heart doesn't pump blood as well as it should.
Congestive heart failure (CHF) and heart failure are chronic progressive conditions characterized by a weakened heart that is unable to pump enough blood to meet the body's energy needs.
Heart failure often refers to early-stage weakening of the heart without congestion. As the damage to the heart progresses, it causes fluid to build up in the feet, arms, lungs, and other organs, which is referred to as congestion, throughout the body. This stage of heart failure is called CHF.
- Decreased ventricular function
- Increased ventricular size
- Reduced EF - less than 35%
- Preserved EF

Left-sided heart failure occurs when the left ventricle, the heart's main pumping power source, is gradually weakened. When this occurs, the heart is unable to pump oxygen-rich blood from the lungs to the heart's left atrium, into the left ventricle and on through the body and the heart has to work harder.

<u>Systolic</u> failure with <u>reduced</u> ejection fraction: Systolic failure occurs when the left ventricle cannot contract forcefully enough to keep blood circulating normally throughout the body, which deprives the body of a normal supply of blood. As the left ventricle pumps harder to compensate, it grows weaker and thinner. As a result, blood flows backward into organs, causing fluid buildup in the lungs and/or swelling in other parts of the body.

<u>Diastolic</u> heart failure with **preserved** ejection fraction: Diastolic heart failure occurs when the left ventricle has grown stiff or thick, and it is unable to fill the lower left chamber of the heart properly, which reduces the amount of blood pumped out to the body. Over time, this causes blood to build up inside the left atrium, and then in the lungs, leading to fluid congestion and symptoms of heart failure.

Right-sided heart failure means your heart's right ventricle is too weak to pump enough blood to the lungs. As a result: Blood builds up in your veins, vessels that carry blood from the body back to the heart. This buildup increases pressure in your veins.

So what should we be also looking for?
    PHTN

Myocarditis

- Inflammation of the middle layer of the heart wall.
- Usually caused by a virus
- Other pathogens may also be the cause
- Inflammation can reduce the heart's ability to pump blood.

Some people with early myocarditis don't have symptoms. Others have mild symptoms. Common myocarditis symptoms include:
- Chest pain
- Fatigue
- Swelling of the legs, ankles and feet
- Rapid or irregular heartbeat (arrhythmias)

- Shortness of breath, at rest or during activity
- Light-headedness or feeling like you might faint
- Flu-like symptoms such as headache, body aches, joint pain, fever or sore throat

Usually, myocarditis goes away without permanent complications. However, severe myocarditis can permanently damage the heart muscle.

Potential complications of myocarditis may include:
- Heart failure. Untreated, myocarditis can damage the heart muscle so that it can't pump blood well. In severe cases, myocarditis-related heart failure may require a ventricular assist device or a heart transplant.
- Heart attack or stroke. If the heart muscle is injured and can't pump blood, the blood that collects in the heart can form clots. A heart attack can occur if a clot blocks one of the heart (coronary) arteries. A stroke can occur if a blood clot in the heart travels to an artery leading to the brain.
- Rapid or irregular heart rhythms (arrhythmias). Damage to the heart muscle can change how the heart beats. Certain arrhythmias increase the risk of stroke.
- Sudden cardiac death. Certain serious arrhythmias can cause the heart to stop beating (sudden cardiac arrest). It's deadly if not treated immediately (sudden cardiac death).

Cardiac functions may be monitored via serial echocardiograms. In general, left ventricular function improves in fulminant myocarditis over the course of approximately 6 months.

Echocardiographic findings in myocarditis include:
- Wall motion abnormalities
- Systolic dysfunction
- Diastolic dysfunction
- Changes in image texture on echocardiogram, i.e. increase in brightness, heterogeneity, and contrast
- Pericardial effusion may be noted in a few patients
- Functional regurgitation through the AV valves may be noted due to ventricular dilation

No single imaging modality has the capability to diagnose myocarditis with absolute certainty
- Echo is used primarily to access function
    - Systolic & diastolic
    - Valves
    - WMA

Pericarditis

A swelling and irritation of the thin saclike membrane surrounding the heart (pericardium).

Causes:
- Idiopathic
- Infection
- Trauma
- Autoimmune
- Comorbidities
- Open heart

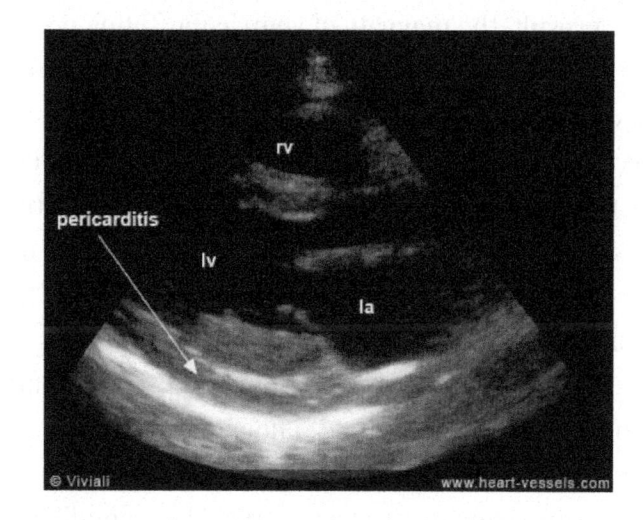

Pericarditis - Symptoms

Chest pain that:
- Can especially be felt behind the breastbone, and sometimes beneath the clavicle (collarbone), neck, and left shoulder
- Is a sharp, piercing pain over the center or left side of the chest that gets worse when you take a deep breath and usually gets better if you sit up or lean forward
- Feels a lot like a heart attack
- Fever
- Weakness and tiredness
- Coughing
- Trouble breathing
- Pain when swallowing
- Palpitations (irregular heartbeats)

A common sign of pericarditis is a pericardial rub. This is the sound of the pericardium rubbing against the outer layer of your heart. Other chest sounds that are signs of fluid in the pericardium (pericardial effusion) or the lungs (pleural effusion) may also be heard. Pericardial effusion is a common complication of pericarditis. However, pericarditis does not always lead to pericardial effusion, and pericardial effusion does not always occur due to pericarditis.

Constrictive pericarditis is the result of scarring and consequent loss of the normal elasticity of the pericardial sac. This leads to impairment of ventricular filling in the mid and late diastole. As a result, the majority of ventricular filling occurs rapidly in early diastole and the ventricular volume does not increase after the end of the early filling period. In patients with constrictive pericarditis, the pulmonary capillary wedge pressure is influenced by the inspiratory fall in intrathoracic pressure, while the LV pressure is shielded from respiratory pressure variations by the pericardial scar. Thus, inspiration lowers the pulmonary capillary wedge pressure, and presumably left atrial pressure, but not LV diastolic pressure, thereby decreasing the pressure gradient for ventricular filling. The less favorable filling pressure gradient during inspiration explains the decline in filling velocity. Reciprocal changes occur in the velocity of right ventricular (RV) filling [2,3]. These changes are mediated by the ventricular septum, not by increased systemic venous return.

Restrictive cardiomyopathy is characterized by a nondilated rigid ventricle, resulting in severe diastolic dysfunction and restrictive filling that produces hemodynamic changes similar to those in constrictive pericarditis. In patients with restrictive cardiomyopathy, inspiration lowers pulmonary wedge and LV diastolic pressures equally, thereby leaving the pressure gradient for ventricular filling and filling velocity virtually unchanged.

Pericarditis - protocol additions
- ❖ Best views
  - ➢ Sub 4C
  - ➢ PLAX
- ❖ Measure effusion
- ❖ Check for tamponade*

CONSTRICTIVE VS. RESTRICTIVE

	constrictive pericarditis	restrictive cardiomyopathy
Doppler ECHO Respiratory variation in ventricular inflow velocities	increase in respiratory variation of the ventricular inflow velocities in patients with compared to a in patients	normal pattern
Hepatic venous flow reversal	usually reverses during expiration in constrictive pericarditis	reverses during inspiration in restrictive cardiomyopathy.
Ventricular end-diastolic pressures	(RVEDP and LVEDP) are equal or nearly equal	LVEDP is usually higher than RVEDP in restrictive cardiomyopathy.

Pericarditis - Complications
- pericardial effusion
- cardiac tamponade*
- constrictive pericarditis

1. Inflammation of the pericardium leads to a pericardial effusion.
2. If the amount of fluid increases quickly, the effusion can keep the heart from working properly. This complication of pericarditis is called cardiac tamponade
3. Chronic constrictive pericarditis occurs when scar-like tissue forms throughout the pericardium. It's a rare disease that can develop over time in people with pericarditis. The scar tissue causes the pericardial

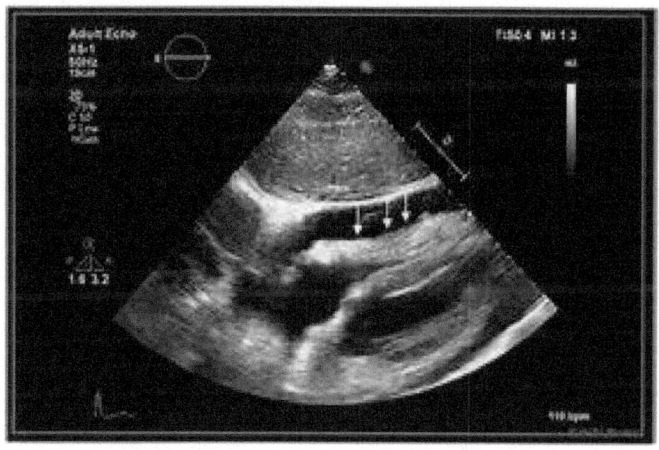

sac to stiffen and not move properly. In time, the scar tissue squeezes the heart and keeps it from working well.

*Cardiac Tamponade **MEDICAL EMERGENCY**

Cardiac tamponade is the result of an accumulation of fluid, pus, blood, gas, or benign or malignant neoplastic tissue within the pericardial cavity, which can occur either rapidly or gradually over time, but eventually, results in impaired cardiac output.
This is to be distinguished from a pericardial effusion, which can be very large but does not necessarily impair cardiac function.
Checking for tamponade:
- M-Mode across RV in PLAX & subcostal

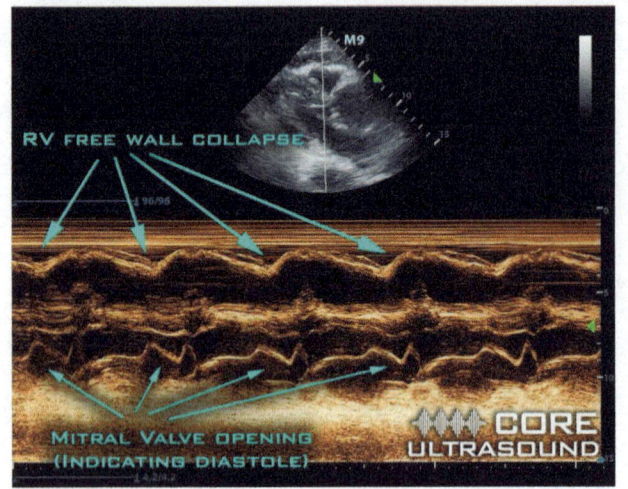

- Observe RV, watch for collapse and relaxation movement
- CW TV & MV in A4C
- Separate from the normal CWs
- Turn speed all the way down
- Watch for respiration differences

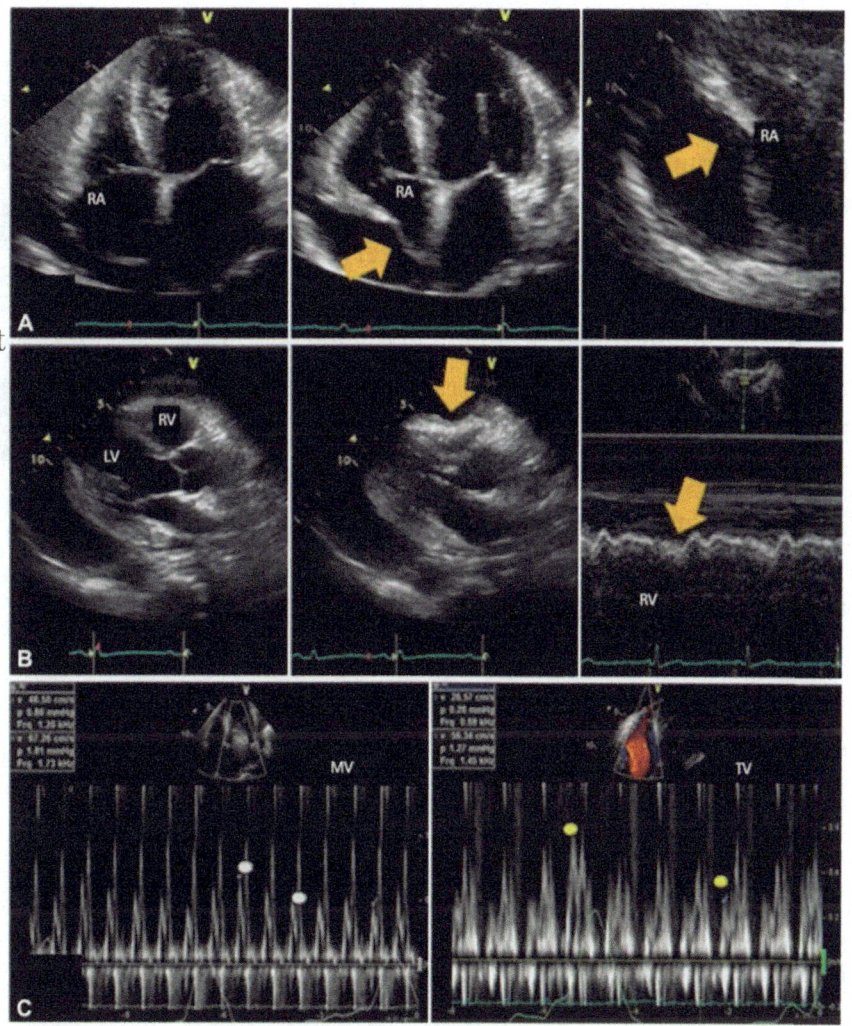

Dressler syndrome, also known as postmyocardial infarction syndrome or postcardiac injury syndrome, is a rare form of secondary pericarditis that occurs when the heart or pericardium is injured. It's believed to be caused by the immune system's response to damage, which can result from a heart attack, surgery, or traumatic injury. Symptoms include: Chest pain, Fever, Pleuritic pain, Pericarditis, and Pericardial effusion.

Tumors, Thrombus & Missiles
Tumors - Benign
A **myxoma** is a myxoid primary tumor of primitive connective tissue.
A cardiac myxoma is a tumor that affects your heart. It's the most common noncancerous primary cardiac tumor.
- 75% of myxomas originate in the left atrium either at the mitral annulus or the fossa ovalis border of the interatrial septum
- 20% arise from the right atrium
- 5% stem from both atria and the ventricle.

Myxoma - Complications
- Embolism
- Valve obstruction
- LVDD
- HF
- Mimics stenosis

Myxoma - Symptoms

- Fever.
- Lethargy (lack of energy).
- Night sweats.
- Raynaud's phenomenon*
- Shortness of breath with physical activity.
- Shortness of breath or fainting when you stand. (This is because gravity pulls the tumor into your mitral valve, causing your blood pressure to temporarily drop.)
- Weight loss.

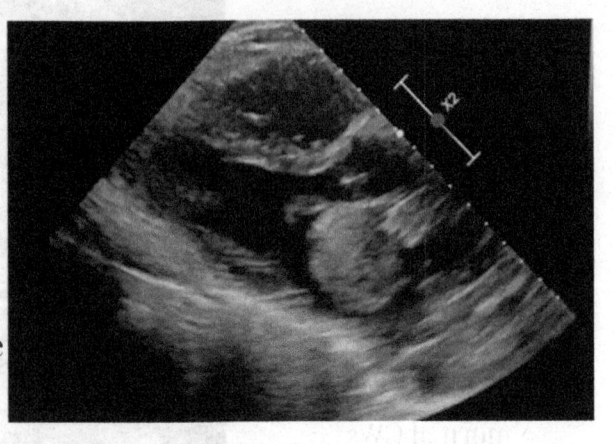

*Raynaud's syndrome causes spasms in small blood vessels in your fingers and toes. This limits blood flow and leads to symptoms like skin color changes, cold skin and a pins and needles sensation. Common triggers of Raynaud's attacks include cold weather and stress. Many people have mild symptoms that they can manage through lifestyle changes.

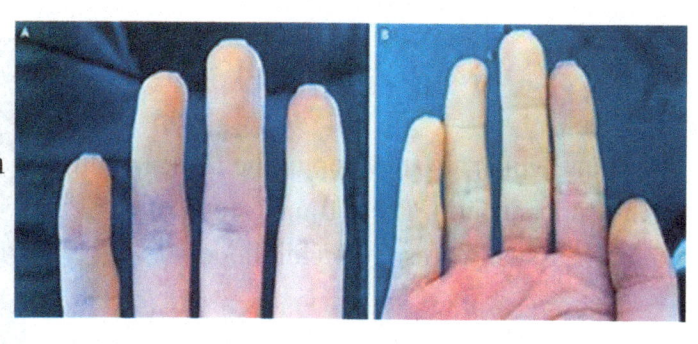

Myxoma - Echo additions

Measure mass in multiple planes
- Cross-sectional measurements
- If able, measure the area - trace

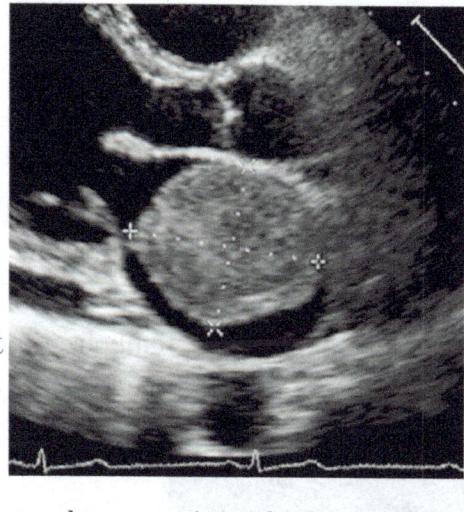

Rhabdomyomas, which develop in the myocardium or the endocardium and account for about one out of every five tumors that originate in the heart. Most of these occur in children or infants and are associated with tuberous sclerosis, adenoma of the skin, kidney tumors and arrhythmias. These tumors tend to occur in multiples inside the wall of the ventricle.

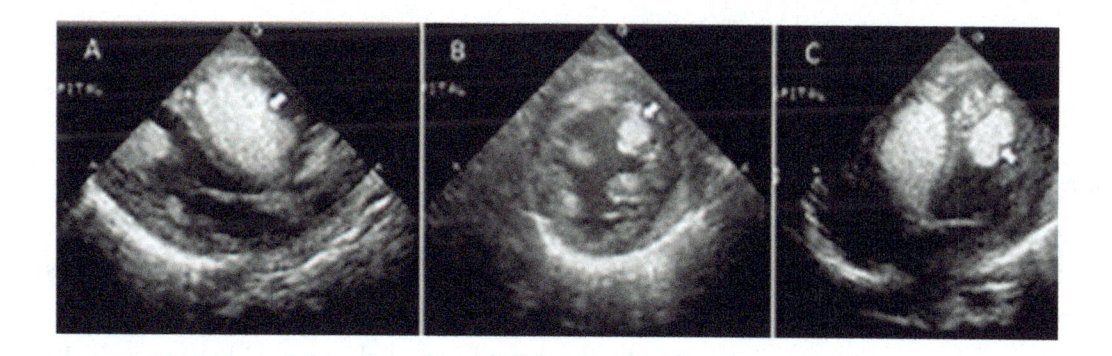

101

Fibromas, which also develop in the myocardium or the endocardium. These tumors tend to occur in the walls. Usually present in childhood.

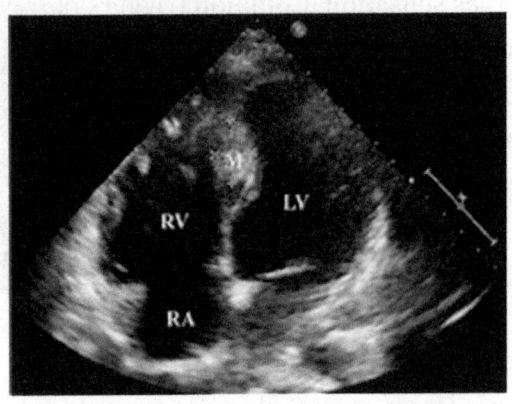

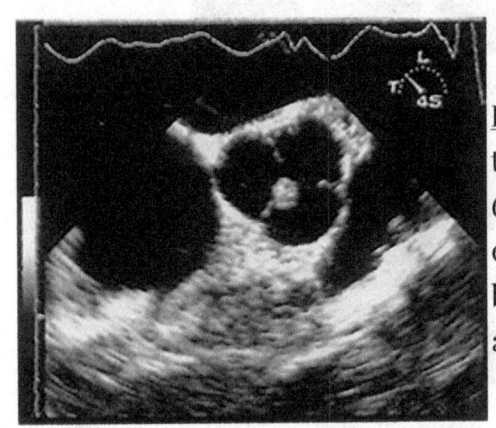

Papillary fibroelastoma – the most common cardiac tumor to affect the cardiac valves. The mean age at diagnosis is 60 years old. These tumors are associated with embolization (breaking off and traveling in the bloodstream) resulting in stroke or less commonly heart attack.

Tumors - Malignant

Nearly all primary malignant cardiac tumors are sarcomas, and the most frequent one is angiosarcoma.
Angiosarcoma is a very aggressive form of cancer made up of abnormal blood vessels. It characteristically originates from the right atrium. The clinical course is rapid with a very high incidence of spread throughout the body (80%). Once the cancer has metastasized the prognosis is poor.

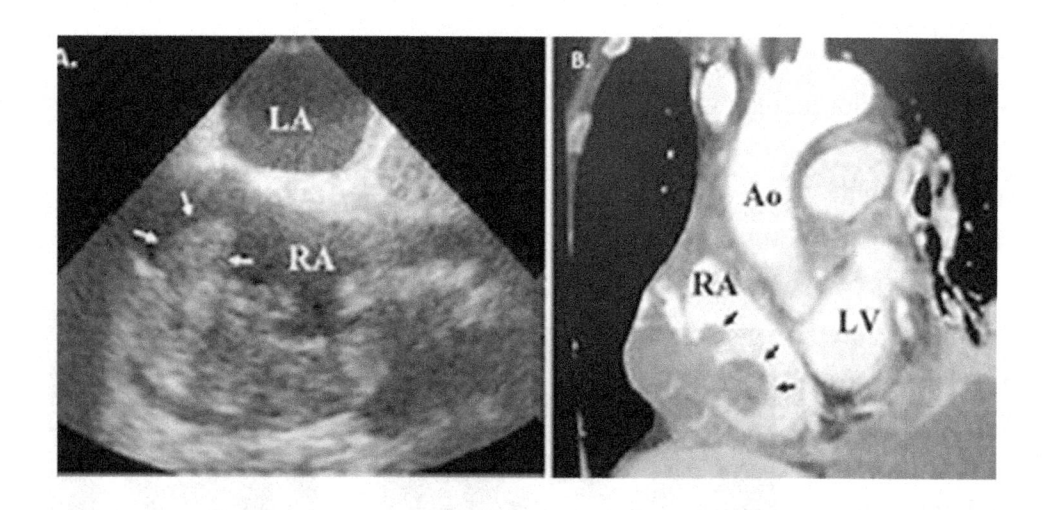

Tumors - Secondary

A term used to describe cancer that has metastasized from the place where it first started to another part of the body.

Appearance depends on type, varies with most

Interrogate as you would any other mass.

Carcinoid heart disease occurs when large amounts of vasoactive substances such as serotonin, tachykinins, and prostaglandins reach the right side of the heart, consequent to reduced hepatic metabolism from extensive metastatic liver involvement of the carcinoid tumor.

Findings may include:
- Fixed/rigid TV
- Severe TR
- PR
- Right HF
- TS and/or PS - rare

Diagnosis & Determination of Mass

Since tumors look almost the same via ultrasound, here are steps used:
- Mass noted on echo
- Alternate imaging
- Blood test
- Tumor markers
- Biopsy

Thrombus – A blood clot formed in situ within the vascular system of the body and impeding blood flow.
- Fixed / attached
- Usually caused by WMA

Thrombus - Types
1. Layered
2. Single
3. Multilobulated
4. Pedunculated

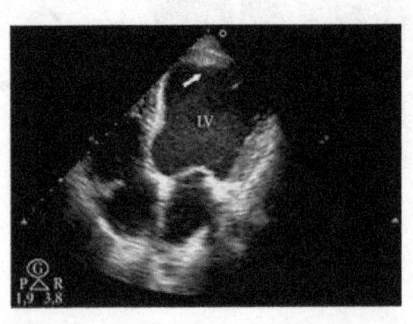

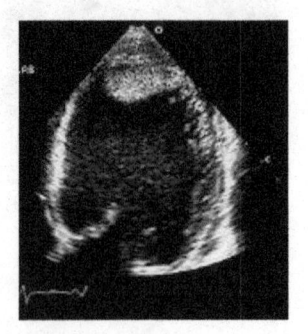

Embolism = a blood clot that is moving throughout the cardiovascular system

Missiles - Foreign bodies
Usually already seen on other imaging. XRAY, CT
Echo used for accessing complications from missile
- Trauma
- Tamponade
- Rupture

Anytime there is a structure whether it be a mass, or foreign body it is imperative that the echo technician captures as many images and in as many views as possible. measure the foreign structure cross-sectionally and trace if possible.

Diseases of the aorta

- Aortic aneurysm
- Aortic dissection
- Marfan
- Sinus of Valsalva aneurysm
- Aortic coarctation

Aortic aneurysm -An abnormal bulge in the aorta which carries blood from the heart to the rest of the body. It can occur anywhere in the aorta and may be in a tube form or round shaped.

Can burst/rupture if not detected.

Given the fact that the aorta runs from the heart all the way down through the abdomen, as an echo technician we can only see an aneurysm of the aortic root, ascending aorta and the beginning of the descending aorta.

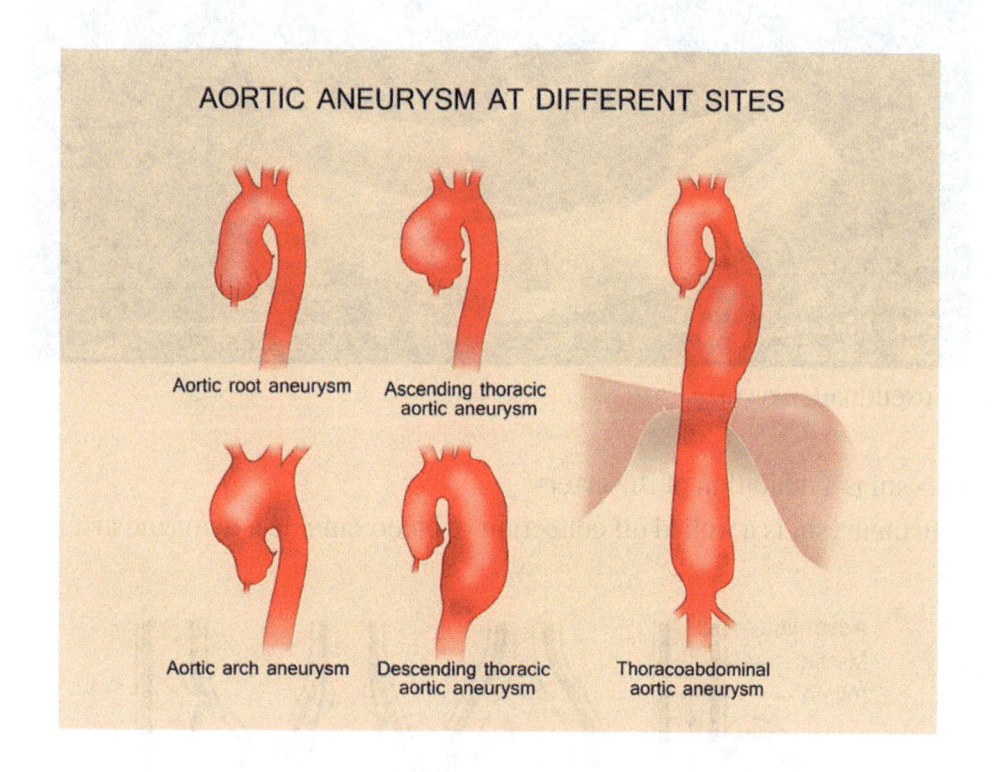

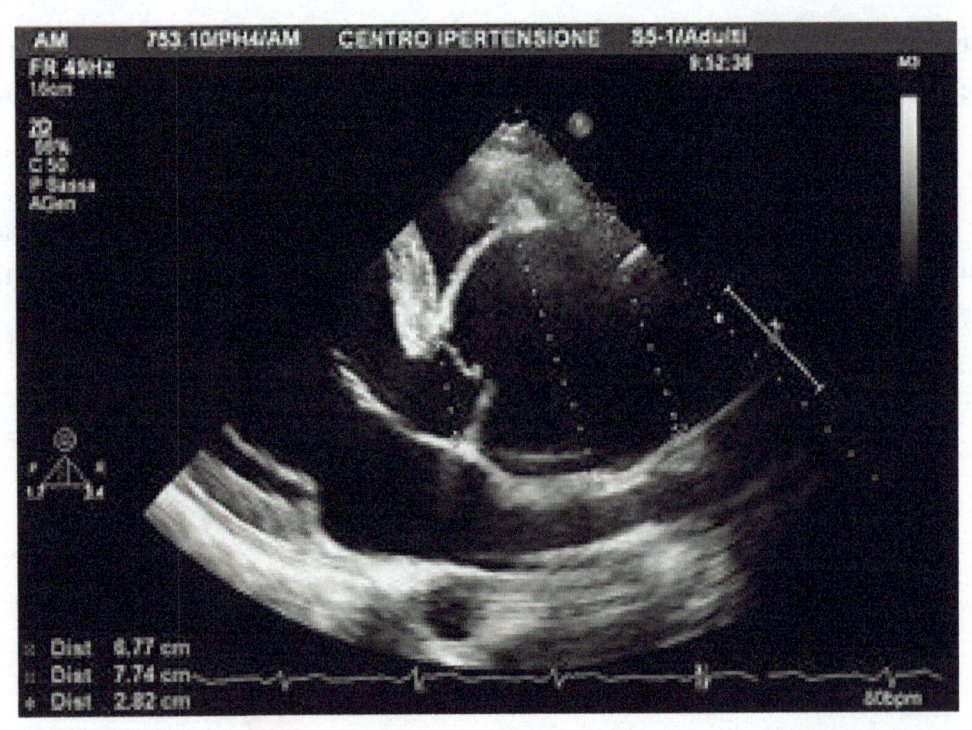

aneurysm vs pseudoaneurysm

- Aneurysm is a dilatation of the artery
- Pseudoaneurysm is a walled off collection of blood outside a damaged artery

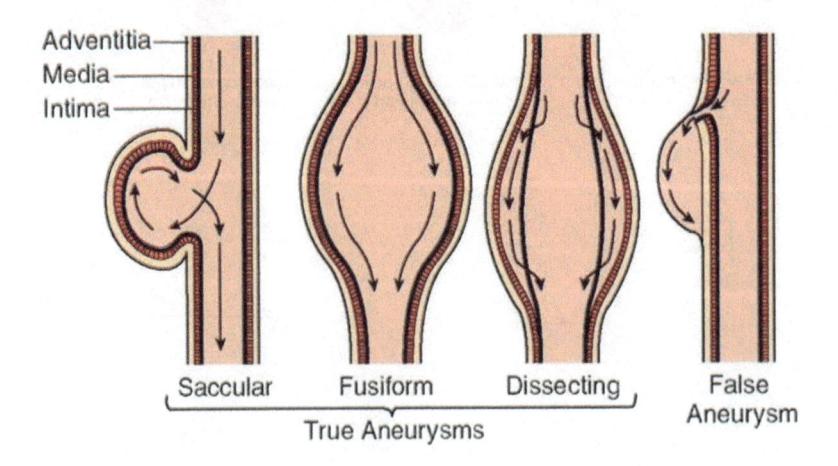

Aortic dissection

A tear in the inner lining

Sudden severe chest or upper back pain, often described as a tearing or ripping sensation, that spreads to the neck or down the back

🚨 MEDICAL EMERGENCY 🚨

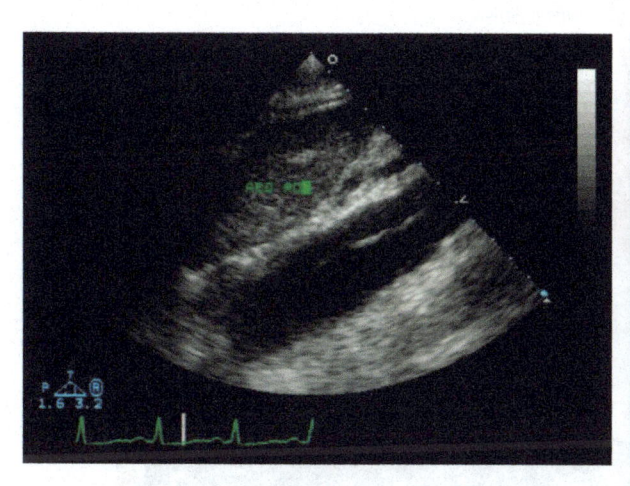

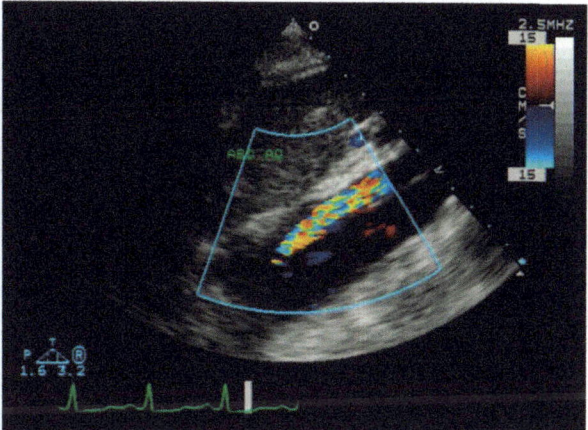

An aortic dissection has a visible echogenic line in the middle of the vessel where the Tunica intima has torn. You will also see a turbulent flow between the torn lining and the original arterial wall.

Marfan - a genetic condition that affects connective tissue, which provides support for the body and organs. Marfan syndrome can damage the blood vessels, heart, eyes, skin, lungs, and the bones of the hips, spine, feet, and rib cage.

An echocardiogram is recommended at the time of diagnosis of Marfan syndrome to not only measure aortic root diameter, but also determine the rate of enlargement of the aorta. Even if no enlargement is detected, it is recommended that the aorta is imaged at least once a year to monitor any changes in size

The most common cardiovascular abnormalities are dilatation of the aorta and mitral regurgitation

- ★ Great vessels - check diameter
- ★ Valves - check diameter & function

Aortic coarctation - is a narrowing of the aorta

The narrowing forces the heart to pump harder to move blood through the aorta. Coarctation of the aorta is generally present at birth (congenital heart defect).

Symptoms can range from mild to severe. The condition might not be detected until adulthood.

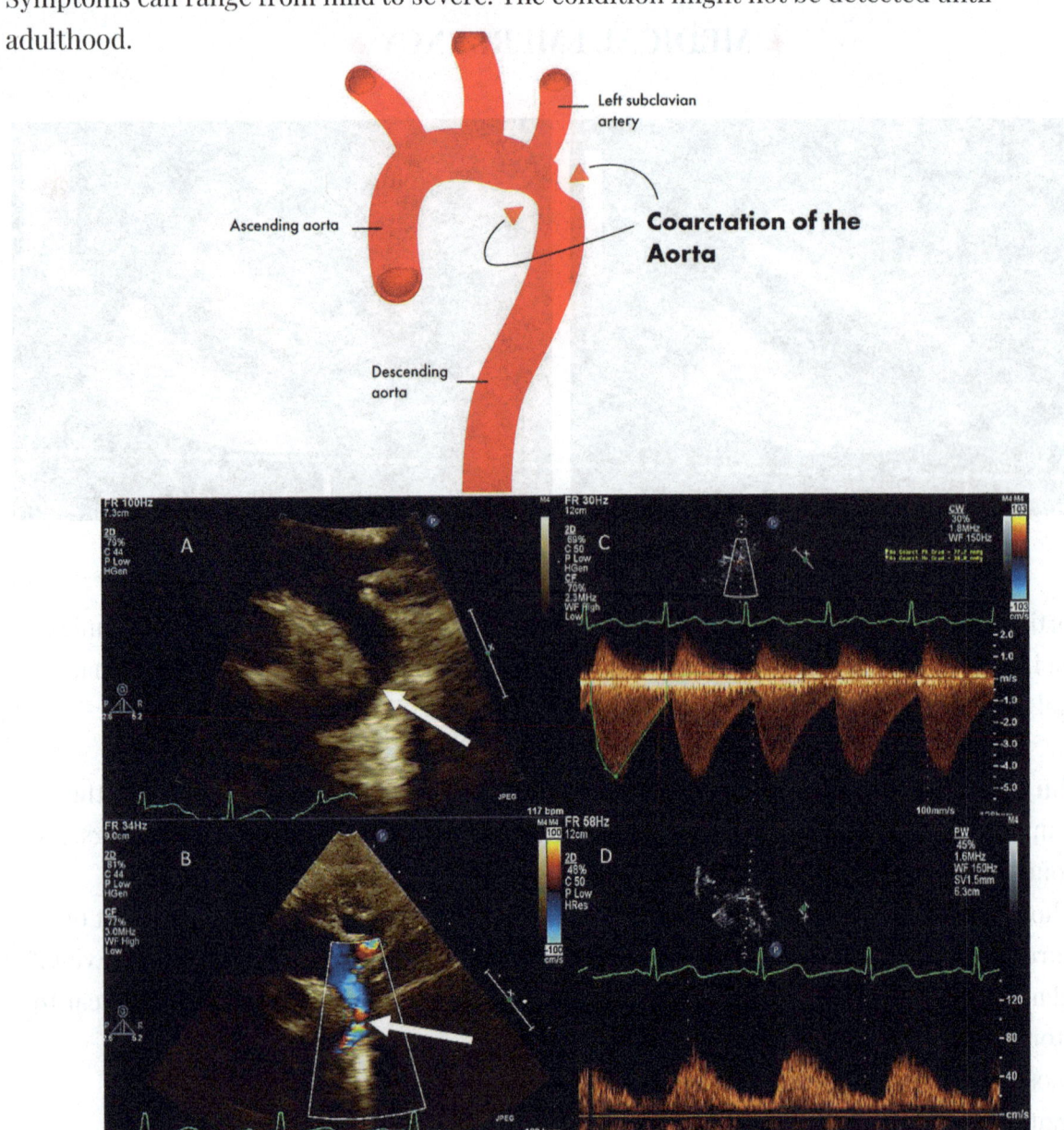

Comorbidities & the TTE

Morbidity: The condition of suffering from a disease or medical condition.
Comorbidity: The simultaneous presence of two or more diseases or medical conditions in a single patient.

Certain cardiac pathologies can affect the heart and or the treatments for them. It is important to know these, so when you are performing an echo you can acquire all of the necessary information.

Cancer- certain chemotherapies are cardiotoxic. If your lab has the availability for strain Imaging, it is highly recommended to do so. strain Imaging shows the deformation of the heart throughout the cardiac cycle, thus, assessing the effects of chemotherapy on cardiac function.

History or indication of a stroke or a TIA or if the exam reason is so most Labs have a mandatory protocol Edition to do a bubble study or agitated Saline study. A bubble study is what is used to check for any septal defects.

Kidney disease - when someone has CKD, their hearts need to pump harder to get blood to the kidneys which can lead to heart failure. This also applies to patients with diabetes who often have corresponding kidney disease.

Liver disease - cirrhosis can lead to systolic and diastolic dysfunction. Liver disease can also cause congestive heart failure and pericardial effusion. be sure to check all views for corresponding pathologies.

COPD- one of the leading causes of death among patients with COPD is comorbid heart failure.

Obesity- overweight and obesity contributes to comorbidities including several cardiovascular conditions such as arrhythmias, coronary heart disease and heart failure.

Chapter 8
Congenital Heart Disease

Congenital heart disease are pathologies and defects that occur while the child is in utero. These are differences that occur when a child is still a fetus, and structures are still forming. In this chapter we will cover some of the most common congenital defects:
- ASD
- VSD
- PDA
- Endocardial Cushion Defect
- Cleft MV
- PV Stenosis
- Ebstein Anomaly
- Tetralogy of Fallot
- Transposition of the Great Arteries
- HLHS

Atrial septal defects

The atrial septal defect is the most common congenital defect. There are four main types of atrial septal defects.

Most common
1. Primum ASD
2. Secundum ASD

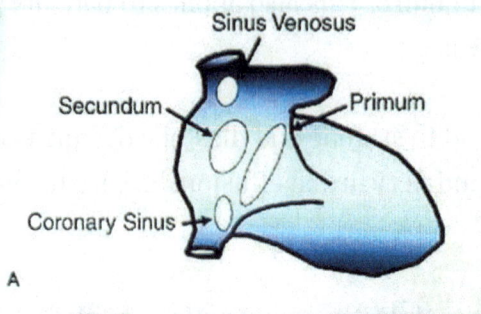

Less common:
1. Sinus venous
2. Coronary sinus

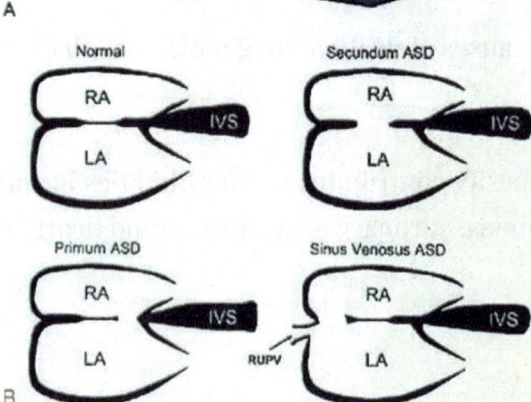

Primum

This type of ASD affects the lower part of the atrial septum and might occur with other congenital heart defects.

Primum ASDs are commonly linked with Down syndrome.

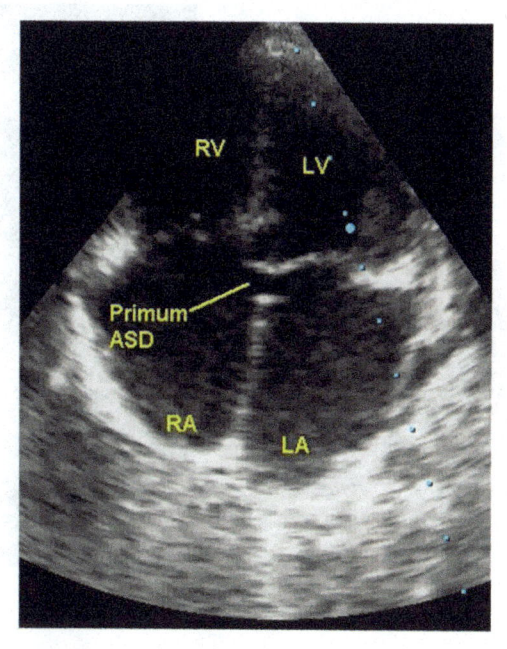

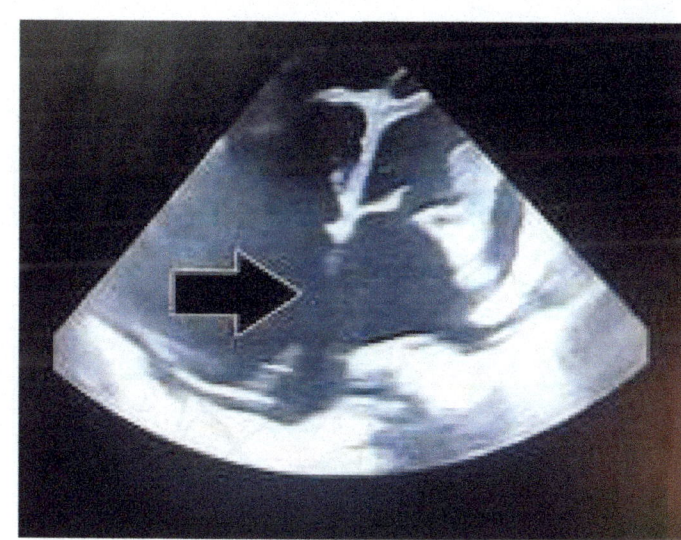

Secundum

In the middle of your atrial septum. This is the most common type of ASD, (80% of all ASDs).

Sinus venous

This rare type of ASD usually occurs in the upper part of the wall separating the heart chambers. It's also associated with other heart structure changes present at birth. After birth, sinus venosus also forms the sinoatrial node and the coronary sinus

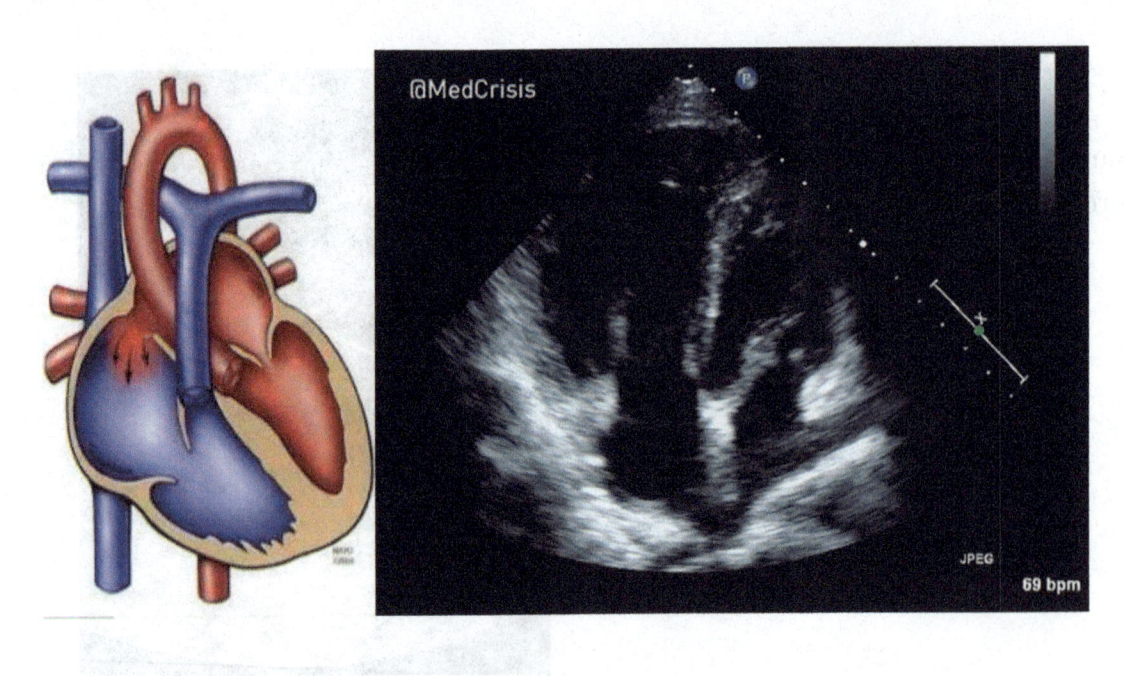

Coronary sinus - Unroofed

The rarest type of ASD (less than 1% of all ASDs).
It involves a missing or incomplete wall between your coronary sinus (a group of veins connected to your heart) and your left atrium

The atrial wall between the coronary sinus and left atrium is either partially or completely absent, resulting in a right-to-left shunt.

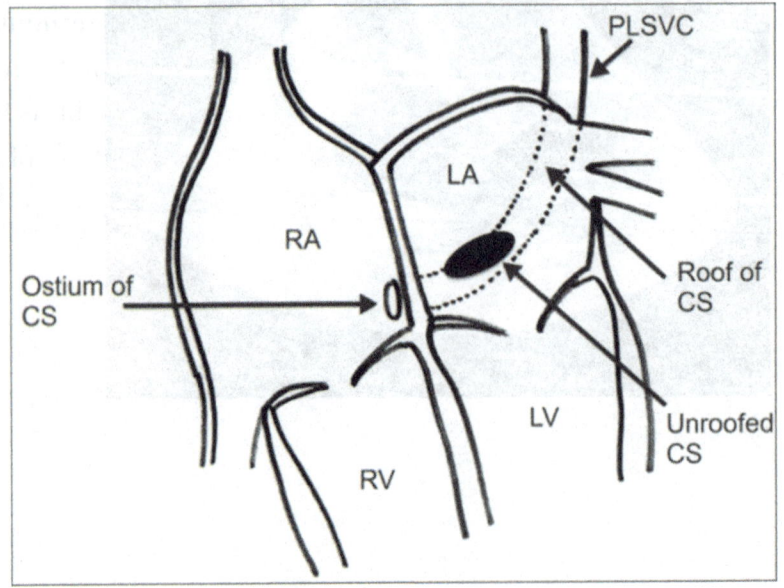

What is the difference between an atrial septal defect and a patent foramen ovale?

An atrial septal defect and a patent foramen ovale are both openings in the atrial septum. But ASD is a congenital heart defect, meaning it's a problem that occurred while a fetus was still in the uterus. Septal tissue should've formed in that part of the atrial septum but didn't.

- A patent foramen ovale isn't a congenital heart defect.
- Tissue isn't missing from the atrial septum.
- Instead, a PFO happens when a normal flap-like opening in a baby's heart (foramen ovale) doesn't seal shut after birth.
- The foramen ovale is normal, and we all have one when we're born.
- A PFO is usually smaller than an ASD

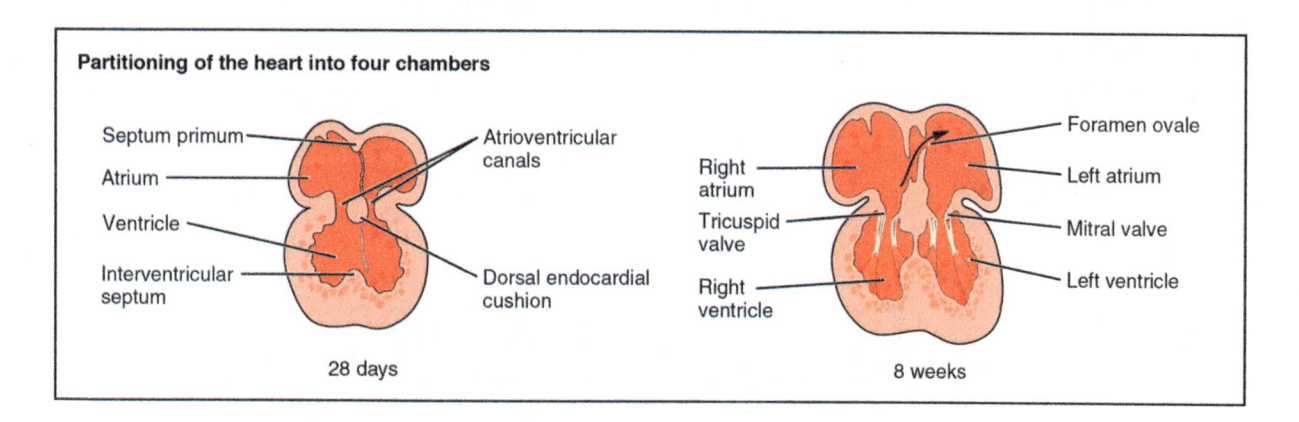

Partitioning of the heart into four chambers

28 days — Septum primum, Atrium, Ventricle, Interventricular septum, Atrioventricular canals, Dorsal endocardial cushion

8 weeks — Right atrium, Tricuspid valve, Right ventricle, Foramen ovale, Left atrium, Mitral valve, Left ventricle

ASD & TTE
- Determining the hemodynamic effect
- Shunt direction
- Imaging planes
- PLAX
- PSAX
- A4C
- SUBC

(shunt) In medicine: a passage that allows blood or other fluid to move from one part of the body to another

ASD - Hemodynamics
Shunt size & direction - How big is the defect & how does it alter flow?
Most ASDs have a R ↠ L direction

The Shunt
Images needed:
- 2D of ASD
- CFD through same image
- CW & PW of RVOT
- CW & PW of LVOT
- LVOT diam
- RVOT diam
- The calculation: Qp/Qs ratio

Qp/Qs ratio
Measurements needed:
1. RVOT diam
2. RVOT VTI
3. LVOT diam
4. LVOT VTI

Traditional Methods of Measuring Qp:Qs

Qp = Pulmonary flow
Qs = Systemic flow
Qp:Qs describes the magnitude of a cardiovascular shunt
  Normally = 1:1
  Left to right shunts >1.0
  Right to left shunts <1.0
Qp:Qs is classically determined with oximetry via cardiac catheterization

Q = Blood Flow
P = Pulmonary
S = Systemic

ASD TTE Gold Standard

BUBBLES

When an ASD is suspected a bubble study is highly recommended. Bubble study is performed by agitating saline and identifying if bubbles come through the atrial septum on to the left side. Obviously if the shunt is left to right a bubble study will not show this.

The Bubble Study
- A4C
- Agitated Saline
- Agitated vigorously
- Push fast
- Turn capture time up to maxim
- Valsalva in the middle

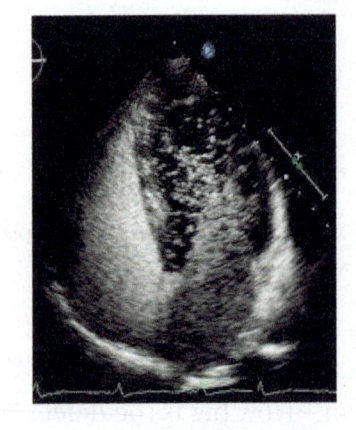

Ventricular septal defects

VSD Types:

- Membranous: This is the most common type of VSD and makes up about 80% of cases. These VSDs happen in the upper section of the wall between the ventricles.
- Muscular: These account for about 20% of VSDs in infants, and there is often more than one hole that's part of the defect.
- Inlet: This is a hole that happens just below the tricuspid valve in the right ventricle and the mitral valve in the left ventricle. That means when blood enters the ventricles, it must pass a VSD that connects the two chambers.
- Outlet (conoventricular): This kind of VSD creates a hole just before the pulmonary valve in the right ventricle and just before the aortic valve in the left ventricle, connecting the two chambers. That means blood has to go by the VSD on its way through both valves.

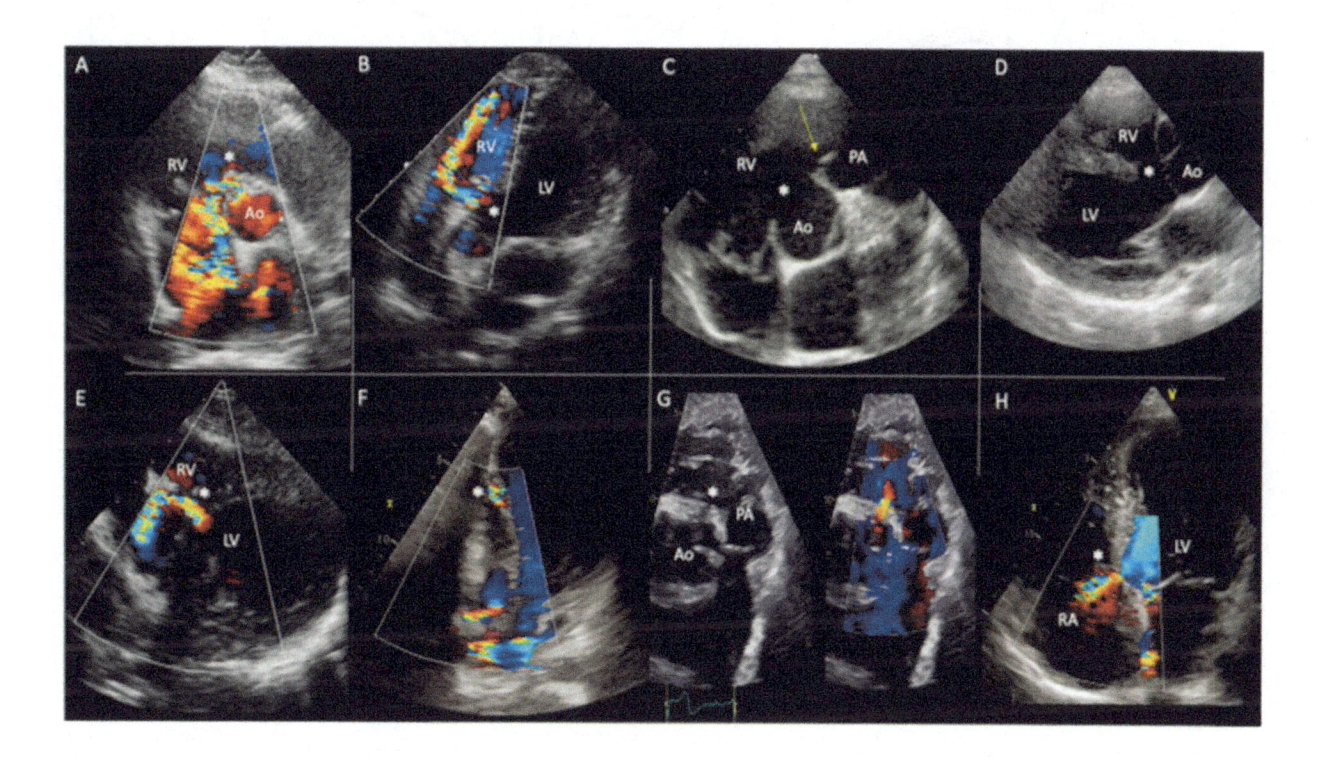

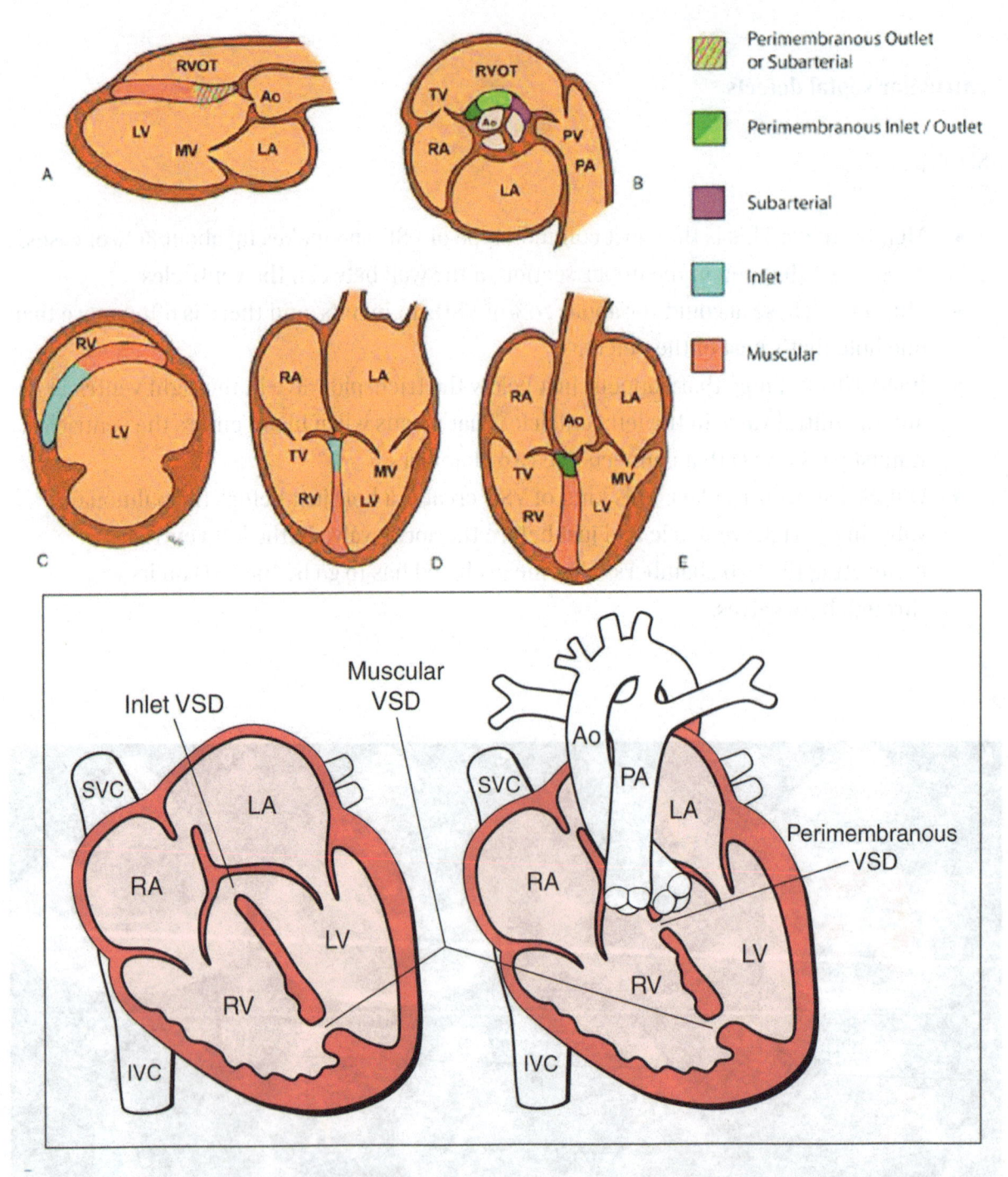

Similar to an ASD, as an echo technician our duty is the same to determine the direction and size of the shunt. Remember when any shunt is visible via 2D Imaging or color Doppler to continuous wave through the opening to acquire pressure gradients throughout.

PDA - Patent ductus arteriosus

The ductus arteriosus, as we know, is a natural occurring shunt in fetal circulation. This should close as the walls contract once the lungs begin to function at birth. When this natural occurring shunt fails to close it becomes a patent opening and therefore a defect. This defect is best seen in the short axis at the aortic level where the Pulmonary artery is in view.

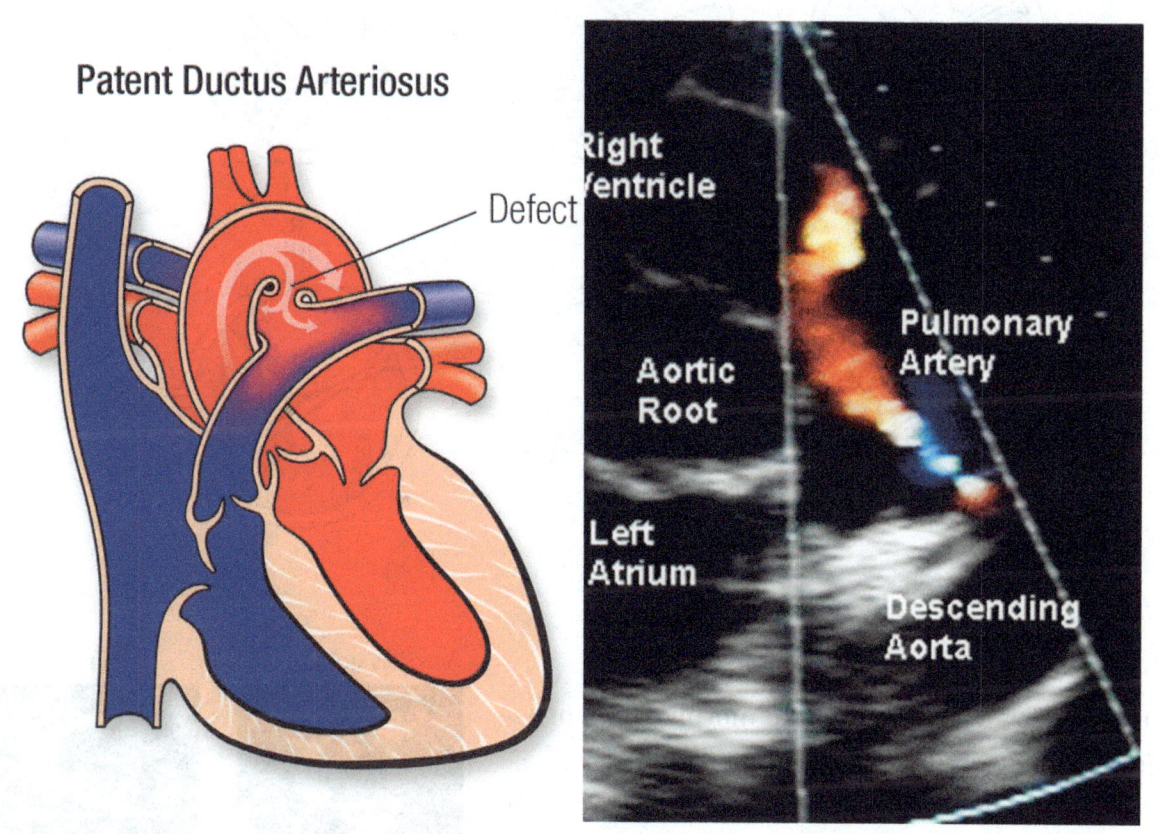

PDAs are usually seen in pediatric studies. They present as a jet between the aorta and the pulmonary artery. color Doppler and spectral Doppler are important to utilize with this pathology.

AoV Defects

A bicuspid aortic valve and other aortic valve defects are either when only two leaflets are formed in the aortic valve, or two of the three leaflets are fused together making up only two functioning leaflets.

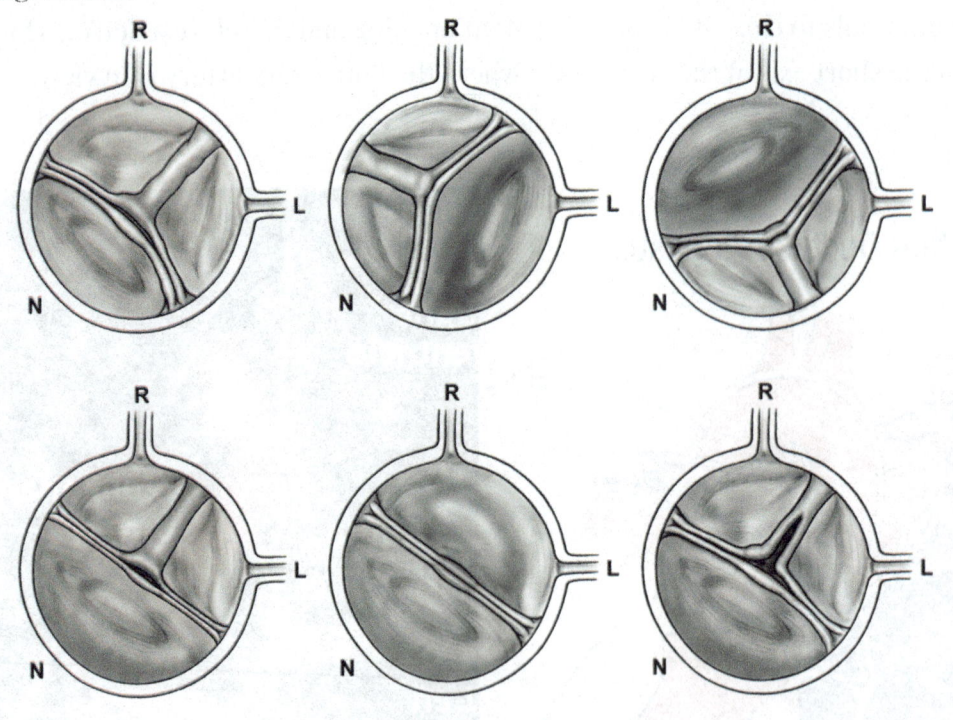

This image shows a few different morphologies of aortic valve defects. The most common visual presence is this systolic opening of the aortic valve. It looks more like a "football" than a "Mercedes symbol."

Notice how when the valve is closed it still may look trileaflet so it's imperative to get an optimal View of the aortic valve in a complete cardiac cycle.

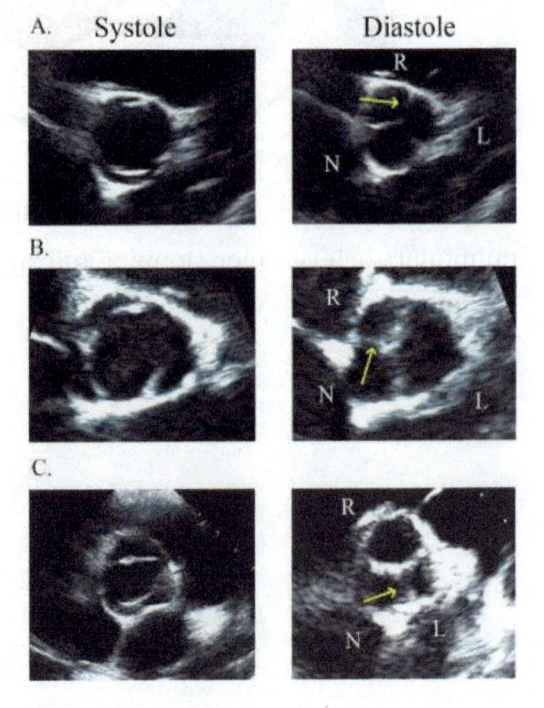

Endocardial Cushion Defect

Congenital heart conditions that occur early in fetal life due to improperly developed heart tissue in the center of the heart (the endocardial cushion area of the heart). This results in a range of defects that are included in this category of endocardial cushion defects

AKA - AV SEPTAL DEFECT

- A hole in the center
- 1 AV valve
- Usually associated with
- Detected in-utero to 6-months
- Surgery is necessary

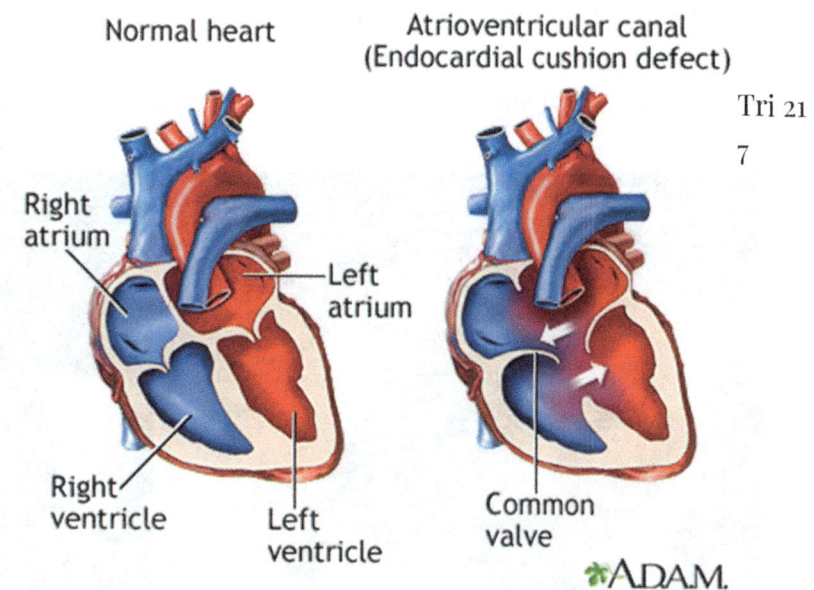

Tri 21
7

Cleft MV

When a leaflet doesn't fully form
Usually AML
Regurg is common
usually associated with congenital heart disease, most notably ostium primum atrial septal defect or other conditions, including MV prolapse, myxomatous MV disease, Marfan syndrome, and malrotation of the papillary muscles

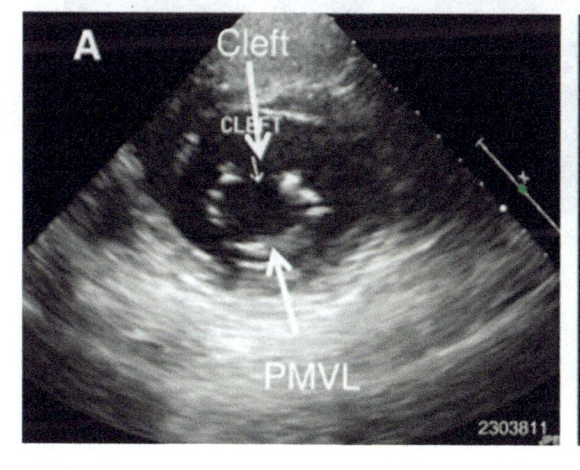

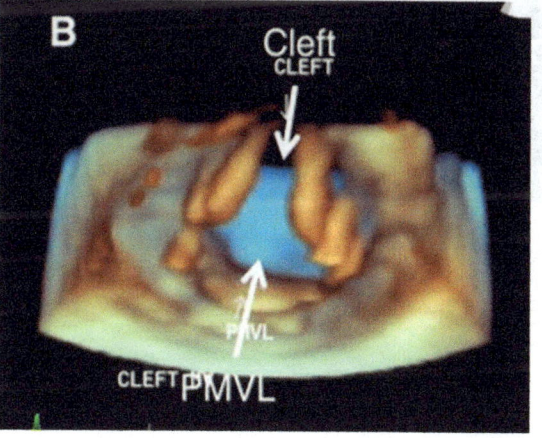

PV Stenosis

If I have to define this, then you should be scared!!!!!

3 Types
1. Valvular - valve itself
2. Subvalvular - RVOT obstruction
3. Supravalvular - stenosis of the MPA

Evaluate as you would any other stenosis and/or obstruction

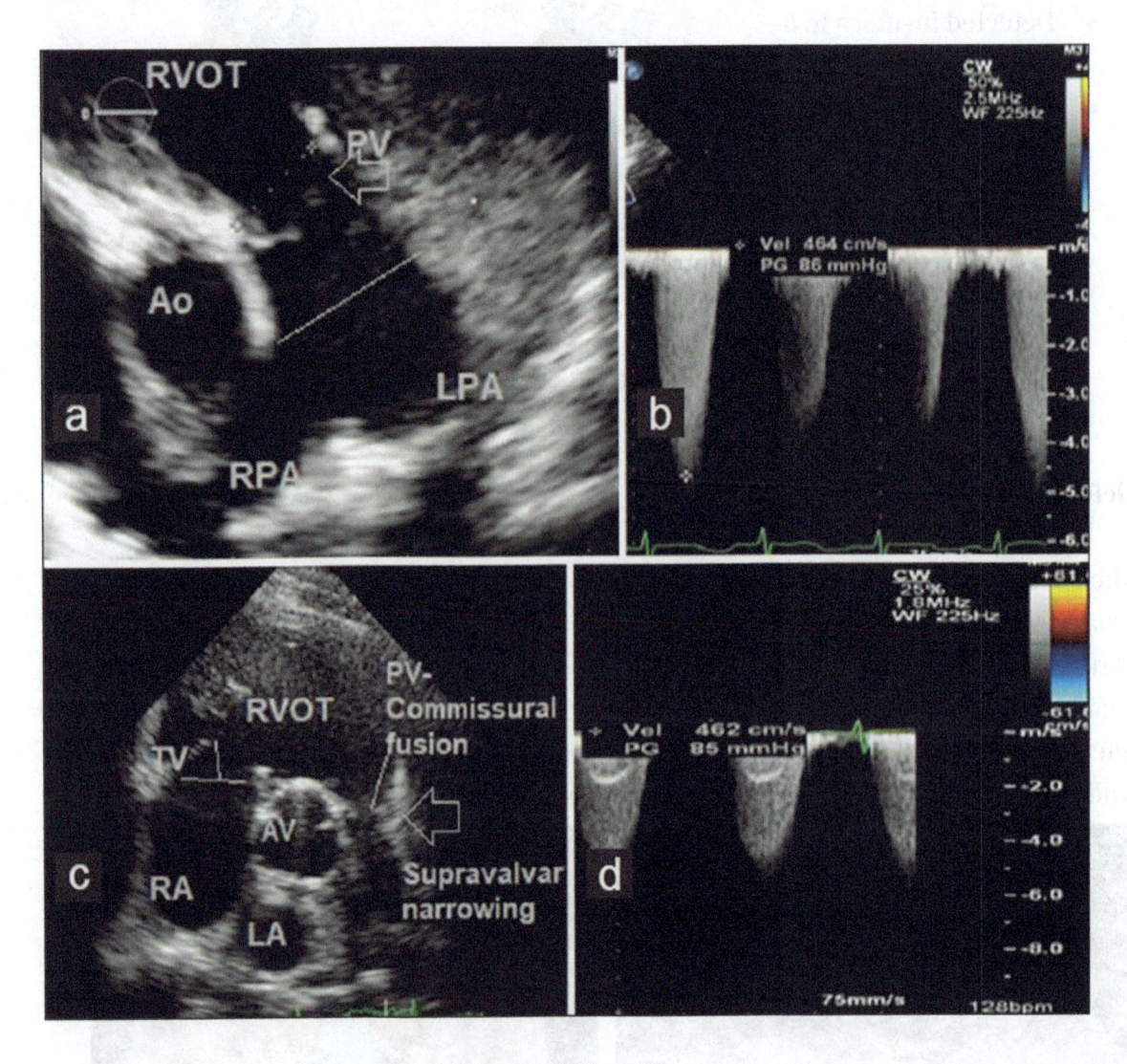

Ebstein Anomaly

In this condition, your tricuspid valve is in the wrong position and the valve's flaps (leaflets) are malformed.
As a result, the valve does not work properly.
Blood might leak back through the valve, making your heart work less efficiently.

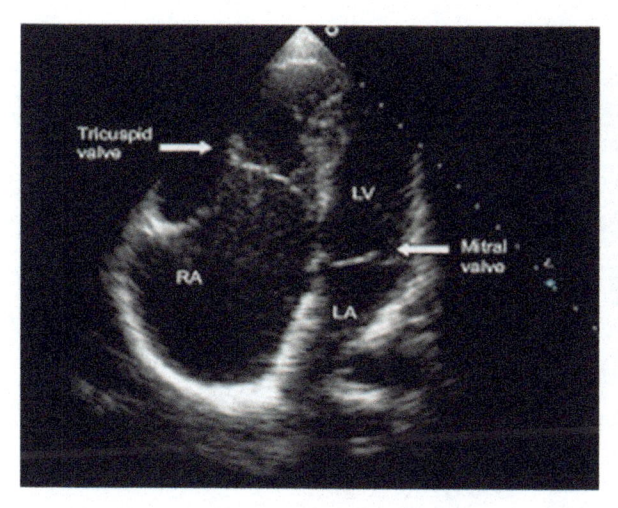

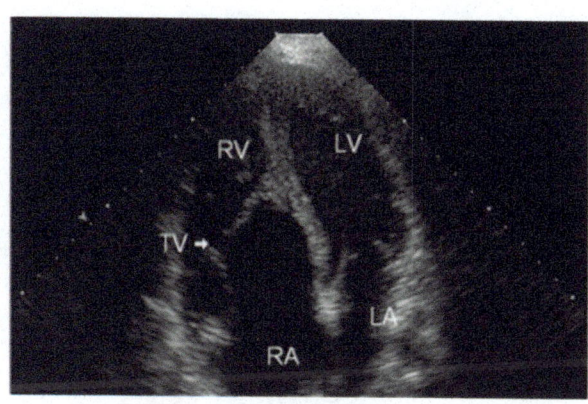

Tetralogy of Fallot

A rare condition caused by a combination of four heart defects that are present at birth.
1. VSD
2. PS
3. Misplaced aorta
4. RVH

Symptoms include blue-tinged skin and shortness of breath. Surgery is typically performed in the first year of life, followed by ongoing care.

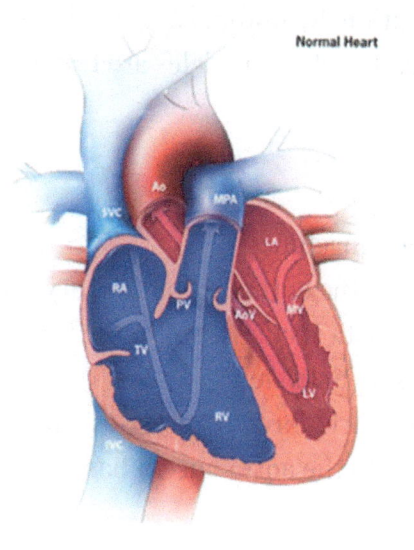

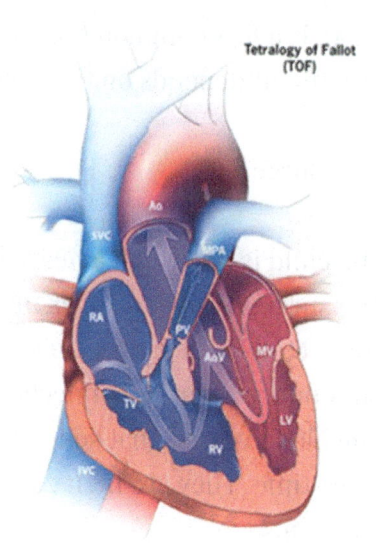

Transposition of the Great Arteries

Dextro-Transposition (pronounced DECKS-tro trans-poh-ZI-shun) of the Great Arteries or d-TGA is a birth defect of the heart in which the two main arteries carrying blood out of the heart – the main pulmonary artery and the aorta – are switched in position, or "transposed."

★ In this case, the natural shunts must remain open

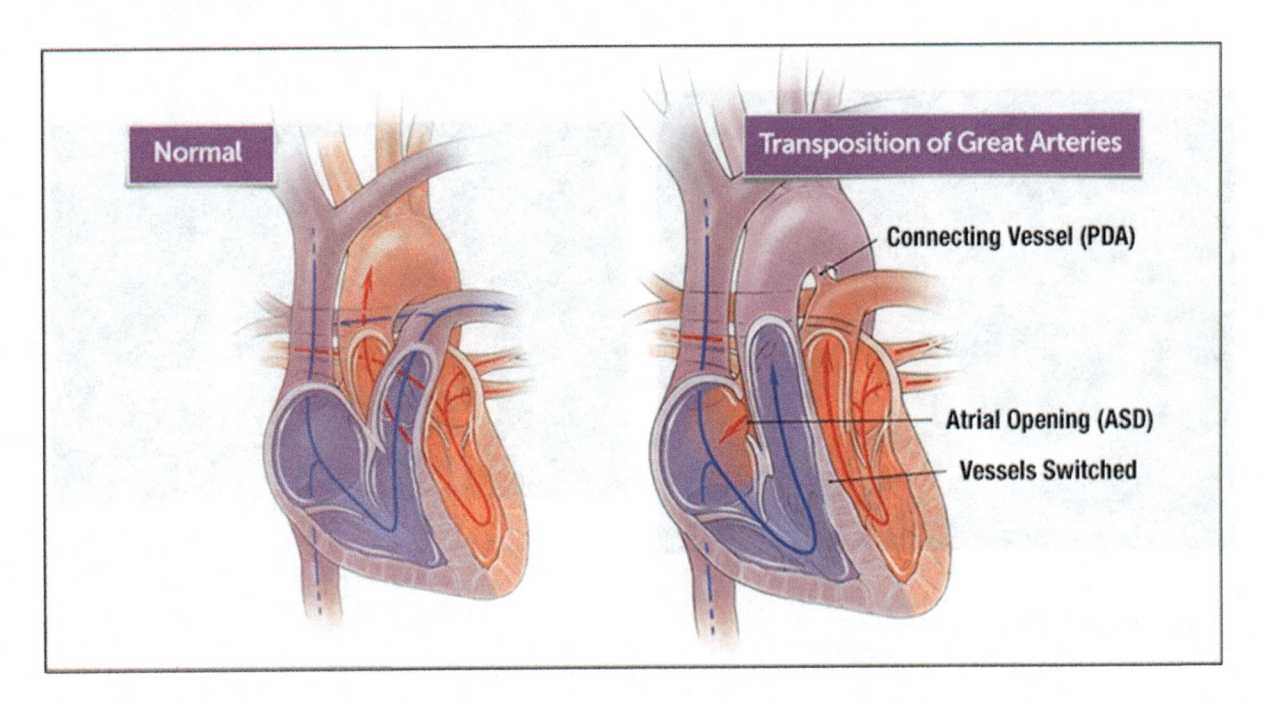

Congenitally corrected transposition, also called levo-transposition of the great arteries (L-TGA), is a less common type of this condition. Symptoms may not be noticed right away. Treatment depends on the specific heart defects. Ventricles are transposed

TGA Surgery

The child is placed on a heart-lung bypass machine.
The surgeon then switches the positions of the aorta and pulmonary artery. They are connected to the correct ventricles. The aorta is connected to the left ventricle. The pulmonary artery is connected to the right ventricle.
The blood vessels that send blood to the heart (coronary arteries) are taken off the aorta for a short time. They are then connected back to the aorta once it has been moved into its correct position.

Hypoplastic Left Heart Syndrome

As the baby develops during pregnancy, the left side of the heart does not form correctly. Most infants die within the first two weeks of life. The medication prostaglandin helps widen the blood vessels and keeps the ductus arteriosus open. Children with hypoplastic left heart syndrome will likely need several surgeries. Surgeons perform these procedures to create separate pathways to get oxygen-rich blood to the body and oxygen-poor blood to the lungs. The procedures are done in three stages.

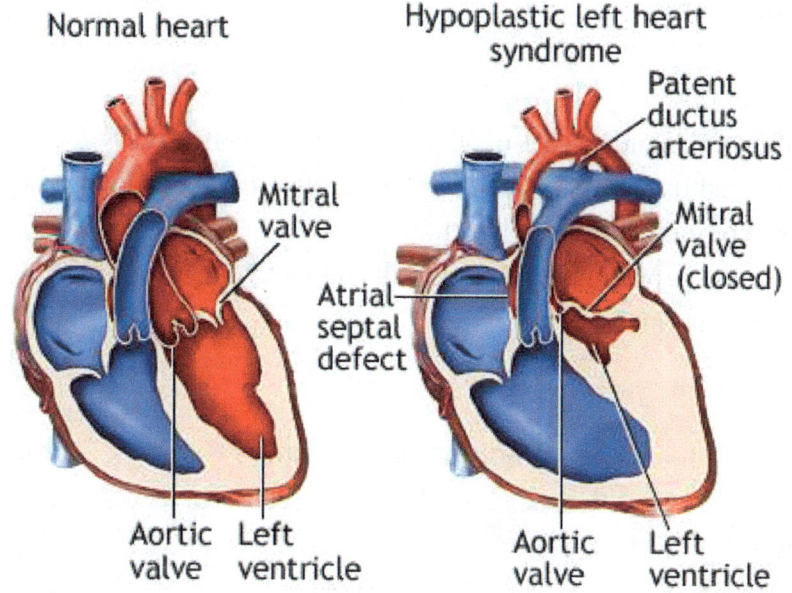

Surgeons perform three separate operations.

Hypoplastic left heart syndrome surgery stages are the 1. Norwood, 2. Glenn and 3. Fontan procedures.

1. Norwood procedure:
    - Babies with HLHS need Norwood surgery within the first two weeks of life. During the procedure, surgeons:
    - Reconstruct your child's underdeveloped aorta to provide blood flow to their body.
    - Place a shunt (tube) to reroute blood either from their right ventricle or aorta to their pulmonary arteries, which go to their lungs.
    - Create a connection between the upper chambers of their heart. This drains oxygen-rich blood from their lungs to supply their body.

2. Bidirectional Glenn shunt operation:
   - At 4 to 6 months of age, babies need a second operation. During the Glenn procedure, surgeons:
   - Remove the old shunt.
   - Place a new shunt to attach your baby's superior vena cava to their pulmonary arteries. The superior vena cava (SVC) is a large vein that carries oxygen-poor blood from their upper body to their heart.
   - Use this shunt to reduce the strain on your child's right ventricle by letting blood flow right into their lungs.

3. Fontan procedure:
   - Between 18 months and 4 years of age, babies need final surgery.
   - This final procedure allows all blood returning from their body to go straight to their lungs instead of mixing in their heart.
   - During a Fontan procedure, surgeons will connect your baby's inferior vena cava (IVC) to their pulmonary arteries.

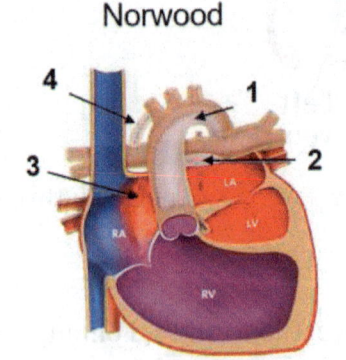

Norwood
Patch to reconstruct the aorta
Patch the Pulmonary artery
Enlarge atrial septal defect
Blalock-Taussig shunt

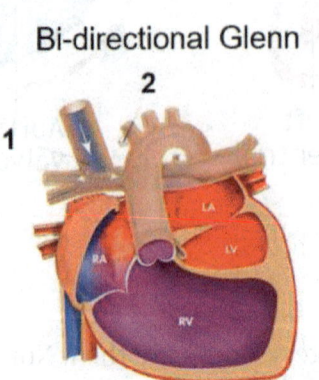

Bi-directional Glenn
Connect the SVC to right pulmonary artery
Sever the Blalock-Taussig shunt to the pulmonary

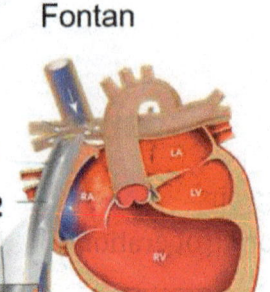

Fontan
Connect IVC to the pulmonary artery via conduit
Create a fenestration through conduit and right atrium

Unit 4

Other Modalities

Chapter 9
The Stress Echocardiogram

The stress echocardiogram is a combination of the stress test and the echo. There are two main reasons why the cardiologist will order this examination. one, because of a low ejection fraction in combination with possible aortic stenosis and two, to check the wall motion abnormalities between Peak and resting states.

Doing your stress echo for wall motion abnormalities is similar to doing a limited echocardiogram. you want to obtain at least four images of the left ventricle at different angles and planes. you want to be able to capture all the wall segments of the left ventricle. The point is to do this while the patient is resting. The patient is then stressed whether it's exercise or pharmaceutical and then the echo is repeated of the exact same images to see if there are any wall motion abnormalities or while motion changes between rest and post stress. protocols for stress Echoes are usually facility dependent, make sure to check with yours before proceeding with the exam.

Stress echos that are ordered for aortic stenosis are done similarly but you're obtaining velocities through the aortic valve in the five an apical long access. Most machines have a preset protocol for stress echoes, make sure to play with the different presets to find out which is best for you and your facility.

For people who can exercise, a treadmill or bike is usually used. These patients are generally checked for wall motion abnormalities and ejection fraction. for those patients who are unable to exercise a pharmaceutical stress test will be ordered instead. The use of Lexi scan or dobutamine are the two most common medicines given to achieve Peak stress.
Keep in mind that a pharmaceutical stress test, while simulating peak stress, does not raise the heart rate. The medicine dilates the blood vessel and tricks the body into thinking it needs more Supply than it actually does.
these medicines have some common adverse reactions:
- Headache
- Nausea
- Dizziness
- feeling of shortness of breath*
- General discomfort

*Before the medicine is injected, I recommend explaining to the patient that they may feel short of breath but assure them that they are getting enough oxygen. When patients feel short of breath they most likely begin to panic and can start hyperventilating.

The stress echo General protocol:
- prep the patient for an Echo
- obtain the fortify views of the left ventricle
    - these are your resting pictures
- if the patient is exercising prep the patient for a stress test if they are pharmaceutical this step can be skipped
- stress the patient
- obtain post stressed images

The hardest part of this exam is obtaining the post stress images in the time frame needed. You have approximately 60 seconds to get the same images you got at rest, as you want to see the heart function at Peak stress.

Like any other stress testing, vitals should be obtained in the same way. at rest, during stress and the stages, and during recovery.

Pay close attention to the optimization of your images during rest. If the endocardium is not fully defined an Imogen agent may be indicated. remember, you have 60 seconds to get your post stress images so if an Imaging agent will help get the image, then it is suggested to us
e it for both sets of pictures.

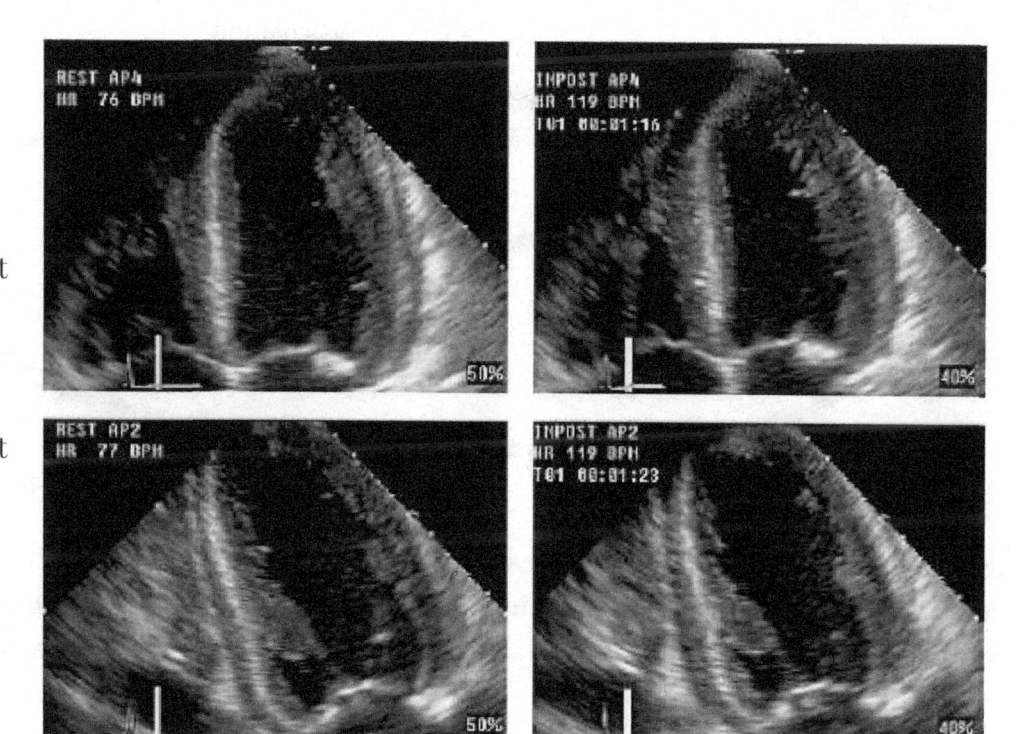

Chapter 10
The Transesophageal Echocardiogram - TEE

The transesophageal echo uses a specialized probe containing an ultrasound transducer at its tip and is passed to the patient's esophagus. With all modern TEE transducers, the transducer beam can be rotated within the probe to generate different beam angles. This is achieved using two buttons on the control module, one button rotates from 0 to 180° while the other button rotates it back from 180 back to 0 °. Using the buttons and combination any desired angle between 0 and 180° can be achieved.

 at zero degrees the transducer beam is in the transverse position, oriented left screen- right patient
 at 90° the transducer becomes longitudinal
 at 180°, the transducer beam is transverse, oriented left screen- left patient

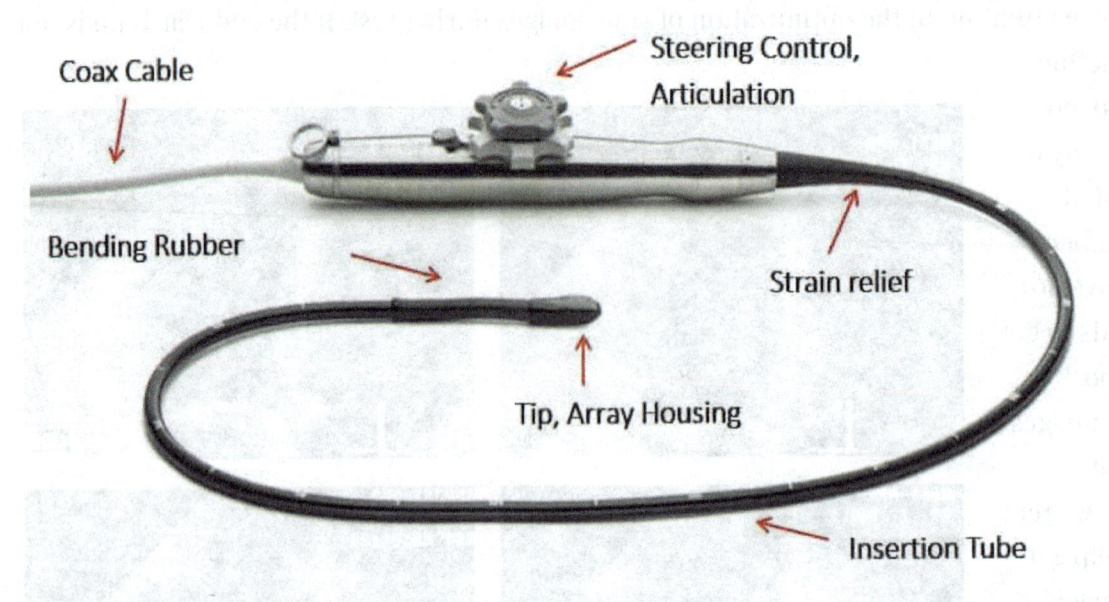

TEE Is considered more sensitive for the detection of major cardiac sources of embolize such as left atrial thrombus, valve abnormalities, atrial septal abnormalities and cardiac tumors. The transthoracic is more suited for the visualization of a left ventricular thrombus.

Complications:
- Bleeding
- Dental injury
- esophageal preparation
- Hoarseness
- mortality

The team usually consists of an Ecotec, a cardiac nurse and a cardiologist. In some situations, an anesthesiologist is present. As an echo Tech our job is to control the machine as a cardiologist is the one that controls the probe while the nurse monitors the patient and injects the medications.

A patient is prepped by:
- starting an intravenous line
- giving a local anesthetic spray that will be applied to the back of the throat. this will numb the back of the throat to make the passing of the probe more comfortable
- a bite protector will be placed in the patient's mouth
- a conscious sedation of Fentanyl and versed is given to put the patient in a twilight sedation

The three windows for a TEE are transgastric, mid esophageal and high esophageal. Cardiologists adjust and rotate the probe in order to get correct views at the different levels. The most difficult part from transitioning between a transthoracic echo and a transesophageal echo is recognizing the structures that are shown on the screen. Once you've mastered the transthoracic images this should be easier than mastering them without knowing the inner cardiac structures and what they look like on an ultrasound. Let's go through some different windows and planes and then we'll attach the structures and Anatomy to the images.

Transgastric
- Best TEE views for evaluating left and right ventricular function
- TG long

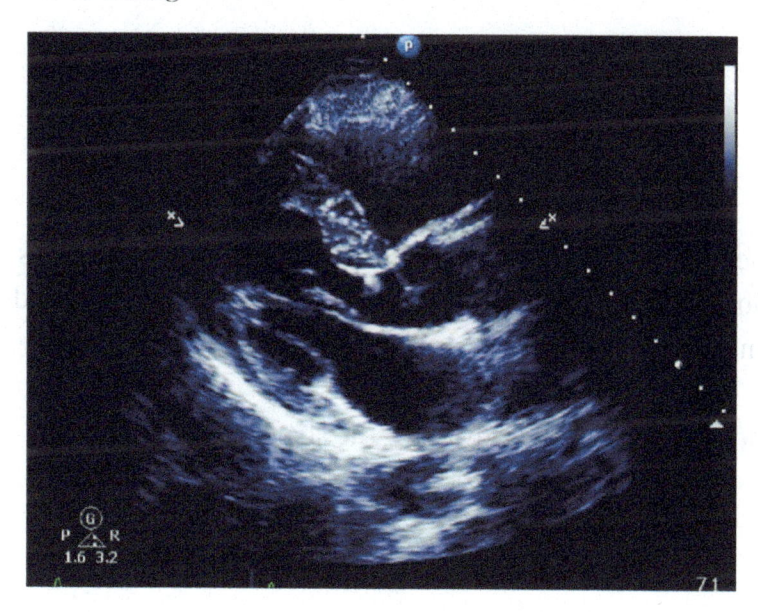

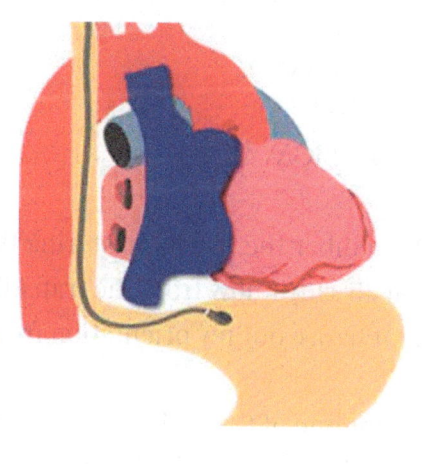

- TG short
    - These views are similar to an inverted parasternal short axis view with the interior wall on the bottom of the screen and the inferior walls at the top.
    - By advancing and withdrawing the probe, short axis slices can be obtained at mitral valve level, papillary muscle level and the left ventricular Apex.
    - In addition, short access views of the right ventricle, tricuspid valve in RVOT can be obtained via clockwise rotation of the probe. These images resemble the parasternal short but slightly off access.
- Deep TG
    - These views are the best for assessing aortic stenosis and regurgitation, because in general, the probe can be oriented parallel to the direction of the LVOT and aortic valve.
    - These views are obtained by advancing the probe deep into the stomach roughly about 50 to 60 cm in most patients and generally anti-flexing the tip.
    - These can be quite challenging to obtain in some patients.
    - This view is similar to the apical five chamber view obtained in a transthoracic echo.

TEE midesophageal views
6 basic and most common views
- 4C
- 5C
- 2C
- LAX
- SAX
- BICAVAL

Remember the trip to mastering these views is to correlate them to the Views and structures you already know from the transthoracic echo. For instance, I always use the aortic valve and then figure out my orientation from there.

All but one of these views you already know, and I already know the structures in them. The bicaval View shows both Atria and both vena cava.

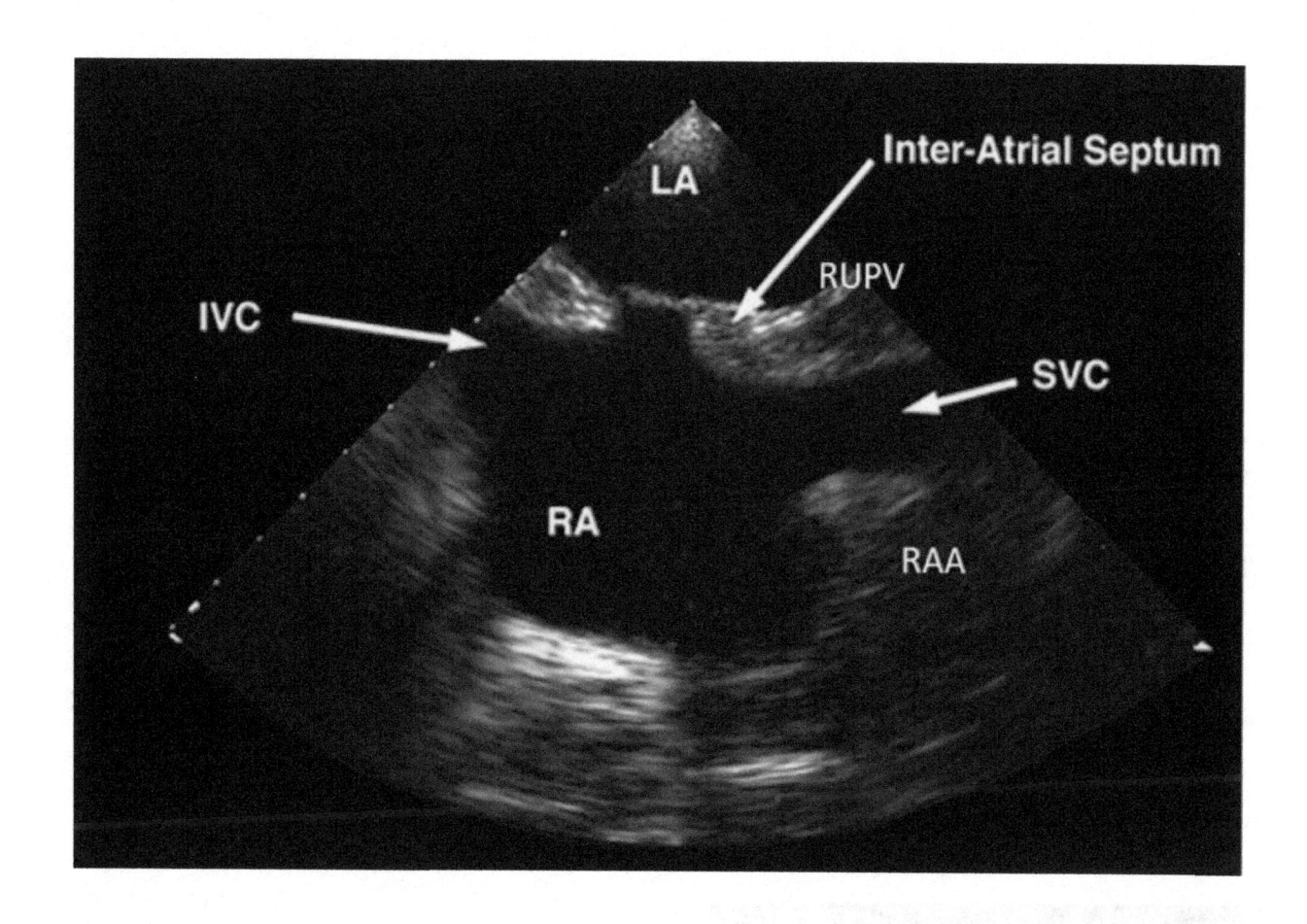

TEE - Core views - INDEX _____ lists all the TEE views

- ME 4C
- ME 2C
- ME LAX
- ME 5C
- ME asc Ao LAX
- ME asc Ao SAX
- ME AV SAX
- ME RV IF-OF
- ME BICAVAL
- TG SAX
- TG LAX
- Des Ao SAX
- Des Ao LAX

Left atrial appendage

The left atrial appendage is a small pouch extending off the side of your left atrium. It acts as a decompression chamber when atrial pressure is high. well, everyone has a left atrial appendage, the size and Anatomy vary, as do the issues it can cause. Certain arrhythmias like atrial fibrillation, can cause blood to coagulate in form little blood clots that sit in the appendage. These clots can embolize and cause a stroke, myocardial infarction or other vascular issues.

The left atrial appendage is a common source of cardiac thrombus formation associated with systemic embolism. The transesophageal echo allows a detailed evaluation of the structure and function of the appendage by two-dimensional Imaging and the capability to interrogate via Doppler.

The LAA:
- Can be seen on a transthoracic but is very uncommon
- Transesophageal is the gold standard for interrogation
- check before cardioversions
- checked in combination with certain arrhythmias

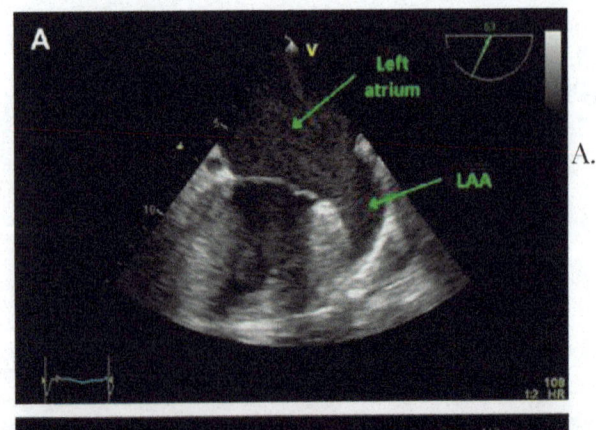

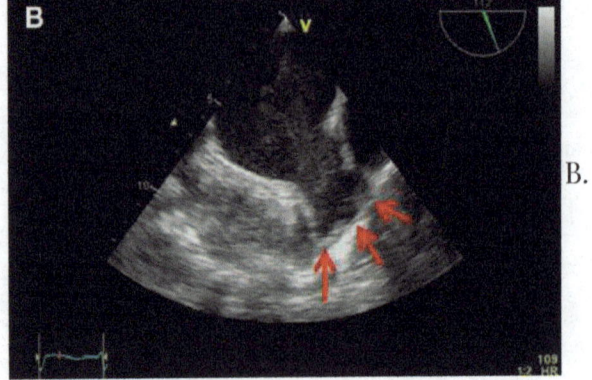

A. Normal LAA

B. LAA with a thrombus

The Watchman

The Watchmen device, a catheter delivered heart implant, is placed at the opening of the left atrial appendage. Because the appendage is a source for stroke causing blood clots The Watchmen device is placed in an ax as a screen to prevent any class from embolizing throughout the system.

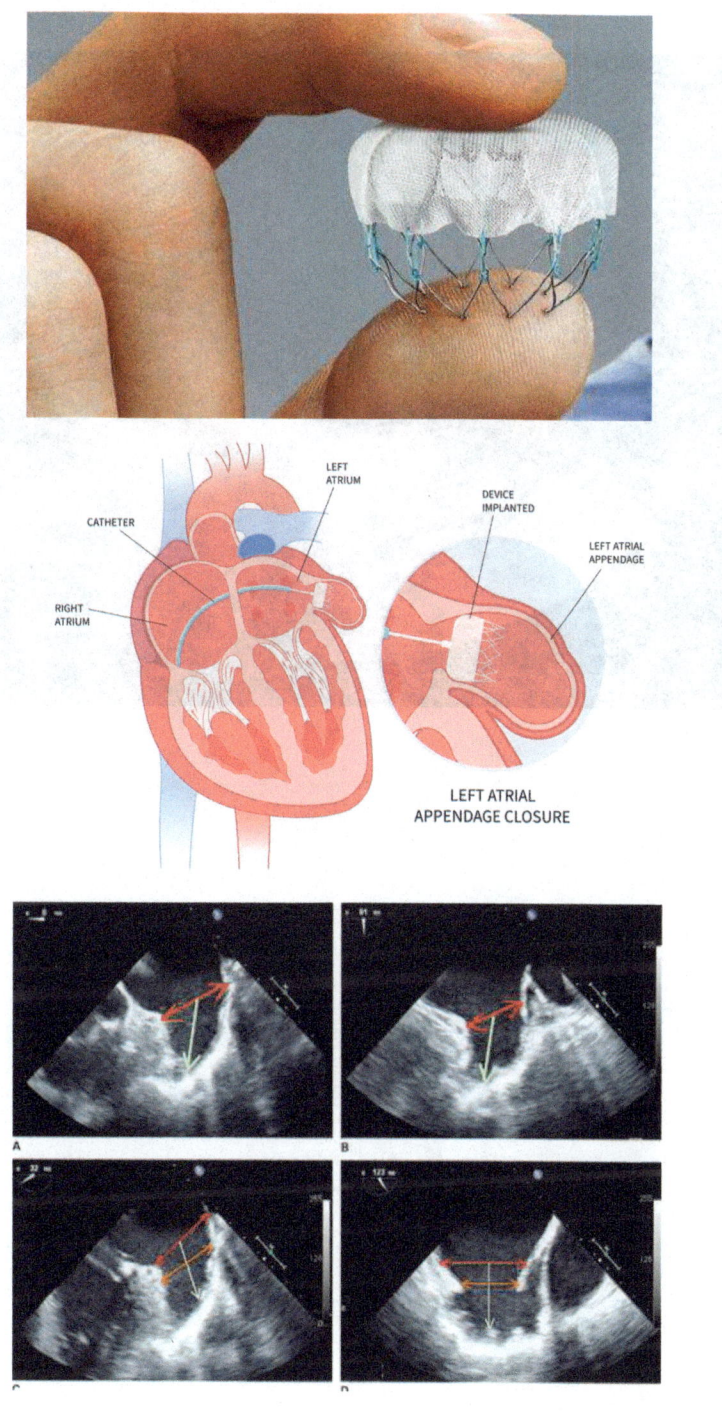

133

TEE & the IAS

The bicaval view is the best TEE view for checking septal defects via bubble study.

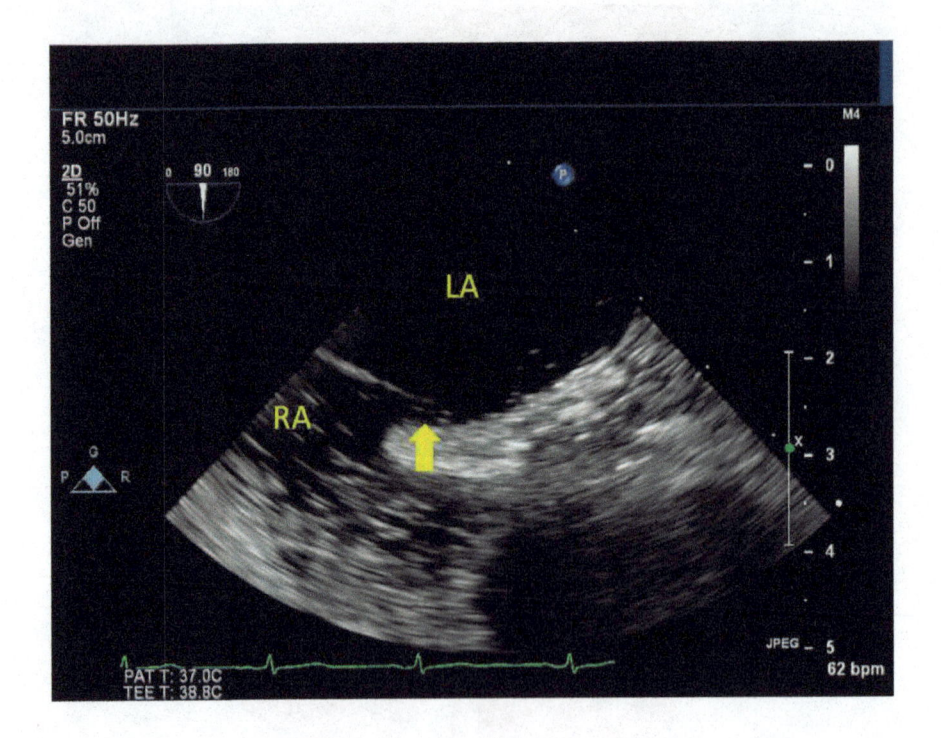

Unit 5

Physics

Chapter 11
Ultrasound Physics

Understanding the physics of ultrasound is critical to applying clinical ultrasound, particularly as it applies to the optimization, interpretation, and clinical integration of images captured at the bedside.

Direct: related so that one becomes larger so well the other
Indirect: related soul that as one becomes larger the other becomes smaller
Proportional: related so that as one increases or decreases the other does so at the same rate

Instrumentation
Instrumentation applies to the equipment used to perform an ultrasound. There's an ultrasound machine in the ultrasound probe. There are many different types of probes that each have their own unique qualities. Some types of probes are linear, phased array, curved linear and Pedoff probes that go inside of the body. In echo we use a phased array probe. Which should be used depends on the depth of the structure being imaged. The higher the frequency of the transducer crystal, the less penetration it has but the better the resolution. So, if more penetration is required you need to use a lower frequency transducer with the sacrifice of some resolution here yet the higher frequency, the less penetration it has but the better the resolution. Ultrasound frequency affects the resolution of the imaged object.

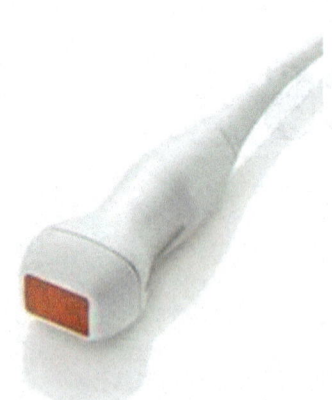

Phased Array Probe: 2 – 12 MHz
5MHz is the most common.

- Sector shaped image with a smaller footprint
- ideal for use between ribs
- Low frequency

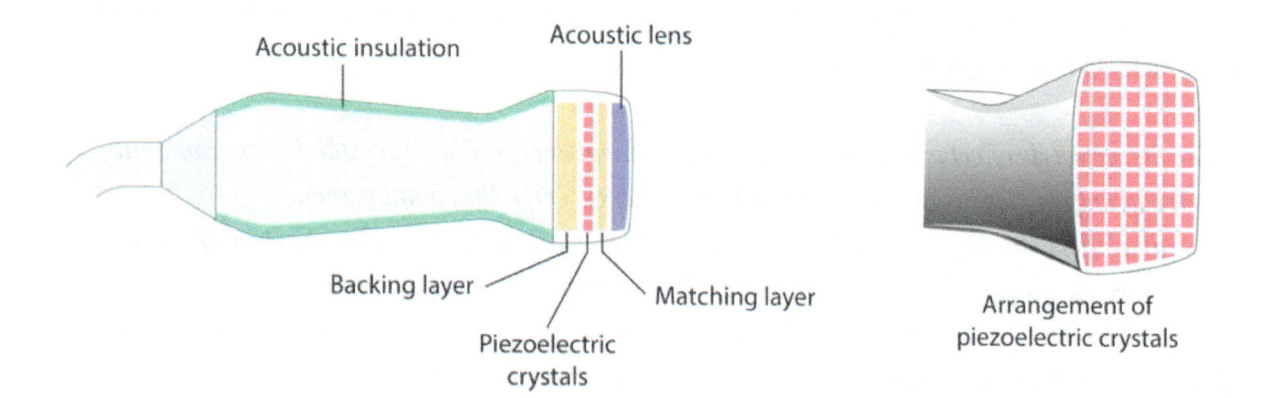

Sound waves

Sound waves audible to the human ear lie within the range of 20 to 20,000Hz. Clinical ultrasound systems use transducers between 2 and 17MHz. Sound waves do not exist in a vacuum and propagation in gases is poor because the molecules are too widely spaced which is why lungs do not image well with ultrasound. A gel is used between the skin of the subject and the transducer face otherwise the sound would not be transmitted across the air-filled gap. The strength of the returning echo is directly related to an angle at which the beam strikes the acoustic interface. The more nearly perpendicular the beam is, the stronger the returning echo.

*** Do not confuse with parallel flow and hemodynamics***

Propagation speed in soft tissue is 1540 m/s.

Speed is if the stiffness is increased, or the density is decreased.
Other propagation speeds:
- Air 331m/s
- Muscle 1585 m/s
- Fat 1450 m/s

The ultrasound transducer generates ultrasound beams. The technician holds the transducer and maneuvers its position and angle to send the ultrasound beam through the body to give an image of the desired structure. The way ultrasound works is by sending rapid transmissions of the ultrasound beam or sound waves, and these beams are reflected back and redirected to the monitor to produce the image that is seen. This is made possible by using specialized crystals called piezoelectric crystals. Thousands of these crystals are attached to the front of the traducer or transducer head. These specialized crystals are unique in the electromechanical properties they possess. When an electric current is applied to these crystals, in altra sound this is done by the power supply, they start to vibrate and generate sound waves with frequencies that are between 1.5 and 8 MHz aka ultrasound. When an ultrasound beam is reflected back to the crystals the signal is then interpreted into the image viewed. This is all possible by the principle of the piezoelectric effect.

"The piezoelectric effect converts kinetic or mechanical energy, due to crystal deformation, into electrical energy. This is how ultrasound transducers receive the sound waves.
The same effect can be used in reverse – inverse piezoelectric effect – whereby the application of an electric field to a crystal causes realignment of the internal dipole structure. This realignment results in crystal lengthening or contraction, converting electrical energy into kinetic or mechanical energy. This is how ultrasound transducers produce sound waves."

Probes use temporal **resolution** to scan multiple successive frames and observe the movement of an object throughout time. Better wise rapidly moving objects like valve leaflets and the fast-beating cardiac structure.
Temporal resolution is enhanced by minimizing depth, line intensity and by reducing the sector angle, thus increasing the frame rate.

Resolutions

Spatial resolution is the ability of the ultrasound system to detect and display structures that are close together
Axial resolution is the ability to see the two structures that are side by side as separate and distinct when parallel to the beam. So, a higher frequency and short pulse length will provide a better axial image
Axial resolution is generally around four times better than lateral resolution
Lateral resolution is the image generated when the two structures lying side by side are perpendicular to the beam. This is directly related to the width of the ultrasound beam. The narrower the beam better is the resolution.
And being increasing frequency and reducing the beam width by focusing. By increasing the frequency, beam width will be decreased, and lateral resolution will be improved.

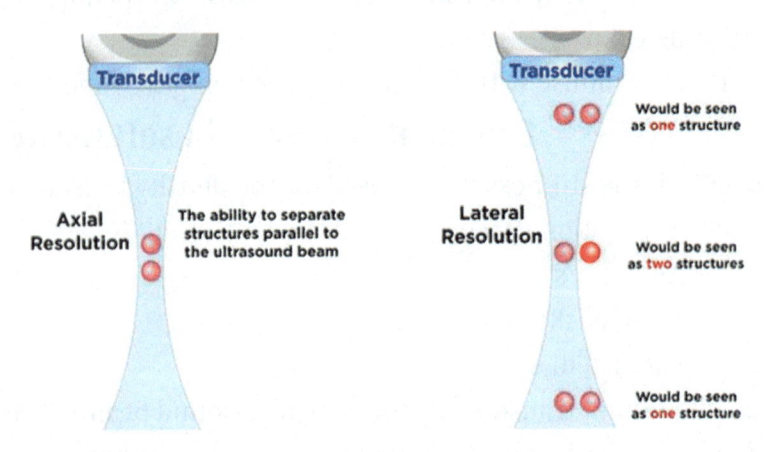

Zones/Fields

Near: zone closest to the probe before the focal zone.
Far: zone furthest from the probe after focal zone.
Focal: the nearest part of the ultrasound beam profile when it's emitted from the transducer. In this region the pulse waves are concentrated resulting in increased beam intensity.

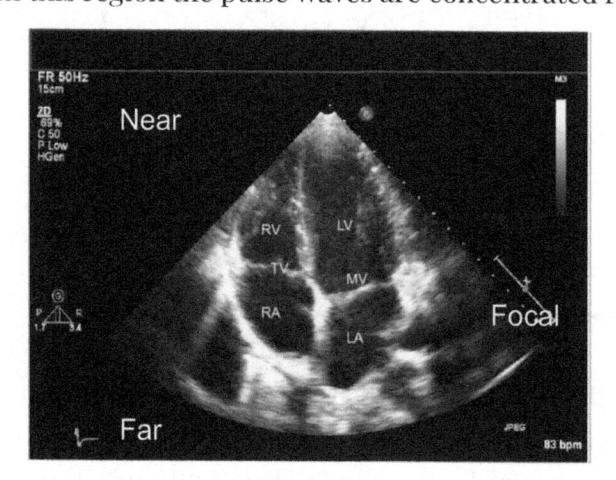

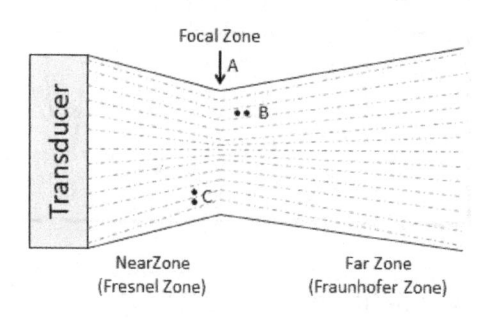

Wavelength: length or distance of a single cycle of a wave.
Amplitude: distance between the resting position and the maximum displacement of the wave
Frequency: number of waves passing by a specific point per second
Period(cycle): it takes for one wave cycle to complete

The equation for Frequency = Speed of sound wave/Wavelength

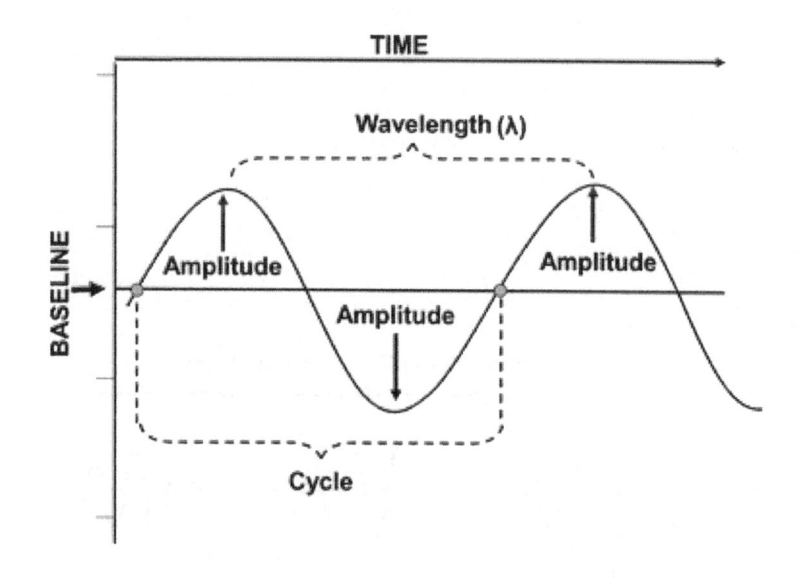

Short Wavelength = High Frequency

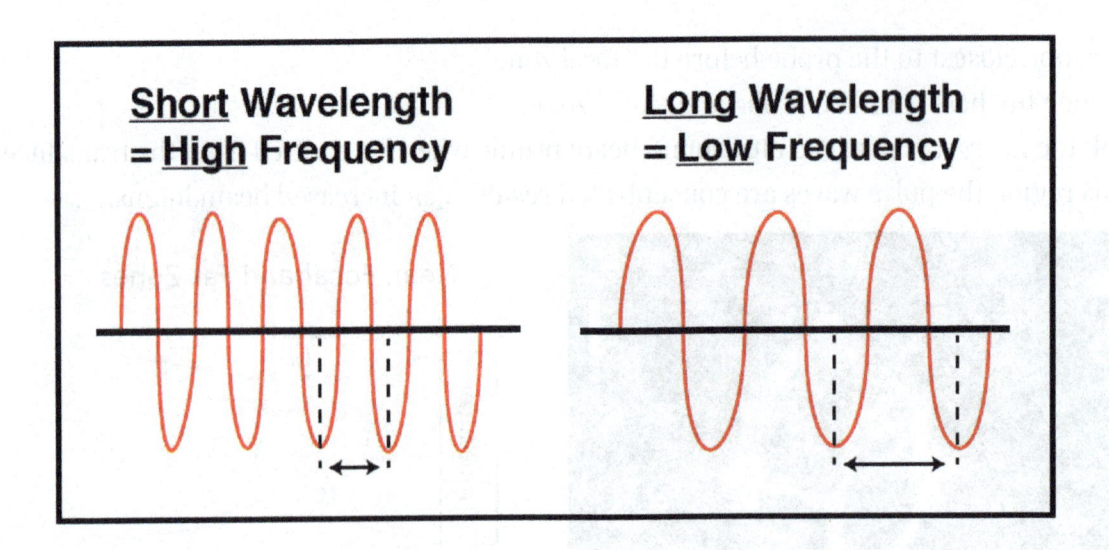

Long Wavelength = Low Frequency

The pulse repetition period or PRP can be defined as the time interval from the beginning of one pulse to the beginning of another pulse. (time)

Pulse repetition frequency (PRF) indicates the number of ultrasound pulses emitted by the transducer over a designated period of time. (Hz)

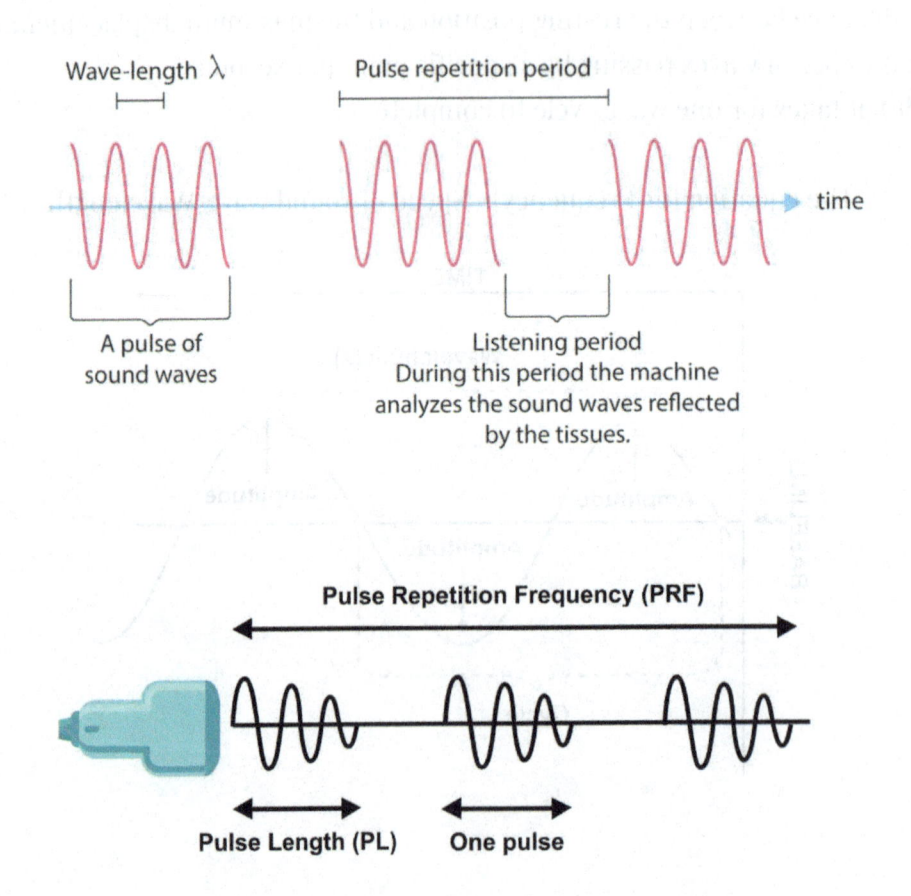

Wave-length λ

Pulse repetition period

A pulse of sound waves

Listening period
During this period the machine analyzes the sound waves reflected by the tissues.

Pulse Repetition Frequency (PRF)

Pulse Length (PL)   One pulse

140

Acoustic velocity is the speed at which a sound wave travels through a medium. It is equal to the frequency times the wavelength.

Speed (c) is determined by the density (ρ) and stiffness (κ) of the medium
$(c = (κ/ρ)1/2)$.

Density is the concentration of a medium.

Stiffness is the resistance of a material to compression.

So, the ultrasound propagation speed from slowest to fastest is:
$$\text{Lung (air)} \ll \text{Fat} < \text{Soft tissue} \ll \text{Bone}.$$
This happens because stiffer mediums have tighter particles to propagate the ultrasound wave and therefore the velocity is greater.

Harmonics - is a wave or signal whose frequency is an integral (whole number) multiple of the frequency of the same reference signal or wave. As part of the harmonic series, the term can also refer to the ratio of the frequency of such a signal or wave to the frequency of the reference signal or wave.

Harmonic imaging is a technique that employs the resonance characteristics of tissue. As images produced with harmonic imaging have a higher resolution and are associated with fewer artifacts. The stronger harmonic signal undergoes considerably less distortion. However, it will reduce axial resolution.

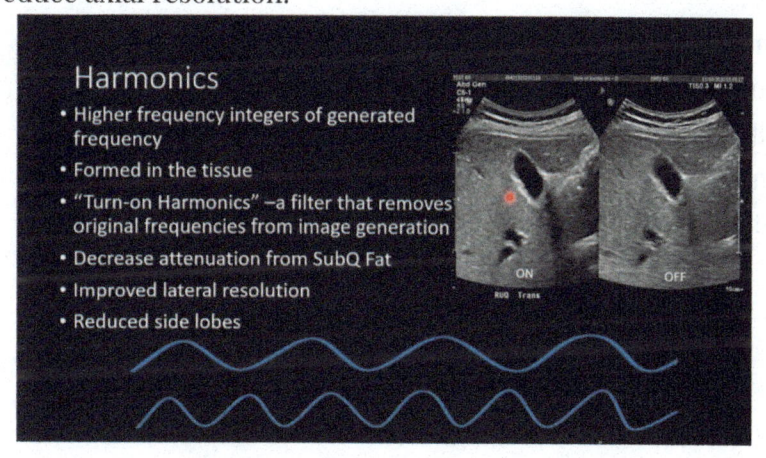

Harmonics
- Higher frequency integers of generated frequency
- Formed in the tissue
- "Turn-on Harmonics" – a filter that removes original frequencies from image generation
- Decrease attenuation from SubQ Fat
- Improved lateral resolution
- Reduced side lobes

Dynamic Range (also known as Compression) allows you to tell the ultrasound machine how you want the echo intensity displayed as shades of gray. A broad/wide range will display more shades of gray and an overall smoother image.

The dynamic range of an ultrasound transducer needs to be wide (typically 60dB) in order to detect both very strong, specular reflections from tissue interfaces, and very weak, scattered reflections from the texture within tissue.

Essentially, dynamic range is how far the brightest spots in your image can vary from the darkest spots in your image and still maintain proper details in a single exposure.

The higher the dynamic range, the more potential shades can be represented, although the dynamic range does not automatically correlate to the number of tones reproduced.

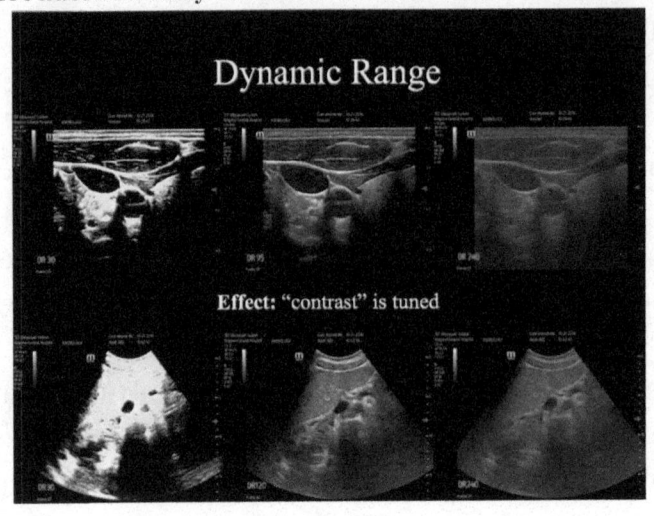

The frame rate of ultrasound is the number of frames produced in quick succession to create the image on the monitor. High frame rates enable us to see rapidly moving structures (such as heart valves) without motion artifacts, and also perform velocity and deformation analysis (i.e. tissue Doppler).

Frame rate determined by:
- Speed of sound in medium
- Sector width
- Depth of image
- Has to wait for each sound wave to return to make another frame

Chapter 12
The Doppler

The principles of Doppler - The Doppler Shift
- Doppler Echocardiography is a method by which one is able to identify the direction and velocity of blood flow
- Doppler shows that the observed frequency of a wave depends on the relative speed of the source and the observer

"The Doppler effect or Doppler shift is the apparent change in frequency of a wave in relation to an observer moving relative to the wave source."

Just think of the sound of an ambulance or a motorcycle as it speeds towards you and then away from you. You will notice that the sound of the vehicle has a higher frequency (pitch) as it comes towards you and a lower frequency as it moves away.

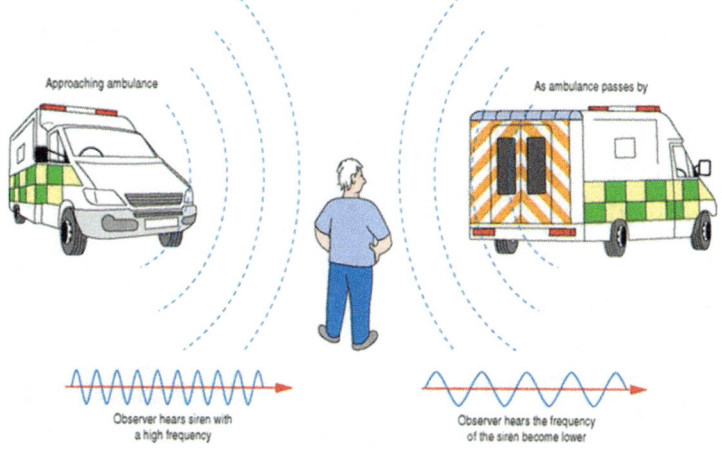

As the Doppler formula shows, the calculated velocity also depends on the angle of insonation (cos α). The angle of insonation greatly influences measurements. The more perpendicular the ultrasound beam is aligned to the direction of blood flow, the greater is the measurement error.

This is a crucial point to be considered when using Doppler. Care must be taken to align the ultrasound beam as parallel to blood flow as possible.

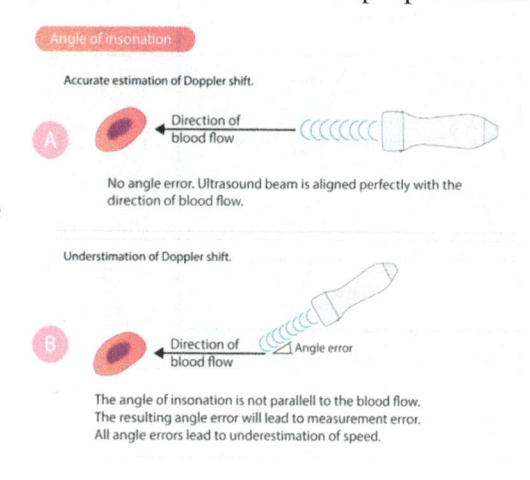

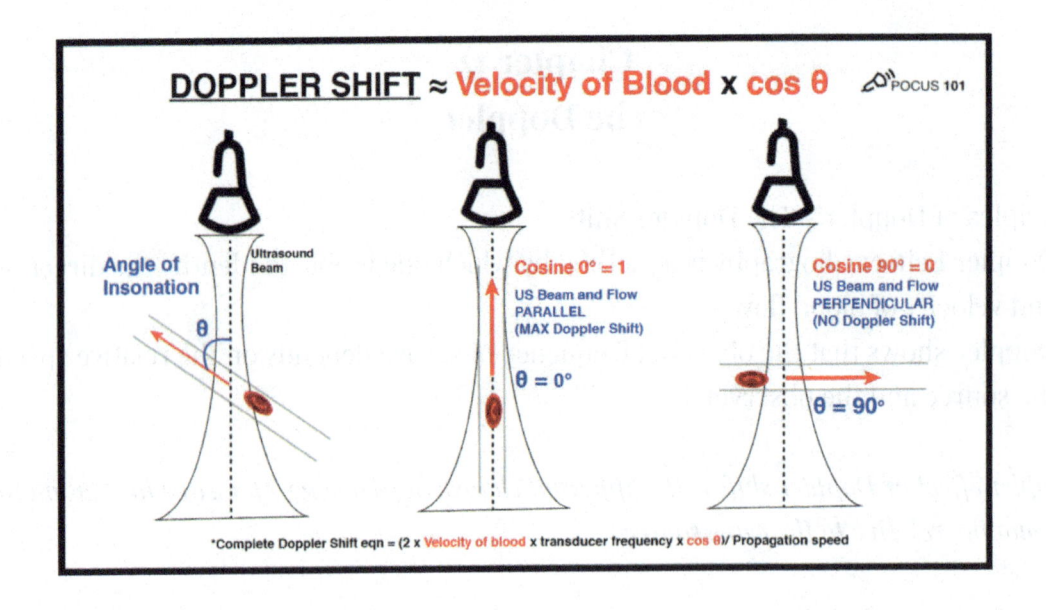

Doppler information can be obtained either with "spectral Doppler" or with color Doppler. Both provide information about blood flow velocity and its direction. However, they employ different display formats, yield different functional information, and can be applied in different situations.

So, the Doppler shift is mainly related to TWO things:
1. The Velocity of the blood cells
2. The Angle of Insonation

Spectral Doppler & The Doppler shift

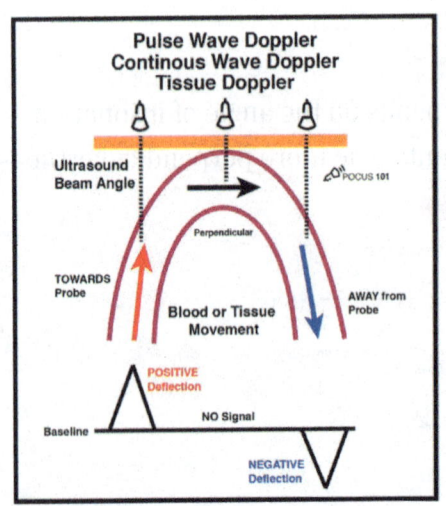

Velocity curves provide information about absolute velocities and the direction of blood flow as well as how velocity changes in a certain region (pulsed-wave Doppler) or along a certain Doppler line (continuous-wave Doppler). The Doppler tracing has an "y axis" which represents velocity (m/sec) and an "x axis" which shows time. Velocities towards the transducer are depicted above, and velocities away from the transducer below, the "zero line". Use color Doppler to guide the positioning of your sample volume (PW Doppler) and Doppler line (CW Doppler). It will help you to observe the location of the flow as well as the direction of the jet. To obtain the best results, align the Doppler wave parallel to flow.

Bernoulli's principle

Bernoulli asserted in "Hydrodynamica" that as a fluid moves faster, it produces less pressure, and conversely, slower moving fluids produce greater pressure.

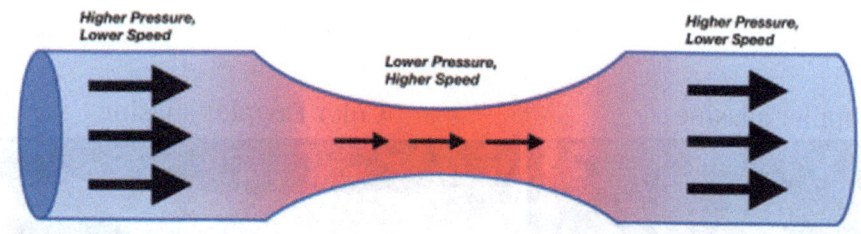

Bernoulli's equation:
P = pressure
Δ = change in 2
V = velocity

$$P_1 - P_2 = 4(V_2) \text{ or } \Delta P = 4(V_2)$$

Color Doppler & The Doppler shift

The most common Doppler mode you will use is color Doppler. This mode allows you to see the movement of blood movement in arteries and veins with blue and red patterns on the ultrasound screen.

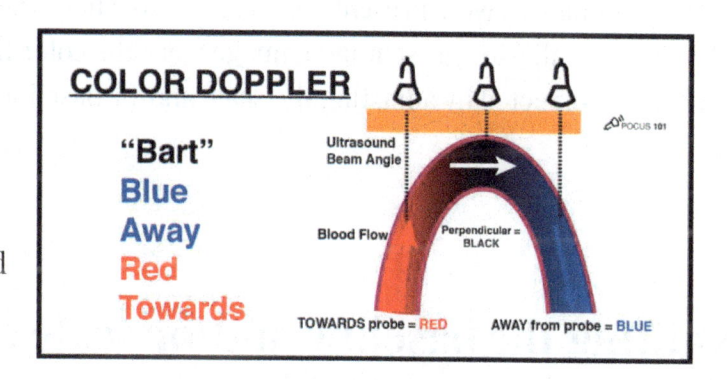

Nyquist limit

Represents the maximum Doppler shift frequency that can be correctly measured without resulting in aliasing in color or pulsed wave ultrasound

If the blood flow velocity exceeds this limit the device will incorrectly register the direction and velocity of the flow, resulting in color or spectral Doppler aliasing artifact

Aliasing phenomena

Happens when the velocity is higher than the **Nyquist** limit.
The Nyquist limit always equals Pulse Repetition Frequency (PRF)/2.
To a certain degree the PRF can be increased to permit higher velocities to be displayed.
However, the maximal PRF depends on imaging depth.

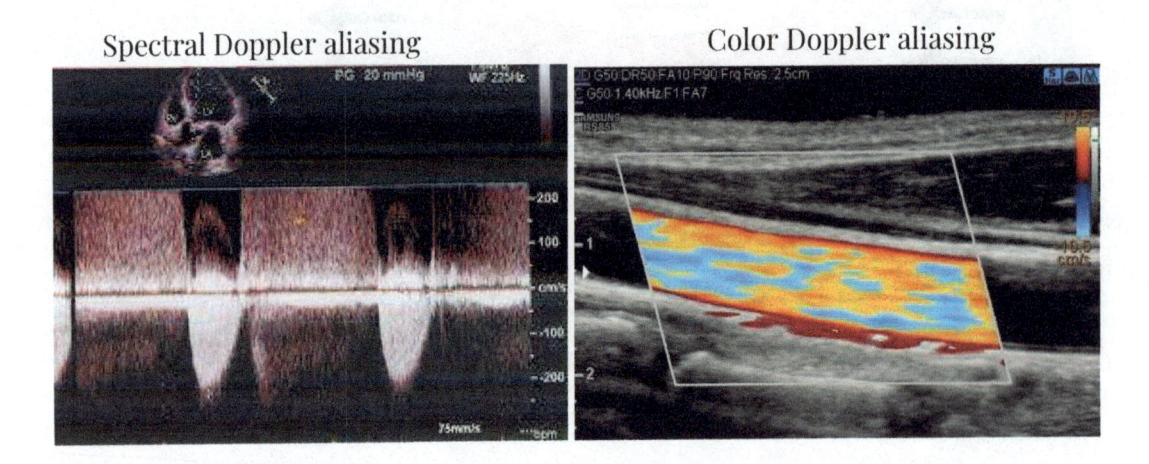

Spectral Doppler aliasing   Color Doppler aliasing

Spectral Doppler aliasing presents in an image to where the waveform isn't completely in view.
Color Doppler aliasing present in an image were the color has a mosaic like pattern.
This can be corrected by adjusting the scale and/or baseline.

Shifting the baseline and/or scale does NOT change the Nyquist limit, only the appearance

Chapter 13
Artifacts & Attenuation

Attenuation of the force or amplitude of a signal. Attenuation and artifacts can occur for a multitude of reasons in creating an impaired image. The major source of attenuation in soft tissue is absorption, the conversion of acoustic energy into heat. Other causes of attenuation are reflection, refraction and scatter. These occur as sound waves encounter a boundary between two different media

Attenuation may also be caused by:
- **Reflection**
- **Refraction**
- **Shadowing**

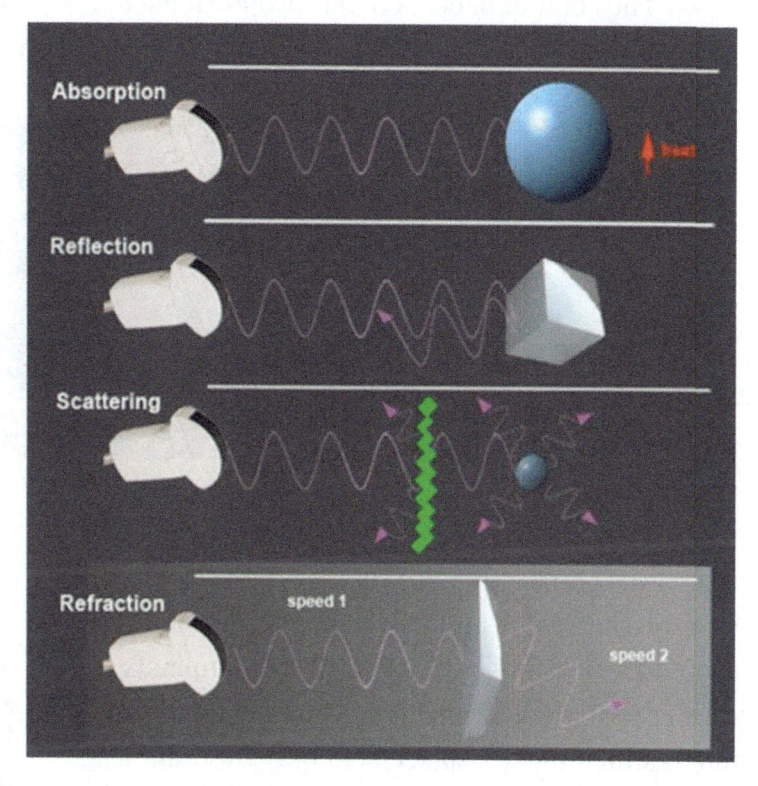

Reflection - mirror image
- Some of the waves bounce back towards the source as an echo
- The angle of approach (incidence) is identical to the angle of the reflection
- The remaining sound wave travels through the second medium (or tissue)
- ❖ Change scanning plane and altering the incident angle of the ultrasound's beam

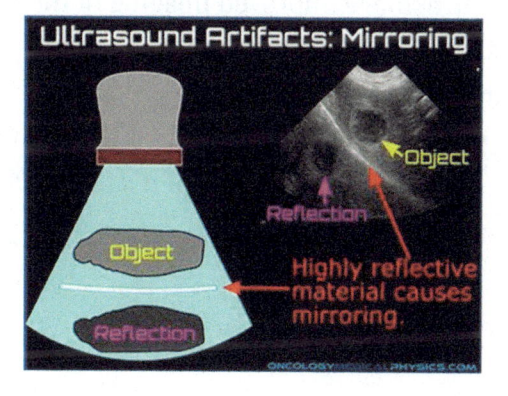

Refraction
- If the two mediums have different "stiffness" the resulting change in propagation speeds will cause the wave to be "bent" from its original path (refraction)
- The angle of incidence will be different from the angle of transmission
- The amount of deflection is proportional to the difference in the two tissues 'stiffness'
- ❖ To eliminate it, you can alter the transducer's angle and position.

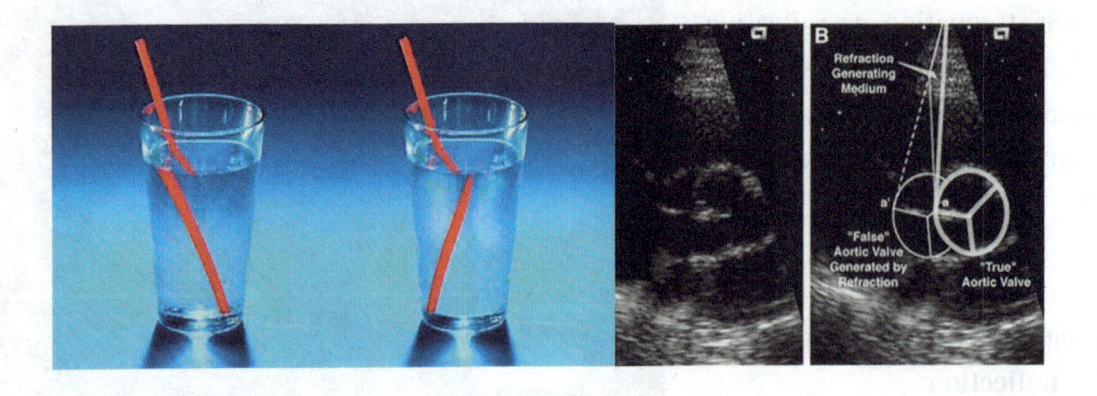

Acoustic Shadowing

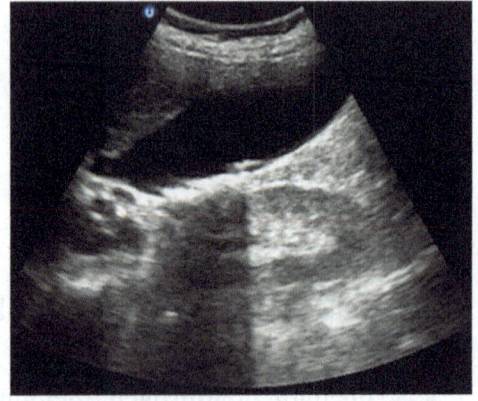

Acoustic shadowing occurs when calcium-containing structures, prosthetic valves, or silicone implants interfere with the imaging process. To prevent the underestimation or displacement of regurgitant jets, you can increase the aliasing velocity to examine them. In addition, you can use a deep transgastric long-axis view to achieve improved imaging of the LVOT and aortic valve and reposition the short-axis view to examine any aortic leaflets.
- ❖ you can alter the angle of the beam to eliminate traces of the artifact if it's interfering with the diagnostic process

Other artifacts

Comet Tail Artifact 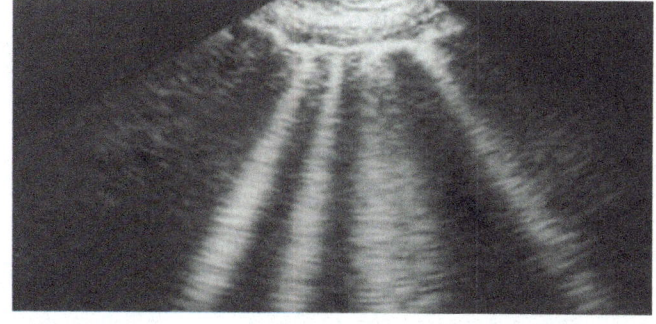
- Comet tail artifacts are produced when the ultrasound's sound wave is reflected by more than one reflector and makes several round trips before returning to the transducer.
- When necessary, they can be prevented by decreasing the TGC near in the near gain, or by changing the beam's angle and switching windows.

Foreshortening 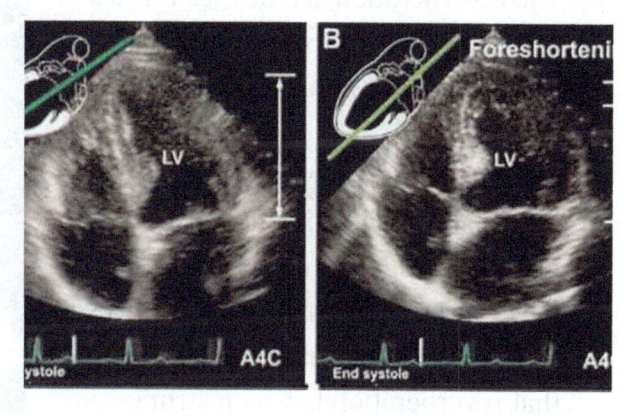
- Foreshortening refers to a situation where the ultrasound plane does not cut through the true apex.
- You can recognize this phenomenon when the apical region looks "rounded".
- However, if echocardiography is performed correctly, the apical region should have a bullet-shape.
- ❖ Foreshortening can be corrected by moving the probe more towards apex (= 1 intercostal space lower) and laterally.

Beam width 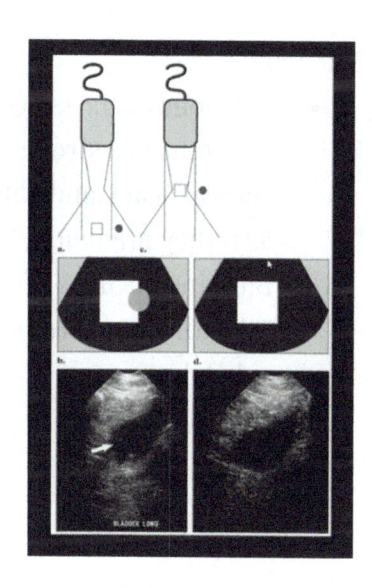
- Beam-width artifact refers to the lateral blurring of a point target that occurs as echoes from the same target are insonated at adjacent beam positions.
- Lateral blurring of image that may result in the overlapping of 2 images, thus appearing as one
- If there is a highly reflective object in the widened base of the beam, the ultrasound system will think that the echo from this object originates from the focal zone. Thus, ghost images of these highly reflective objects can become visible along the same plane of the real image.
- ❖ Move the focal zone to the area of interest to correct

Near field clutter
- Clutter is a noise artifact in ultrasound images that appears as diffuse echoes overlying signals of interest.
- It is most easily observed in anechoic or hypoechoic regions
- It involves the near field and may hinder identification of structures that are close to the transducer - such as the apex - on a 4-chamber view (i.e. thrombus).
- ❖ Corrected by utilizing TGC

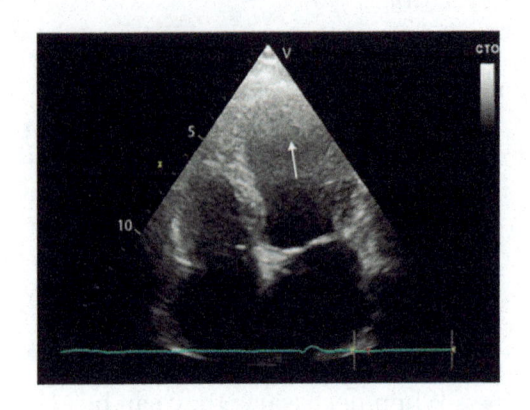

Reverberation
- The reverberation artifact occurs as a result of repetitive reflection back and forth between two highly reflective surfaces.
- Reverberation is created when a sound or signal is reflected. This causes numerous reflections
- ❖ Reverberation artifacts can be improved by changing the angle of insonation so that reverberation between strong parallel reflectors cannot occur

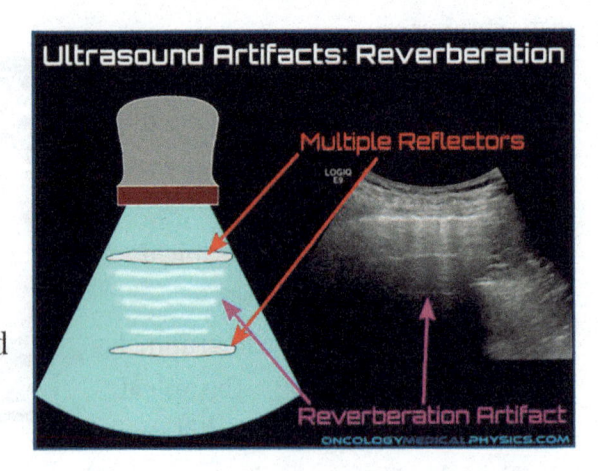

Side lobe
- Side lobe artifacts occur where side lobes reflect sound from a strong reflector that is outside of the central beam, and where the echoes are displayed as if they originated from within the central beam.
- Blurring of edges of an image
- ❖ Adjusting the harmonic frequency will minimize side lobes

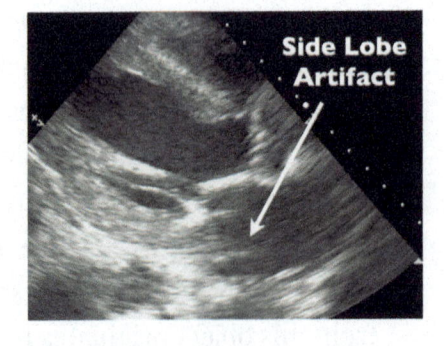

Chapter 14
Optimization

Optimization checking that the sonographer can do to make sure the images are the most optimal they can be. This can be done by altering the settings that the machine provides.

Settings & Controls
- Focus
- Depth
- Zoom
- Gain
    - 2-D
    - Color
    - CW / PW
- TGC
- Scale
    - Grey
    - Color
    - CW / PW

Gain
- Refers to the amount of amplification of the returning echoes
- The image on the screen is whitened by a uniform margin, as though the returning signal is stronger than it is, to make it easier to see
- Adjusts entire screen

TCG - Time Gain Compensation
- Equalizes differences in received reflection amplitudes because of the reflector depth. Reflectors with equal reflector coefficients will not result in equal amplitude reflections arriving at the transducer if their travel distances are different.
- TGC allows you to adjust the amplitude to compensate for the path length differences.
- The longer the path length the higher the amplitude. The TGC is located on the right upper hand corner of the monitor and is displayed graphically.
- The goal of TGC is to make the entire image look evenly lit from top to bottom

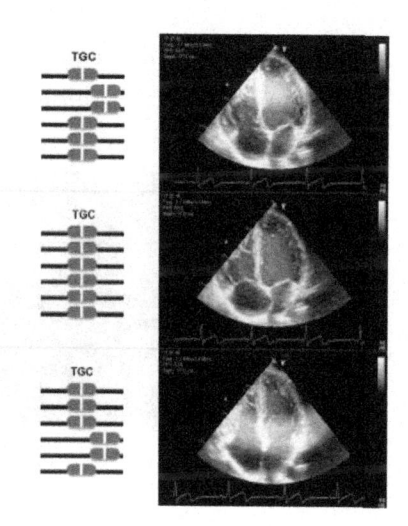

Gain vs TGC

Unlike TGC, overall gain alters the amount of amplification applied to signals from any depth. This is used to increase or decrease the overall brightness of the image. Overall gain amplifies the return signal and has no effect on the transmitted pulse. Therefore, gain cannot compensate for inadequate penetration.

Scale - Grey 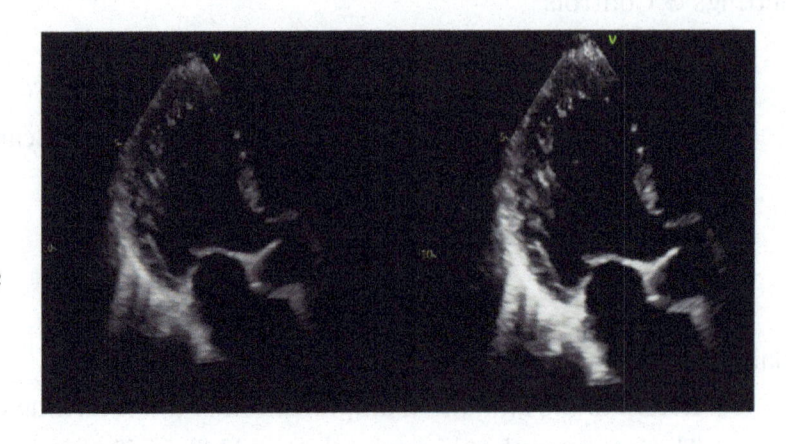
- The image grey scale can be changed by adjusting the Grey Scale Map (Grey Map/Map).
- This permits the brightness of the B-Mode dots to be displayed in various shades of gray to represent different echo amplitudes.
- This is one of the first changes to make with optimizing a custom preset.
- Adjusting gray maps on your image has a similar effect on an ultrasound image as changing the dynamic range, but they are different.

Scale - Color - Velocity Scale
- Color display of Doppler velocity and flow direction

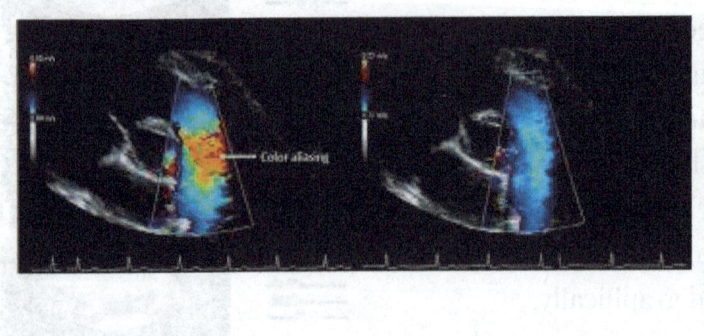

Scale & Baseline- CW/PW - Velocity Scale
- Adjust size of waveform

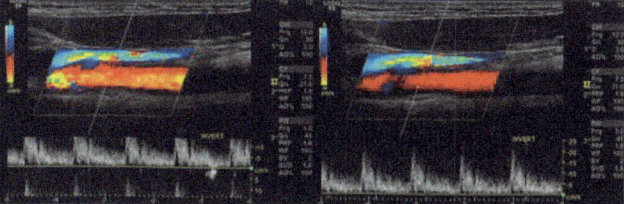

Focus Position / Focus Depth
- The focal position tells the ultrasound the depth at which you'd like the highest resolution
- The image resolution improves in the area of the selected focal position

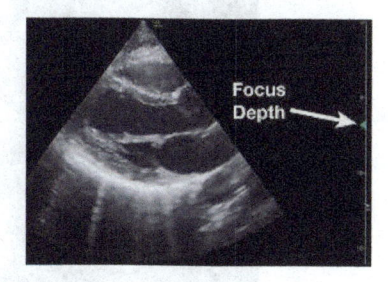

Zoom vs Depth
- The zoom is used for magnifying the area of interest.
- Unlike the depth which magnifies by moving the area of interest closer, the zoom actually magnifies by making the region of interest appear bigger.
- The depth determines how "deeply" into the body one wishes to image

Sector width
- Selecting the sector width is always a trade-off between the field of view on the one hand and frame rate and image resolution on the other.
- Therefore, keep sector width at a minimum.

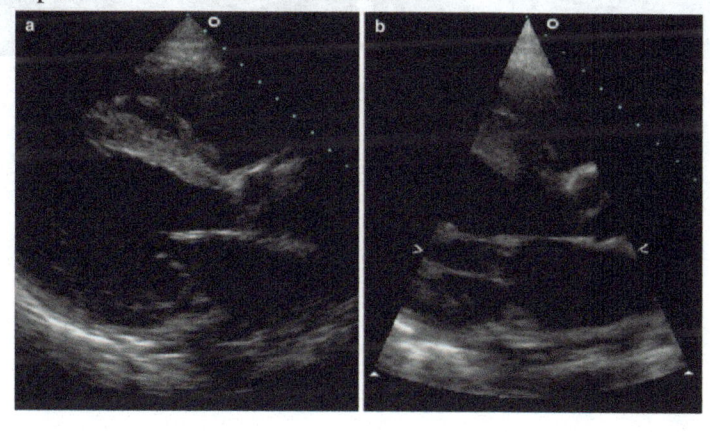

Contrast

Contrast is an imaging agent used when endocardium is not defined enough to observe wall motion or to obtain accurate measurements of the left ventricle. The most widely used imaging agent is called Definity.

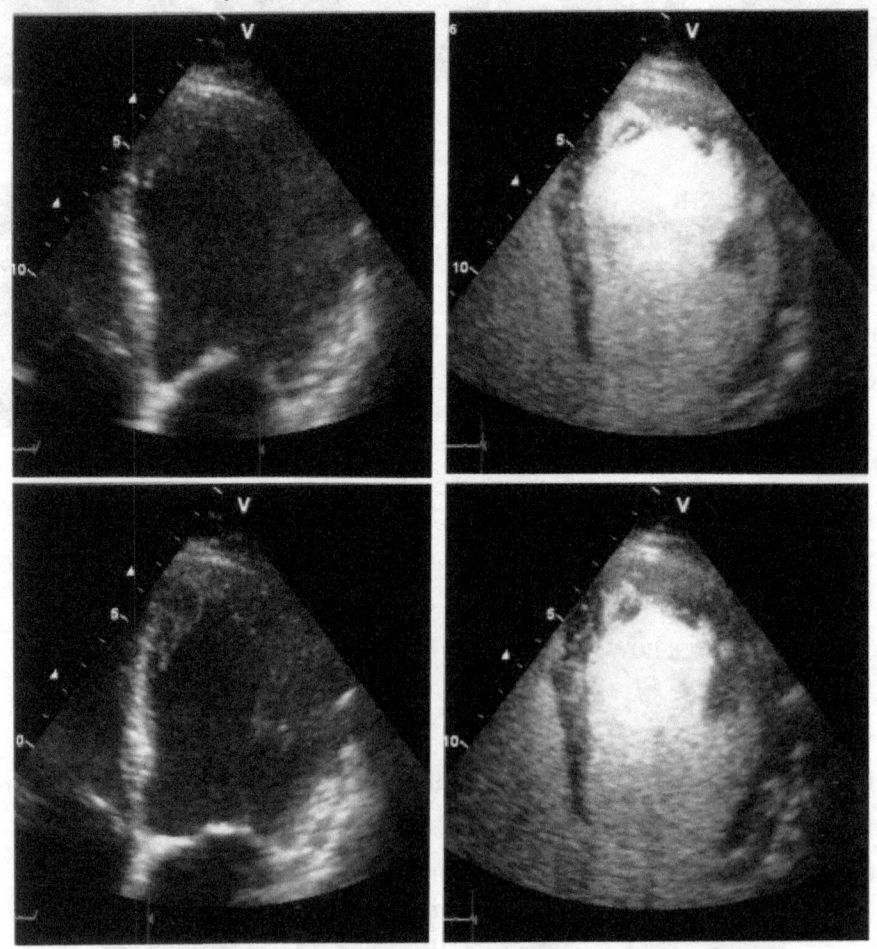

In Memory of Diane Fushi DeFries

INDEX A
Equations

VALUE	EQUATION
Area by PHT	220/PHT
Bernoulli	$(P_1-P_2) = PG = 4V^2$
Body surface area	$0.007184 \times (Height(cm)^{0.725}) \times (Weight(kg)^{0.425})$
Cardiac index	CO/BSA
Cardiac output	SV X HR
Continuity equation	$(A_1 \times V_1)/V_2$
Cross-sectional area	$0.78 \times d^2$
Ejection fraction	(SV/EDV) x 100%
Index values	X/BSA
RVSP	$4(V)^2 + RAP$
Stroke volume (LV)	EDV - ESV
Stroke volume (VALVE)	VTI X CSA

GLOSSARY

Acoustic impedance: describes how much resistance an ultrasound beam encounters as it passes through a tissue

Acoustic shadowing: occurs when calcium-containing structures, prosthetic valves, or silicone implants interfere with the imaging process. To prevent the underestimation or displacement of regurgitant jets, you can increase the aliasing velocity to examine them. In addition, you can use a deep transgastric long-axis view to achieve improved imaging of the LVOT and aortic valve and reposition the short-axis view to examine any aortic leaflets.

Acoustic velocity: is the speed at which a sound wave travels through a medium. It is equal to the frequency times the wavelength

Action potential: An action potential is a rapid sequence of changes in the voltage across a membrane. The membrane voltage, or potential, is determined at any time by the relative ratio of ions, extracellular to intracellular, and the permeability of each ion

Acute: In medicine, describing a disease as acute denotes that it is of recent onset; it occasionally denotes a short duration.

Agitated saline: Agitated saline, also known as an echo bubble study, is a technique that uses sound waves and saline injections to create images of the heart. The saline is agitated with air to create micro-bubbles that reflect ultrasound into a vein, reaching and opacifying the right heart chambers.

Akinetic: without motion or unmoving

Aliasing: a phenomenon in ultrasound that occurs when the velocity of measured flow goes beyond the limits of the set scale or PRF

Amplitude: distance between the resting position and the maximum displacement of the wave

Anechoic: a term used in medicine to describe body parts that appear black on ultrasound scans because they do not produce echoes

Aneurysm: a bulge or abnormal widening of a blood vessel wall, usually more than 50% of the vessel's normal width.

Angina: a condition marked by severe pain in the chest, often also spreading to the shoulders, arms, and neck, caused by an inadequate blood supply to the heart.

Angiogram: is a medical imaging technique used to visualize the inside, or lumen, of blood vessels and organs of the body, with particular interest in the arteries, veins, and the heart chambers

Annulus: a ring-like structure that supports the tissue of a heart valve

Apex: bottom of the heart

Apical: relating to the tip of a rounded or pyramid-shaped structure, usually facing opposite the base of the heart

Arrhythmia: an abnormality in the heart's rhythm or rate

Artery: blood vessel the moves blood away from the heart

Artifact: a feature in an ultrasound image that doesn't accurately represent the examined area. Artifacts can be caused by technical imaging errors or result naturally from the complex interaction of the ultrasound with bodily tissues and organs

Asymmetric: having parts that fail to correspond to one another in shape, size, or arrangement; lacking symmetry.

Atrium(atria): receiving chambers of the heart

Attenuation: is the loss of absorption through a medium

Auto: The prefix auto- means "self."

Axle resolution: is the ability to see the two structures that are side by side as separate and distinct when parallel to the beam. A higher frequency and short pulse length will provide a better axial image. Axial resolution is generally around four times better than lateral resolution

B mode: brightness mode; also known as 2D mode, is a type of ultrasound that uses an ultrasound signal to create points that are made up of bright dots

Base: top of the heart

Baseline: a control that moves the center of the velocity scale up or down to show a greater range of velocities in one direction. The total velocity range remains unchanged

Beam steering: a technique that alters the angle of an ultrasound beam without moving the probe

Bernoulli's principle: a physics equation that uses the law of conservation of energy to calculate pressure gradients between two points from a velocity

Bicuspid: two cusps or leaflets

Bifurcate: to divide into two branches or parts

Bioprosthetic: a medical device made from animal tissue or an animal part

Bovine: tissue from a cow

Bowing(valve): also known as floppy valve syndrome, is a condition where the mitral valve flaps bulge backward into the left atrium of the heart during contraction; prolapse

Carcinoma: a cancer arising in the epithelial tissue of the skin or of the lining of the internal organs.

Cardiomegaly: abnormal enlargement of the heart.

Cardiomyopathy: a general term for diseases that affect the heart muscle, causing the heart's walls to thicken, stretch, or stiffen

Chordae tendineae: are fibrous connections in the heart that connect the papillary muscles to the tricuspid and mitral valves.

Cleft defect: a gap or split in the respective tissue that is present from birth

Clutter: is a noise artifact in ultrasound images that appears as diffuse echoes overlying signals of interest. It is most easily observed in anechoic or hypoechoic regions

Color flow Doppler: an ultrasound technique that uses sound waves to measure blood flow. It uses Doppler technology to track changes in sound waves as particles pass the probe, which is then converted into an image that shows blood flow direction

Color map: a display feature that allows the user to change colors while in color flow Doppler

Color scale: Color display of Doppler velocity and flow direction

Comorbidity: the simultaneous presence of two or more diseases or medical conditions in a patient.

Compression: see **Dynamic range**

Concentric: concentric remodeling of the left ventricle (LV) is when the thickness of the LV's posterior wall or septum is divided by the LV's radius at the end of diastole and is greater than or equal to 0.45

Congenital: a condition or trait that exists at birth.

Continuity equation: The continuity equation, also known as the principle of continuity, states that the volume of blood flowing into a chamber must be equal to the volume flowing out of the same chamber. In ultrasound, the continuity equation is used to calculate the valve area, which equals the cross-sectional area of the left outflow tract times the velocity time integral (VTI).

Continuous wave Doppler: a type of ultrasound that uses two transducers, one to transmit and one to receive sound, to determine frequency shifts along a path

Contrast imaging agent: involves the administration of intravenous contrast agents consisting of microbubbles/nanobubbles of gas. These substances that improve the echogenicity of targeted tissue by changing how ultrasound waves

Cusp: valve leaflet

Cycle(waveform): One cycle of a wave is one complete evolution of its shape until the point that it is ready to repeat itself.

Deceleration slope: the rate at which the E wave decreases in m/s2

Deceleration time: the time between the peak of the E-wave and its projected baseline, and is a marker of diastolic left ventricular (LV) chamber stiffness

Dehiscence(valvular): Valve dehiscence is a rare complication that occurs when the sutures of a prosthetic cardiac valve break down, causing partial or complete detachment from the annulus.

Density: is the concentration of a medium

Depolarization: an electrical activity that occurs in the heart when cardiomyocytes, or heart cells, increase their membrane potential to become more positive of the heart muscle; causing contraction; systole

Depth: determines how "deeply" into the body one wishes to image

Dextrocardia: a rare congenital heart condition that causes the heart to be located on the right side of the chest, instead of the left

Diaphoresis: sweating, especially to an unusual degree as a symptom of disease or a side effect of a drug.
Diastole: the phase of the heartbeat when the heart muscle relaxes and allows the chambers to fill with blood.
Doppler: Doppler ultrasound is a noninvasive test that can be used to measure the blood flow through your blood vessels. It works by bouncing high-frequency sound waves off red blood cells that are circulating in the bloodstream. A regular ultrasound uses sound waves to produce images but can't show blood flow.
Doppler shift(effect): The Doppler effect is described as the effect produced by a moving source of waves in which there is an apparent upward shift in frequency for observers towards whom the source is approaching and an apparent downward shift in frequency for observers from whom the source is receding.
Ductus arteriosus: a blood vessel that connects the fetal pulmonary artery to the aorta, allowing oxygenated blood to bypass the lungs and provide nutritional blood directly into the systemic circulation
Ductus venosus: a vascular shunt that allows oxygenated blood from the umbilical vein to bypass the liver and enter the heart
Dynamic range: allows you to tell the ultrasound machine how you want the echo intensity displayed as shades of gray. A broad/wide range will display more shades of gray and an overall smoother image
Dyskinetic: a condition that occurs when a segment of the heart's ventricle wall moves outward during systole, causing blood to flow between systole and diastole
Dyspnea: an uncomfortable feeling of not being able to breathe well enough; short of breath
Dysrhythmia: see **Arrythmia**
Echogenic: something has the ability to bounce an echo, or reflect sound waves. For example, in medical ultrasounds, echogenicity refers to the ability of tissue to reflect or transmit ultrasound waves. Echogenicity is higher when the surface bouncing the sound echo reflects increased sound waves.
Edema: swelling
Ejection fraction: a measurement of the percentage of blood leaving the heart each time it squeezes.
Embolism: obstruction of an artery, typically by a clot of blood; mobile blood clot
Embryology: the branch of biology and medicine concerned with the study of embryos and their development.
Endocardial: of or relating to the endocardium; inner layer of the heart muscle
Endocarditis: a rare, life-threatening condition that causes inflammation of the lining of the heart's chambers and valves, known as the endocardium

EROA: Effective regurgitant orifice area (EROA) is a measurement used to estimate the severity of mitral regurgitation.
Far zone: In the far zone (also called the Fraunhofer) sound pulses spread out as they move away from the crystal; furthest from the probe
Field: see **Zone**
Focal zone: The narrowest part of the ultrasound beam profile when it is emitted from the transducer. In this region, the pulse waves are concentrated resulting increased beam intensity
Foramen ovale: a muscular opening in the heart wall that allows blood to flow from the right atrium to the left atrium during fetal development
Foreshortening: when the ultrasound beam does not cut through the true apex of the left ventricle but transects above and anterior of the true apex. It leads to a geometric distortion of the image of the left ventricle, making the apex look "rounded" instead of the normal "bullet" shape.
Frame rate: is the number of frames produced in quick succession to create the image on the monitor
Frequency: number of waves passing by a specific point per second
Gain: Refers to the amount of amplification of the returning echoes. The image on the screen is whitened by a uniform margin, as though the returning signal is stronger than it is, to make it easier to see
Grey map: see **gray scale**
Grey scale: The image grey scale can be changed by adjusting the Grey Scale Map (Grey Map/Map)
Harmonics: is a wave or signal whose frequency is an integral (whole number) multiple of the frequency of the same reference signal or wave. As part of the harmonic series, the term can also refer to the ratio of the frequency of such a signal or wave to the frequency of the reference signal or wave
Hemodynamics: the study of blood flow and the physical structures that blood flows through, such as arteries. It's also a branch of physiology that deals with the circulation of blood, and the forces or mechanisms involved in circulation.
Hetero: is a prefix that means "different", "other", or "dissimilar
Homo: refers to the genus of primate mammals that includes modern humans, or Homo sapiens, and several extinct related species
Hyperkinetic: a clinical condition that occurs when the heart beats faster than normal, with an increased rate of blood ejection with each beat
Hypertension: high blood pressure
Hypertrophy: thick/enlarged or stiff walls or chambers

Hypoechogenic: not many echoes". In medical imaging, hypoechoic structures appear darker than surrounding structures because they don't reflect or bounce back ultrasound waves as well

Hypokinetic: a clinical condition that occurs when the heart beats slower than normal, with a decreased rate of blood ejection with each beat

Hypoplastic: incomplete development or underdevelopment of an organ or tissue.

Idiopathic: a disease or condition with no known cause

Index: a value or measurement that uses the body surface area in its calculation

Insufficiency: see **Regurgitation;** usually associated with the semilunar valves

Ischemia: a condition in which blood flow to a part of the body is reduced, preventing tissues from getting oxygen.

Isovolumetric relaxation time: (IVRT) is a measurement of the time between the closure of the aortic valve and the opening of the mitral valve, which is measured in milliseconds

Kinetic: movement

Laminar flow: flow in which the fluid travels smoothly or in regular paths, in contrast to turbulent flow, in which the fluid undergoes irregular fluctuations and mixing.

Lateral resolution: is the image generated when the two structures lying side by side are perpendicular to the beam. This is directly related to the width of the ultrasound beam. Narrower the beam better is the resolution

M mode: motion-mode

Mass: 1. is the amount of matter that makes up an object. 2. a lump in the body that can be benign (not cancer) or malignant (cancer)

Medium: a substance that allows an effect to be obtained, or a substance that transmits impulses

Missile: foreign body

Mono: A prefix that means "one, only, single,"

Morbidity: the condition of suffering from a disease or medical condition

Morphology: shape

Murmur: extra heart "sound; a series of vibrations that can be heard with a stethoscope at the chest wall and are caused by turbulent blood flow in the heart or blood vessels. Murmurs can be systolic, diastolic, or continuous. A systolic murmur starts during or after the first heart sound and ends before or during the second heart sound. A diastolic murmur occurs when the heart relaxes between beats to fill with blood. A continuous murmur occurs throughout the heartbeat.

Myocardial infarction: heart attack; injury to the cardiac tissue due from prolonged ischemia

Myxoma: is a benign, non-cancerous tumor that grows in the heart, most commonly in the left atrium

Myxomatous degeneration is a valvopathy that causes a progressive, non-inflammatory disarray of the valve structure

Near zone: The region located close to the transducer surface; closer to the probe

Nyquist limit: The Nyquist limit states that the sampling frequency must be greater than twice the highest frequency of the input signal to be able to accurately represent the image. If the velocity of the flow is greater than the Nyquist limit, the Doppler shift exceeds the scale and "wrap-around" aliasing occurs.

Ostium: opening

Outflow tract: A ventricular outflow tract is a portion of either the left ventricle or right ventricle of the heart through which blood passes in order to enter the great arteriesOutput power

Palpitation: a noticeably rapid, strong, or irregular heartbeat due to agitation, exertion, or illness.

Parasternal: situated close to the sternum

Patent: something is open, unobstructed, or affords free passage

Pathology: is the study of disease and injury

Pedoff probe: a very basic ultrasound transducer which only has 2 large piezoelectric crystals. One crystal is for transmitting and the other one is for receiving. The Pedoff probe is a non-imaging continuous wave Doppler transducer.

Period: it takes for one wave cycle to complete

PISA: PISA stands for Proximal Isovelocity Surface Area, and it's a measurement used in echocardiography to calculate the area of an orifice that blood flows through. It's also known as the "flow convergence" method.

Planes: the plane that contains the projected image of an object and is located beyond the back focal plane.

Poiseuille law: Poiseuille's law shows the enormous influence that vessel diameter has on the blood flow rate that circulates through the vessel, which is the basis of many pathological and physiological phenomena

Poly: multiple

Porcine: tissue from a pig

Power Doppler: a technique that uses color to show the strength of a Doppler signal, rather than its direction and speed

Primum: Ostium primum defect is a congenital malformation involving atrial septum contiguous with atrioventricular valve annulus; it is accompanied by abnormalities in the development of the endocardial cushions, often resulting in associated atrioventricular valves malformations

Pressure halftime: the time it takes for the pressure gradient across an obstruction to decrease to half of its maximum value

Prolapse: a displacement of a part or organ of the body from its normal position, usually downward or outward, often resulting in it protruding from an orifice

Propagation speed: the rate at which waves pass through a medium. The ultrasound waves' speed is accepted to be 1540m/sec in soft tissue, known as acoustic impedance. Propagation speed depends on the characteristics of the medium that waves are traveling through and is independent of the frequency.

Pseudoaneurysm: , also known as a false aneurysm, is a vascular abnormality that occurs when an artery is damaged, causing blood to leak into the surrounding tissue

Pulse reputation frequency: indicates the number of ultrasound pulses emitted by the transducer over a designated period of time. (Hz)

Pulse reputation period: defined as the time interval from the beginning of one pulse to the beginning of another pulse

Pulse wave Doppler: the range is estimated by binning the returns of the individual pulses by their time of arrival, which is proportional to the range

Reflecting: Some of the waves bounce back towards the source as an echo. The angle of approach (incidence) is identical to the angle of the reflection. The remaining sound wave travels through the second medium (or tissue)

Refraction: If the two mediums have different "stiffness" the resulting change in propagation speeds will cause the wave to be "bent" from its original path (refraction). The angle of incidence will be different from the angle of transmission. The amount of deflection is proportional to the difference in the two tissues 'stiffness'

Regurgitant flow: the product of the surface area of the isovelocity shell and its velocity. The formula for regurgitant flow rate is $(2\pi r^2)v$, where r is the radius of a hemispheric shell

Regurgitation: occurs when the flaps of a heart valve do not close properly, causing blood to flow backward; leaky valve

Repolarization: a crucial step in cardiac electrical activity consisting of a recovery period with the return of the ions to their previous resting state, which corresponds with the relaxation of the myocardial muscle; diastole

Resolution: Image resolution determines the clarity of the image

Reverberation: The reverberation artifact occurs as a result of repetitive reflection back and forth between two highly reflective surfaces. Reverberation is created when a sound or signal is reflected. This causes numerous reflections

Rheumatic fever: an abnormal immune response to an untreated group A Streptococcus infection in the throat

Rheumatic heart disease: a permanent damage to the heart valves that can occur after a person recovers from acute rheumatic fever (ARF)

Scattering: The reflected echoes propagate at various directions; it occurs when the reflector has a small surface

Secundum: a congenital abnormality that occurs in the middle of the atrial septum, the wall between the upper chambers of the heart
Sector: the window that is displayed on the monitor, size and shape differs with each probe
Side lobe: Side lobe artifacts occur where side lobes reflect sound from a strong reflector that is outside of the central beam, and where the echoes are displayed as if they originated from within the central beam.
Sigmoid: curved like the letter C
Sinus: a cavity, space, or channel in the body, such as the hollow spaces in the skull's bones, or channels for blood and lymph nodes
Spatial resolution: the ability of the ultrasound system to detect and display structures that are close together
Spectral Doppler: a type of ultrasound that displays blood flow information graphically over time in spectral form
Speed: (c) is determined by the density (ρ) and stiffness (κ) of the medium ($c = (\kappa/\rho)1/2$).
Stenosis: narrow or narrowing
Stiffness: is the resistance of a material to compression
Stroke volume: the amount of blood ejected from the ventricle with each cardiac cycle
Subvalvular: below the valve
Subcostal: below the ribs
Suprasternal: above the sternum
Supravalvular: above the valve
Systemic: affecting the entire body, rather than a single organ or body part.; the flow of oxygenated blood from the heart to all body parts and deoxygenated blood from the tissues back to the heart.
Systole: the phase of the heartbeat when the heart muscle contracts and pumps blood from the chambers into the arteries.
Temporal resolution: in ultrasound represents the extent to which an ultrasound system can distinguish changes between successive image frames over time
Thrombus: a gel-like clump of blood that forms on a blood vessel wall or in the heart; fixed blood clot
Time gain compensation: Equalizes differences in received reflection amplitudes because of the reflector depth. Reflectors with equal reflector coefficients will not result in equal amplitude reflections arriving at the transducer if their travel distances are different. TGC allow you to adjust the amplitude to compensate for the path length differences.
Transgastric: through the stomach, or through the muscular wall of the stomach
Transcatheter: performed through the lumen of a catheter

Transducer: a device that converts variations in a physical quantity, such as pressure or brightness, into an electrical signal, or vice versa.
Transesophageal: passing through or performed by way of the esophagus
Transposition: the act of moving an organ, especially a viscus, to the opposite side
Transthoracic: passing through or performed by way of the thoracic cavity
Turbulent flow: describes a situation in which blood flows in all directions.
Ultrasound vacuum: a space entirely devoid of matter.
Vegetation: an abnormal growth on a body part, especially a wart-like projection made of fibrin, platelets, and infecting organisms.
Vein: vessels that carry blood towards the heart
Velocity: the speed of something in a given direction.
Vena Contracta: the narrowest part of a fluid jet, located downstream of the orifice, and reflects the size of that orifice
Ventricle(s): pumping chambers of the heart
Views: different imaging planes within the same imaging window
Wavelength: length or distance of a single cycle of a wave
Wigger's diagram: clearly illustrates the coordinated variation of these values as the heart beats, assisting one in understanding the entire cardiac cycle.
Windows: An imaging window refers to an anatomic position on the patient's body where an ultrasound transducer is placed to visualize specific structures
Zone: The beam is three-dimensional and is symmetrical around its central axis. It can be subdivided into three regions, near, focal and far
Zoom: used for magnifying the area of interest. Unlike the depth which magnifies by moving the area of interest closer, the zoom actually magnifies by making the region of interest appear bigger

References

Diagram of the human heart (cropped).svg - Wikipedia

https://cveducation.mayo.edu/store/mayo-clinic-echocardiography-board-review-course

https://ecgwaves.com/topic/left-ventricular-segments-echocardiography-cardiac-imaging/

https://ecgwaves.com/topic/ultrasound-physics/

https://iaconlineaccreditation.org/webdriver/login.aspx

https://images.app.goo.gl/7Eth239yFbPevG9c9

https://images.app.goo.gl/CfeaFyRmyUoPnHpt9

https://images.app.goo.gl/EnyHVifaCZbBwHAq9

https://images.app.goo.gl/G57FgNejZLA5oDtS6

https://images.app.goo.gl/iL4YJNoRzkm5RRqHA

https://images.app.goo.gl/jBuJeEPBQ1m4votY8

https://images.app.goo.gl/jtDgxEMV4Kz6AGqNA

https://images.app.goo.gl/ZGZ6aa6NdvU3TMkk9

https://medlineplus.gov/ency/article/007669.htm#:~:text=An%20echocardiogram%20is%20a%20test,not%20expose%20children%20to%20radiation.

https://neonatology.pediatrics.med.ufl.edu/files/2016/05/Cardiac-embryology.pdf

https://schaberg.faculty.ucdavis.edu/wp-content/uploads/sites/604/2021/05/Heart-Pathology.pdfhttps://www.merckmanuals.com/professional/cardiovascular-disorders/cardiovascular-tests-and-procedures/echocardiography

https://training.seer.cancer.gov/anatomy/cardiovascular/heart/structure.html

https://www.asecho.org/

https://www.gcus.com

https://www.jacc.org/doi/10.1016/j.jcmg.2020.06.049

https://www.ncbi.nlm.nih.gov/pmc/articles/PMC9578224/

https://www.sciencedirect.com/topics/medicine-and-dentistry/cardiac-pathology

https://www.texasheart.org/heart-health/heart-information-center/topics/what-is-a-cardiovascular-pathologist/

https://www.uptodate.com/contents/echocardiography-essentials-physics-and-instrumentation

https://images.app.goo.gl/HDYAmfs7VcDRZg7cA

https://nephropocus.com/2020/06/04/what-is-lv-foreshortening/#:~:text=Foreshortening%20occurs%20when%20the%20ultrasound,the%20normal%20%E2%80%9Cbullet%E2%80%9D%20shape.

https://www.ncbi.nlm.nih.gov/pmc/articles/PMC4958049/#:~:text=In%20medical%20contexts%2C%20the%20term,it%20flows%E2%80%9D%20(64).

Resources

https://intersocietal.org/programs/echocardiography/standards/

https://www.asecho.org/

https://ecgwaves.com

https://cci-online.org/

Made in the USA
Monee, IL
03 June 2024